TO TEACH, TO LOVE

Books by Jesse Stuart

MAN WITH A BULL-TONGUE PLOW

HEAD O' W-HOLLOW

BEYOND DARK HILLS

TREES OF HEAVEN

MEN OF THE MOUNTAINS

TAPS FOR PRIVATE TUSSIE

MONGREL METTLE

ALBUM OF DESTINY

FORETASTE OF GLORY

TALES FROM THE PLUM GROVE HILLS

THE THREAD THAT RUNS SO TRUE

HIE TO THE HUNTERS

CLEARING IN THE SKY

KENTUCKY IS MY LAND

THE GOOD SPIRIT OF LAUREL RIDGE

THE YEAR OF MY REBIRTH

PLOWSHARE IN HEAVEN

GOD'S ODDLING

HOLD APRIL

A JESSE STUART READER

SAVE EVERY LAMB

DAUGHTER OF THE LEGEND

MY LAND HAS A VOICE

MR. GALLION'S SCHOOL

COME GENTLE SPRING

TO TEACH, TO LOVE

For Boys and Girls

PENNY'S WORTH OF CHARACTER

THE BEATINEST BOY

THE RED MULE

THE RIGHTFUL OWNER

ANDY FINDS A WAY

A RIDE WITH HUEY THE ENGINEER

JESSE STUART

TO TEACH,
TO LOVE

THE WORLD PUBLISHING COMPANY
New York and Cleveland

Published by The World Publishing Company, 2231 West 110th Street, Cleveland, Ohio 44102. Published simultaneously in Canada by Nelson, Foster & Scott Ltd. FIRST PRINTING—1970. Copyright © 1970 by Jesse Stuart. Copyright 1936, 1938, © 1960 by Jesse Stuart. All rights reserved. No part of this book may be reproduced in any form without written permission from the publisher, except for brief passages included in a review appearing in a newspaper or magazine. Library of Congress Catalog Card Number: 79-88596. Printed in the United States of America.

The author wishes to acknowledge with gratitude the cooperation of the publishers of the magazines in whose pages the stories and articles in this book, in somewhat different form, first appeared:

Reprinted from the Ball State College *Forum*, "A Mother's Place is With Her Son," Spring, 1964, © 1964 by the Ball State College *Forum*.

Reprinted From the *Educational Forum*, "Apple Thief," November, 1942, © 1942 by Kappa Delta Pi, An Honor Society in Education, West Lafayette, Indiana.

Reprinted from the *Educational Forum*, "The Sensible Six Per Cent," November, 1960, © 1960 by Kappa Delta Pi, An Honor Society in Education, West Lafayette, Indiana.

Reprinted from the *Educational Forum*, "The Reason for Dropouts," March, 1965, © 1965 by Kappa Delta Pi, an Honor Society in Education, West Lafayette, Indiana.

First published in *Esquire* Magazine, © 1944—"My Father is an Educated Man," © 1946—"How Sportsmanship Came to Carver College," © 1959—"Earth Poet."

Reprinted from *Kentucky School Journal*, "Saving Brains," November, 1930, © 1930 by the Kentucky Education Association.

Reprinted from the *Kentucky School Journal*, "Questions Students Have Asked Me," December, 1942, © 1942 by the Kentucky Education Association.

"Earth Is His Book" was first published in *The Land*, Volume XI, No. 3, January, 1953; reprinted by permission.

The material on the following page constitutes
an extension of the copyright page.

"Education and American Démocracy," reprinted by permission of the National Association of Secondary School Principals. Copyright 1952, by the National Association of Secondary School Principals.

Reprinted from *Today's Education*, the National Education Association Journal, "Grassy," December, 1965, © 1965 by the National Education Association.

Reprinted from *Today's Education*, the National Education Association Journal, "Challenge in Cairo," May, 1962, © 1962 by the National Education Association.

Reprinted from *Today's Education*, the National Education Association Journal, "Confronted in Crisis," December, 1943, © 1943 by the National Education Association.

"The Teaching Example," reprinted by permission from *The PTA Magazine*, November, 1955, © 1955 by the National Parent-Teacher Association.

Reprinted from the *Peabody Reflector*, "The One Room School Was Accelerated Too," September-October, 1965, © 1965 by the *Peabody Reflector*.

Reprinted from the *Peabody Reflector*, "Harry Kroll as I Knew Him," July-August, 1967, © 1967 by the *Peabody Reflector*.

"Lesson in a Liberal College Education" was first published in *The Saturday Review of Literature*, February 16, 1946; copyright 1946 by The Saturday Review Associates, Inc.

"Teaching Creative English in the High School" and "My Fourteen Originals" were first published by *Scholastic* Magazine. Copyright 1936, by Scholastic Magazines, Inc.; Copyright © 1965 by Scholastic Magazines, Inc.

"The English Teacher Who Helped Me Most," from *The Secondary School English Notebook*, Vol. II, No. 3, 1963. D. C. Heath & Co., Boston, Mass. Reprinted by permission of the publisher.

"What College Meant to Me," reprinted from *Together*, June, 1962. Copyright © 1962 by The Methodist Publishing House.

Previously published material copyrighted by the author includes excerpts from *Head O' W-Hollow*, published by E. P. Dutton & Co., 1936; from *Beyond Dark Hills*, published by E. P. Dutton & Co., 1938; and from *God's Oddling*, published by The McGraw-Hill Book Company, Inc., 1960.

In fond and grateful memory
To all my teachers
Whose praise
Was my greatest encouragement

Preface

SCHOOLS AND CHILDREN AND ATTITUDES
have changed since I was a happy boy in the classroom many
decades ago, and even since I was a high-school principal only
a few years ago. I'm old-fashioned, I don't claim to be anything else. But I can still talk to kids and they listen. I still love
schools and teaching, as I love my memories of one-room
schoolhouses and walks in the Kentucky hills with my students.

I don't claim to know all of what's wrong with our schools
and our kids and our teachers today. Maybe nothing. Maybe
historians, looking back, will simply say that this was a period
of revolutionary change and we were living through the normal upsets—in the schools as well as in the homes and in the
streets—of such a period. I loved school. I loved school as a
barefoot kid, I loved it as a teacher. We never called our kids
from the Kentucky hills "culturally deprived," though many
of their folks couldn't read or write; we just taught them and
they learned.

This much I know: Love, a spirit of adventure and excitement, a sense of mission has to get back into the classroom. Without it our schools—and our country—will die. I am all in favor of schoolteachers getting better pay. For centuries they were paid pennies. I am not in favor of their walking out of the classroom, closing the schools, leaving the children. A teacher is a human being—that is, a self-seeker—like anyone else. But once that self-seeking dominates, and the sense of mission and excitement becomes secondary, that teacher should seek another way of life, become a businessman, a stockbroker. I am not suggesting for one moment that business is not an honorable pursuit. It is. Our country is based on it. But a businessman has a different mission.

I believe, too, that young people should have a greater say in what goes on in the classroom, that teachers and principals and trustees have to listen to them more. I believe many of the changes modern youth are demanding are long overdue. We must not prepare students for our world of the past, but for theirs of the future. For it is a new world, one that will be newer still by the time the youth now in school are as old as we are.

We are now leaving this world for the unexplored universe. Educated people are firing missiles into millions of miles of space and these missiles are returning the data we want. Human beings will be traveling in rockets, from space station to space station, to visit on a planet or a star. In the future an electronic brain will store knowledge of every symptom of every disease, thus making diagnosis and method of treatment instantly available to all physicians. Who says our life-span won't average one hundred years?

To live in this new world, our youth need education—the best that we can give them—not only in science and technology, but in poetry and beauty and perhaps most of all in character. If such education is to prevail, the teacher-student relationship must remain what the words suggest. *The teacher teaches, the student studies.* The assumption that the teacher has something to say, something to give that is of value to the student—that the teacher knows more and is capable of making it interesting—I still hold to be valid. (A lot of teachers should have been retired years ago; a few should never have been hired; but that doesn't change the basic principle.)

Violence in the classroom or the school halls? Well, I handled it in my own way, and sometimes with my own fists, years ago. Students showing how liberal they are, or how patriotic, by burning down libraries, beating professors? Hitler burned books, and had professors beaten—and even jailed. Is this what our young people think liberal, or patriotic?

The answer, of course, is "no." Only a few self-styled radicals on one issue or another think these antics are smart. The tragedy is for the many honest, hard-working youths on riot-torn campuses to be deprived of days or weeks or months of precious educational time because of violence provoked by a few.

But I do not believe this irresponsible minority will dominate the future. In the public schools where I have worked —where all may enter and not be selected for any particular reason—I learned to agree with Thomas Jefferson. I, too, have faith in the masses. No one will know from which family genius will come. Educating all is the only way to discover genius.

This is the way I see most of the youth of today—the ones who will save us tomorrow. Modern youth is a river of clear shining water that is flowing endlessly out into a vast new world. Some impure drops are bound to get into this river, but in its constant flow and surge, these impure drops will be purified in the crystal immensity of the whole. Not any part of young humanity's flow that can be purified should ever be lost.

Jesse Stuart
Greenup, Kentucky
1969

Chapter 1

WHEN I WAS THREE YEARS OLD, PA
carried me three miles to show me a schoolhouse. He carried
me on his back with my arms around his neck; he told me
that he was the horse and I was the rider. Pa was a small horse
for me to ride. The sweat on his neck wet my arms; the sweat
that ran down his body wet his clothes and my legs.

The building was painted white. Pa lifted me from his back
to the ground—the first schoolground that I ever put my feet
on. Pa pulled a bandanna from his overalls pocket and wiped
the sweat from his face and neck.

"I got this house for you, son," he said. "Since I didn't get
any education, I don't want my youngins to grow up in this
world without it. They'll never know what they're missin'
until they don't have it. If I could only read and write!"

Though Pa couldn't read and write, he served for twenty
years as school trustee for the Plum Grove district. I don't
believe that a man with a good education could have done
better. Pa left his corn in the weeds to go over the district
getting the people to petition for the new schoolhouse. He
cleared off the schoolhouse and built the toilets. He built a

cistern. There wasn't anything within his power that he wouldn't do for the Plum Grove school.

Once, when he was plowing around a steep mountainside, where only a sure-footed mule and a wiry mountain man could stand, Pa rested his mule under a beech. While he rested he made me a small wooden plow with his pocketknife out of a papaw sprout. When Pa started his mule around the mountain slope, I tried to follow him and make a furrow with my small plow. But I couldn't keep up with him.

The rows around this mountainside were long to me; they were long rows for the mule, too. But Pa was in his twenties and tough as hickory bark.

That evening at sundown he walked beside the tired mule and talked to me about going to school soon as the corn was laid by. "There's not a surer way on earth to make a livin' than between the handles of a plow," Pa said. "But I want you to learn to read, write, and cipher some, more than anything else in this world."

Pa said: "You must have book-learning, son. You must not grow up like a weed. You must not grow up like I have. I can't write my name till you can read it." I remember seeing Pa try to read the words on tobacco pokes. He would spell the word first. Then he would call it something. He would work and work with a word like a dog at a groundhog hole gnawing roots and rocks to get the groundhog.

Uneducated though he himself was, my father was really my first teacher. Many people thought my father was just a one-horse farmer who had never got much out of life. They often saw the beard long on his face. And they saw him go away and just stand and look at something. They thought he was moody. Well, he was that, all right, but when he was standing there seemingly just looking into space, he was actually observing a flower, plant, mushroom, or a new bug he'd discovered. And every time he looked up into a tree, he wasn't searching for hornets' or birds' nests. And he wasn't trying to find a bee tree. He was just looking at the beauty in one of a million trees. Among the millions of trees, he always found one different enough to excite him.

My father was an earth poet who loved the land and everything on it. He liked to watch things grow. From the time I was big enough for him to lead me by the hand, I went with him over the farm. If I couldn't walk all the way in those early days, he'd carry me on his back. I learned to love many of the things he loved.

I went with him to so many fields over the years and listened to him talk about the beauty and growth of plants, I know now that my father had some wonderful thoughts which should have been written down. And thoughts came to him faster than hummingbirds go from one flower to another.

Somewhere in the dim past, among the unforgotten years of childhood, I remember my father's unloading me from his back under a white oak tree, just beginning to leaf.

"Look at this hill, son," he said, gesturing broadly with a sweep of his hand. "Look up that steep hill toward that sky. See how pretty that new ground corn is."

This was the first field I can ever remember my father's taking me to see. The rows of corn were like dark green rainbows around a high slope, with a valley and its little tributaries down through the center. The ground was clean of woods, and the young corn was dark, stalwart, and beautiful. The corn blades rustled in the wind, and the reason I remember this is that my father said he could understand what the corn blades were saying. He told me they whispered to each other, and this was hard for me to believe. Although I was a child, I thought before anything could speak or make a sound, like a cow, horse, or chicken, it had to have a mouth. When my father said the corn could talk, I got down on my knees and looked a stalk over.

"This corn's not got a mouth," I told him. "How can

anything talk when it doesn't have a mouth?"

And he laughed, and to me it sounded like the wind in the corn.

Then, on a Sunday, when my mother and sisters were at a country church, he took me by the hand and led me across two valleys and the ridge between them to a cove where giant beech timber once had stood. He was always restless on Sundays, eager to get back to the fields in which he worked all week. He had cleared a piece of this land to raise white corn, which he planned to have ground for meal to make our bread. He thought this cove was suited to white corn, which he called Johnson County corn. Someone had brought the seed from the Big Sandy River, in the country where my father was born and lived until he was sixteen. And when he had cleared this cove, set fire to the giant beech tops, and left ash over the new ground, he thought this earth would pro- duce wonderful cornfield beans too. In every other hill of corn, he had planted beans. Now these beans ran up the cornstalks and weighted them with hanging pods of young tender beans. Pictures I saw later in life of Jack and the beanstalk always reminded me of this tall corn with bean vines winding around the stalks up to the tassels.

But what my father had brought me to see that delighted him most were the pumpkins. I'd never seen so many pump- kins, with long necks and small bodies. Pumpkins as big around as the bottom of a flour barrel were sitting beneath the tall corn, immovable as rocks in the furrows. There were pumpkins, and more pumpkins, of all colors—yellow, green and white, and green and brown.

"Look at this, won't you?" my father said. "Look what corn, beans, and pumpkins! Corn ears so big they lean the cornstalks. Beans as thick as honey-locust beans on the honey- locust tree. And pumpkins thicker than the stumps of this new ground. I could walk all over that field stepping on pumpkins. I could go all the way over it and never step on the ground. It's something to see, don't you think? Did you ever see anything as pretty?"

He looked upon the beauty of this cove he had cleared and his three crops growing there before he figured how many bushels of corn and beans and how many pumpkins he would have. He never figured a field in dollars and cents, although he was close and frugal with money. He never wasted a dollar. But dollars didn't mean everything to him. He liked to see pictures of growing things on the land. He carried these pictures in his mind.

Once, on a rainy Sunday afternoon when we were walking between cornfields, he motioned for me to step up beside him and look. He pointed to a redbird on its nest in a locust tree. Here sat a redbird with shiny red feathers upon the dark background of a nest. It was just another bird's nest to me, until he whispered, "Ever see anything as pretty as that redbird sitting on that dark nest in the white drops of rain?" From this time on, I have liked to see birds, especially redbirds, sitting on their nests in the rain. My father was the first one ever to make me see the beauty in these little things about me.

He taught me how to tell a stud terrapin from a female, a male turtle from the female, a bull blacksnake from a female. My father knew all of these things. He learned them in his own way. He observed so closely that he could tell the male from the female in any species, even the gray lizard, which was most difficult.

"A blacksnake is a pretty thing," he once said to me. "He is so shiny and black in the spring sun after he sheds his winter skin."

He was the first man I ever heard say a snake was pretty. I never forgot his saying this, and the sumac thicket where we saw the blacksnake.

He saw more beauty in trees than any man I have ever known. He would walk through a strange forest laying his hand upon the trees, saying this oak and that pine, beech, or poplar was a beautiful tree. Then he would single out trees and say they should be cut. He would always give his reasons for cutting a tree: too many trees on a root stool; too thick; one damaged by fire at the butt; one leaning against another tree; too many on the ground; or the soil not deep enough above a ledge of rocks to support them.

Then there were the hundreds of times my father took me to the hills just to see wildflowers. I thought it was silly at first, but as I continued to go with him, I learned more about wildflowers, and appreciated their beauty.

He could sit on a dead log somewhere under the tall beech trees, listen to the wind in the canopy of beech leaves above, and just sit on that log and enjoy himself indefinitely. He didn't want to get up and move. He wanted to sit there and look and love the color in the wildflower's blossom and the noises the wind made rustling the green beech leaves.

So many times when I went with him, we sat on a log, maybe one covered with wild moss, looked at a wildflower for hours, listened to the wind in the leaves, and then got up from the log when the sun went down, and started for home.

He always had a lot of feeding to do—livestock, mules, horses, hogs, chickens, and dogs. These animals looked forward to seeing him at feeding time. And he was always there to feed them.

My father wouldn't break the Sabbath by working unless it was an emergency. Often he followed a cow that was overdue to calve. And he watched over ewes in the same manner. He followed them to the high cliffs and sometimes helped them deliver their lambs to save their lives. He did these things and fought forest fires on Sunday, when he had to. But he always said he could make a living working six days in the week.

I've been with him many a time going to the field when we'd cross a stream. He'd stop the horse, sit down on the bank in the shade, and watch the flow of water. He'd watch minnows in a deep hole. He wouldn't say a word, and I wouldn't either. I'd look all around, for I'd wonder what he'd seen to make him stop.

But I never would ask him. Sometimes he'd tell me why we had stopped. Sometimes he wouldn't. Then we'd go on to the field together, and he'd work furiously to make up for the time he had lost while we sat beside the stream and watched the cool, clean water flowing over the sand and gravel to some far-off destiny beyond his little hill world.

My father didn't have to travel over the country like other people searching for something beautiful to see. Not until very late in his life was he ever over a hundred miles from home. He found beauty everywhere around him. He had eyes to find it. He had a mind to know it. He had a heart to appreciate it. He was an uneducated poet of this earth. He didn't know that he was a poet either. If anybody had told him in so many words that he was, he wouldn't have understood. He would have turned and walked away without saying anything.

Early on a winter morning, I might go out with my father, and he would show me Jack Frost's architecture, which lasted only until the sun came up. This used to be one of the games my father played with me on a cold, frosty morning. He showed me all of those designs that I would never have found without him. Today I cannot look at white fields of frost on winter mornings and not think about him.

He took me to the first persimmon grove I ever saw. This was after frost, and the persimmons had ripened and had fallen from the trees. "They're wonderful," he said. "The persimmon is a candy tree. It really should have been called the gumdrop tree." His saying this to me, a small boy then, has made me see ripe persimmons after frost as brown gumdrops and the persimmon as the gumdrop tree.

I didn't get the notion that dead leaves can be golden ships on the sea from a storybook. And neither did my father, for he couldn't read. He'd never had a book read to him either. It was in October, and we were sitting on the bank of W-Branch. We were watching the blue, autumn water slide swiftly over the slate rocks. My father picked up leaves that were shaped like little ships and dropped them into the water, and we both watched their graceful movement.

"These are ships on swift water," he told me. "These are going to far-off lands and strange places where strangers will see them."

I never forgot this. I never forgot his love of autumn leaves and the many species he'd pick up when we were out walking and ask me to identify. He'd talk about how pretty each leaf was and how a leaf was prettier after it was dead than it was when it was alive and green and growing.

And no one who knew him as I did would have ever felt sorry for my father in his small world. The feeling of sorrow would have turned to envy. For my father had a world of his own. This world went beyond the vast earth that world travelers know. He found more beauty in his acres than poets who have written a half-dozen books. Only my father couldn't write down the words to express his thoughts. He had no known symbols with which to declare his thoughts. If he had, I don't know what he would have done. But I do know that he would have written something.

If he was not a poet, an earth poet, who lived his life and never left a line of poetry, there never was one.

* * *

At the age of five I started to the new schoolhouse at Plum Grove. Every afternoon when I came home Pa would ask me how I was getting along. I'd tell him I was getting along all right. We didn't get any report cards in those days. Pa was pleased that I liked to go to school so well. When we possum-hunted at night with our hounds, all the time he talked to me about school. I was so filled with the idea, I could hardly wait to get to school in the morning, and I hated to leave in the afternoon. Saturdays and Sundays my sister and I played school.

I walked three miles out of the Hollow with my sister to school after the corn was laid by. We met the foxes in our path many a morning. We saw the squirrels play over our heads in the tall timber. Sawmills had not come to the Hollow yet. We saw the rabbits hop across our path. We met other children. They were strange children to us and we were strange to them. I wanted to outlearn the boys I was in class with. I wanted to turn them down in spelling and get the prize for the most headmarks. When I turned one of the boys down, I laughed. When one turned me down, I cried. My sister and I would hold school before we got to school to see if I had the spelling words down pat. I wanted to outrun anybody in school. I wanted to tell them what to do. I fought with them, whipped and was whipped. It was a great place to be. I loved school—no beans to pick, no corn to cut, no hogs to feed, no wood to get. I learned fast because I worked hard.

The school terms lasted only five months in Kentucky then. And I'll declare it was the finest place to me I'd ever been up to that time. It was a place where I saw a lot of people. Thirty or thirty-five people were a multitude for me to see together. And the things called words and ideas—there was something fascinating about both. Words are marvelous things. They are something which you can do anything with but take hold of with your hands. You can put them on paper, and they mean something. I tried them out first by writing notes. I wrote one to a girl and was severely whipped for it. The girls sat on one side of the schoolhouse and the boys on the other, and I threw the note across to Mabel Jones.

"I can do something you can't do," I said to Pa, long before the first school year was over.

"What's that, son?" he asked me.

"I can read and write my name."

My father sat looking at the fire. I didn't know that I had hurt him. And then he got my mother to teach him a memorized signature. My mother could well do it; she had finished the second grade.

I remember the first poem I ever memorized. It was in an old primer. I loved these words, and they have been with me since I was five years old.

> *Oh Mother look at the moon,*
> *She's riding so high,*
> *For tonight she looks*
> *Like a lamp in the sky.*
> *Last night she was smaller*
> *And shaped like a bow,*
> *But now she is larger*
> *And round like an O.*

Mr. Calvin Clarke was my first teacher at Plum Grove. My father, in his position of trustee, took one look at Mr. Clarke and recommended him to John Prichard, superintendent of Greenup County schools, who recommended him to the Greenup County School Board, and he was hired. When my father was trustee of the Plum Grove district there was only one trustee to each local school district, but later a bill was introduced into the Kentucky legislature to change to the three trustees for each district, a bill that passed both "the house" and "the senate."

When people at Plum Grove saw Calvin Clarke, my father was criticized for hiring him. He was eighteen years old, a graduate of Greenup High School, and he weighed one hundred and ten pounds. He had straight black hair and eyes so black they sparkled. "Mick Stuart's hired a boy to teach Plum Grove," Uglybird Skinner said. "Mighty small, mighty small, Mick, to handle them big boys up there," Annis Beeler told my father. "I'll just stay in school long enough to run him off the hill," Rodney Darter said. He was Plum Grove's bad boy at the time.

When people who had voted for my father for school trustee, which was always a heated and contested election, spoke unfavorable comments about the young small teacher my father had recommended, his answer was: "I liked the looks of Old John Newsome's grandson. The Newsomes have good stuff in them, and they don't run. He's a chip off the old block. They're smart people too. You just wait and see if little Calvin Clarke don't straighten that school out. Last year they built fires up on the schoolground and chased each other with burning sticks. They won't do it this year. I've got a real teacher for Plum Grove."

When we went to school that July morning, Mr. Clarke was up front by his desk. "I've been hired to teach the school," he told his fifty pupils. "And I am sure I will succeed." And succeed he did. He allowed no whispering without permission. And one had to hold his hand up to get attention and ask permission. Only one girl or one boy could leave the room at the same time—to stop jamming the outdoor toilets. There was one girls' outside toilet on one side of the hilltop, and one for the boys on the other side. There had been vulgar things written and vulgar drawings on the walls before Mr. Clarke came. He cleaned it up. If a boy stayed too long, Mr. Clarke often got up and went out and inspected the toilet to see what if anything had been written.

Once when Rodney Darter stayed a little long, Mr. Clarke went out after he came back to the schoolroom. When he returned, his face was red and his black eyes snapped. "Rodney, did you write all that stuff about me out there on the walls?" he asked. "I sure did," Rodney replied. Mr. Clarke ran toward him in the schoolroom, and Rodney ran outside and got a stick. Mr. Clarke, who was smaller and younger, ran outside and got a longer stick. These sticks were dead branches that the winds had blown from one of the oaks nearby. All of the pupils at Plum Grove came outside the building. We saw Mr. Clarke striking at Rodney, and Rodney backing down the hill waving his stick in front of him. He's no coward," Fred Young said. "We have a teacher who will fight." Fred Young, a studious teenager, was larger than Mr. Clarke. And Fred Young's seatmate was my first cousin, Everett Hilton. He was larger too than Mr. Clarke.

When Mr. Clarke and Rodney Darter reached the foot of the hill, each was still trying to get the right lick on the other with his stick. Mr. Clarke had backed Rodney down to Shacklerun Valley. Then Rodney Darter turned quickly and started running down the road. Mr. Clarke larruped him a lick across the shoulder when he turned. And then was at his heels, running him down the road and striking at him. He ran him to the small white cottage, where Rodney cleared the paling fence with a broad leap. This was where Rodney lived. Mr. Clarke had struck at him all the way. He didn't go into his yard after him. He turned and walked back all the way to the schoolhouse. And when he appeared back on the schoolground without his stick, all of his pupils clapped their hands. Rodney wouldn't be back in school. His day of chasing teachers away had ended. He wouldn't build any more fires on the schoolground and play the game of Torch and Fire against the teacher's wishes, either. Calvin Clarke was in firm control of the school. It has been fifty-five years since Mr. Clarke taught me and my sister Sophia. She has kept her report card that has his beautiful handwriting and figures.

I hadn't been in school a week until I had a fight with Tom Lewis, two years older than I. He jerked my straw hat off my head. And I went after him. The fight ended in a throwing duel. He threw a rock at me and missed. I hit him square on the nose and bloodied it with a hard green apple I was trying to eat. Mr. Clarke took us inside. He asked us if we knew the penalty for fighting on the schoolground. We nodded our heads we did. "But, Mr. Clarke, I didn't hit him with a whole apple," I said. "I had taken bites from it. I ought not to get a whole whipping." Everybody in the school laughed. Mr. Clarke smiled. I averaged being disciplined once a week. It was all for fighting.

We never had another teacher at Plum Grove who was as versatile as Mr. Clarke. At noon or after school, he cut our hair. We sat under a giant white oak in front of the schoolhouse, where we sat upon a large gnarled brace root while he used hand clippers and scissors. Some of the older boys he shaved for the first time. He got plenty of practice for he wouldn't permit us to let our hair grow long. And he gave us Plus Merits when we wore clean clothes. He also kept a medicine kit in his desk. We went barefooted to Plum Grove through July, August, September, and into October, until frosts fell and the ground froze. At my home we got one pair of shoes a year. This was true of all the other families in our district. And when we played the fox and hound, we went through brier thickets, woods, across the Wheeler pasture fields, over the Young and Cooper farms. These three large farms surrounded our Plum Grove school. And in that area there were the honey-locust trees that had the dangerous thorns. A sticker from a sawbrier or a blackberry brier would never stop us. We might stop long enough to pull it out and go on chasing the fox. But when we got a honey-locust thorn in our foot, we had to stop. We had to go back to the school to get Mr. Clarke to take it out. He had a pair of tweezers he used for pulling thorns. Then he had antiseptics in his medicine case which he put on the torn flesh, and then he bandaged.

I had two wonderful years and part of another of schooling under Mr. Clarke. First year I learned my multiplication tables. I learned words—to read, spell, and write them. I could read my primer forward and backward. There was no library in our school where I could get more books. I sat and listened to others in grades above me recite until I learned something from their books too. But I couldn't go to school every day. There were days I had to stay home and help my parents.

Mr. Clarke married a young woman in the neighborhood, and they went to Washington, D.C., where he found employment with the U.S. Tax Department. He went to George Washington University at night and worked during the day. He finished college, then the law college, and passed the bar examination that permitted him to practice before the Supreme Court of the United States. The father of four children, he moved to Portsmouth, Ohio, and went into business for himself. When he died at sixty-five, he was a multimillionaire.

"Why didn't you continue teaching, Mr. Clarke?" I later asked him. "Jesse, I couldn't make a living by teaching then," he said. "I made forty-five dollars a month at Plum Grove for five months a year. What could I do with the rest of my time?"

The teaching profession lost a great teacher when it lost Mr. Clarke. He was also a wonderful human being and made a lasting impression on everyone he taught.

* * *

After my sister and I started school, we had something new to talk about at the supper table. If I had been wild at school and got switched, Sophia couldn't wait to get to the supper table to tell it. But if I got a headmark and turned Carrie Burkhardt down in spelling, I couldn't wait to tell it. If I won in an arithmetic match, I never stopped talking about it at supper. We told Pa and Mom about everything we had seen on our way to and from school. Our parents were good listeners.

Our way to school led over a desolate country path. We had to go through two old orchards, two patches of red-oak timber, and one long pasture field where we dared not wear red. There was a bull in the pasture. My sister Sophia became my boss—too much so. She was three years my senior. I couldn't let my hands get dirty; she told on me. Every time I tried to do some miraculous thing before the other students, she told on me—things like jumping off the highest fencepost or eating the most apples. It was a daily thing to hear her tell at home, "Mom, Jesse got a whippin' today. He hit Bill Weaver with an apple core. He tore down the girls' playhouse. He tore down a doodle of Mr. Wheeler's cane hay by running and tumbling over it. He even said a bad word." She was the direct cause of my mother examining my neck and ears every morning before I went to school. And I have heard Mom say so many times: "Son, even if your clothes are a little bad, I'll keep them clean for you, and you must keep your neck and ears and face and hands clean."

To get to Plum Grove school we had to cross a high ridge of hills. Our house was down in W-Hollow, and we had to go beyond the range of hills that enclosed W-Hollow to get our education and to bury our dead. There is neither graveyard nor school within the borders of W-Hollow. Nor is there a churchhouse.

We had to cross the Collins' hill, a pretty hill except for the mouth of an ugly coal mine by our path. There were chestnut trees. We would run night and morning to these trees and pick up the big brown chestnuts that had fallen from the cracked burrs from these giant trees. We would pick them up from the brown leaves that covered the ground. On early autumn mornings these leaves would often be white with frost. When we went to school, we often filled our pockets until they bulged with chestnuts. Afternoons when we came from school, we often filled our empty dinner buckets. Many times we did this without stomping the big chestnut burrs into our brogan shoes when they failed to open and give up their chestnuts.

The top of this hill was covered with fruit trees. There was a fine apple orchard on top of Collins' hill, where there were many kinds of apples. There were plum trees, pear trees, and peach trees. But when we started to school, the last of July or the first of August, the peach trees and the plum trees had already given up their fruit. These trees stood with gold-turning leaves in August, and by the middle of September they had shed their leaves. They were bare trees, standing leafless in the dirges of wind that hit the hilltop. But the pear trees were filled to capacity in good seasons. The apple trees were always loaded.

"Grandma" Collins owned this big hill that had the coal mine and the orchards of luscious fruit. She wasn't our Grandma. All of us schoolchildren in W-Hollow called her "Grandma" because we liked her. To us she was one of the finest women on earth.

In the wintertime when snow covered the hills, "Grandma" Collins would come down where the path came off the steep hill and passed her big white barn. She would bring a bushel basket of apples. She would put them before us. "Help yourselves, children," she would say. We would dive into the basket of apples if "Grandma" Collins turned her back. If she watched us, we lifted them rather politely from the basket. Often she brought us apples in her checked apron.

"Now, children," "Grandma" Collins said, "I'll give you apples, but you must not bother my orchard until I'm through gathering apples. Then I don't care how many apples you get. There's always a lot of apples left on the ground and on the trees. You can help yourselves to them. You must not bother my pears either. You can have all we leave when we are through gathering them. We always leave pears for you."

What she said was true, but when we crossed the hills, I would look at the bright red apples on the trees in the autumn sun. I would look at the big juicy golden pears on the tall pear trees. My eyes would get big, and my mouth watered. Pangs of hunger gnawed at my stomach. It was awfully hard to pass these trees. Instead, I'd get persimmons from the tall twin trees that grew on the top of the hill.

I had ideas about the apples. I would leave my sister and my cousins. I would go to school before they did. Then I would eat all the apples I wanted. I would fill my pockets with these bright red apples. One morning I started early. It was just breaking day.

"Where are you going, Jesse?" Mom asked.

"To school," I said.

"Wait for your sister," Mom said. "Don't you know that bull in Wheeler's pasture field is dangerous?"

The Wheeler pasture field was on the other side of Collins' hill on the slope that led down to the Plum Grove school-house. There was the bull in that pasture and when he bellowed how it made us shudder with fright! How good the girls would be to me! Other times they would say mean things to me, but never when we started across the pasture. We had heard wild tales about how this bull would run trespassers until they fell! We heard that he had run Mr. Wheeler from the pasture. Through this pasture was the only way we had to get to school.

I was the biggest boy in the crowd, and I had to carry the club for the bull. When we got to the pasture field in the morning, I got my club where I left it the night before. It was a pretty hickory club with the bark peeled from it. It was seasoned and hard like an ax handle. I walked across the pasture with it in my hand. I would kill the bull if he ever showed fight. I said that I would, and the girls thought I would. They hugged close to me going down the path through the Wheeler woods—and out across the open grass-fields where we thought the bull would be. I laid the club down when we crossed the fence just as we reached the Plum Grove church. When I came back in the afternoon from school, I picked up my club. The girls were always with me. I couldn't get away from them to get into "Grandma" Collins' apples.

Mom would fix plenty of food in my dinner bucket. It was a five-pint bucket. She would fill it to the top with food. In August and until frost I would take four ears of boiled corn, eight biscuits with cooked apples spread on them, a piece of pie or cake—always a slice of buttered cornbread and a bottle of milk. At the first recess, fifteen minutes we got for play in the morning, I always ate a couple of biscuits. At noon I ate the boiled corn and all of my appled biscuits but two. I kept them for the last recess. When school let out at four o'clock, I was always hungry, and the apple orchard looked inviting when I passed.

One afternoon after we passed through Wheeler's field and I had hidden my club for the bull, I let the rest of the students walk ahead, for I was hungry. When the girls walked up the path, I walked over among the apple trees. I had never seen as many apples in one orchard that had fallen to the ground. They were big red, soft, mellow apples that tasted like meal. Then there were big red apples with plenty of sweet juice in them hanging on the trees. I helped myself; I filled my pockets. Before the girls got home, I caught up with them. I walked home with the rest of the students as if nothing had happened. I had thought of this plan long ago. I had waited long in the autumn before I did it. Why hadn't I done it long ago?

Afternoon after afternoon, I let the students walk on and I went to the orchard. I would see "Grandma" Collins coming down the little path that led from her beautiful painted house. Her house was the only painted house in W-Hollow. She would be wearing a slat bonnet. She would be holding her checked apron filled with apples for us. I would take my share of the apples, though I was getting better apples in the orchard.

"Jesse," my sister said to me one morning when we started to school, "I know why you hang back before we get to Collins' orchard. I'm not going to tell on you, but somebody is if you don't watch. You are getting into "Grandma" Collins' apples. You know you are."

One day when I got home Mom was standing in the yard. She didn't speak. There was a frown on her face. There was a long willow switch in her hand. She looked at me, for I couldn't look at her. I knew that she had found out what I had been doing. Someone had told her. Maybe one of my cousins had told her. I don't know. I never found out.

"You've been gettin' in "Grandma" Collins' apples," Mom said. "Have you got any in your pockets?"

"Two."

"Pull that coat off!"

I pulled off my coat.

"Are the apples in your coat pocket?"

"Yes."

"Get 'em out!"

I got the apples out. I held them in my hand.

"I didn't think I was raising a boy up to steal!"

"But the apples were on the ground," I said to Mom. "The rabbits are eating the mellow ones. The foxes are eating them. The possums are eating them. The crows are eating them. The polecats are eating them. Why ain't I as good as a fox, possum, polecat, rabbit, or crow?"

"They don't know any better, but you do know better," Mom said. "You've been raised not to steal. After "Grandma" Collins has been as good to you children as she has been, then to think you would steal her apples!"

Mom hit me around the legs with the long willow switch. She hit me again and again. I started to cry. I still held the two apples in my hand.

"What must I do with these apples?"

"Take them to "Grandma" Collins and tell her you stole them!"

"I can't!"

"But you will!"

Mom switched me again, and I started down the road. As I walked, Mom switched me. I started to run. Mom kept at my heels and switched me harder as I ran. I couldn't get away. I slowed down and took the beating. We went down the sandy path by the two sweet-potato bottoms. I was crying and wishing that I was dead, and Mom was sorry but kept switching. Through tear-misted eyes I looked at the frostbitten sweet-potato vines covering the dark sweet-potato ridges. I looked at the leaves on the sycamores along the little creek as I ran and walked while Mom whipped me.

It was nearly half a mile to "Grandma" Collins' house. Mom whipped me down to the main W-Hollow road. She let up on me when we crossed the creek. When we had gotten over the footlog, she lit in on me again and whipped me up the little creek nearly to "Grandma" Collins' house.

"Go on up there now and give her them two apples," Mom said. "Tell her you stole them. I'll wait here for you."

Mom stood under the two butternut trees where an old mowing machine was left to rust. I can see Mom yet as she stood there, with her arms folded, the worn-out willow stub still in her hand. My legs, where she had hit me low, were streaked with red whelps—with blood almost oozing through the skin.

I thought once I'd take to the hills. I would leave. They would never hear from me again. I had all sorts of wild thoughts as I walked up alongside the white-painted fence around "Grandma" Collins' lawn. When I got to her gate, just somehow I turned in. I couldn't take to the hills. I walked inside the yard. I cried harder. "Grandma" Collins heard me crying. She ran to the door before I had time to knock.

"What is wrong?" "Grandma" Collins asked. "Is someone dead?"

Her faded blue eyes looked from behind her glasses. Her slat bonnet was pulled low over her forehead. Wisps of her gray hair straggled below her bonnet. She wore her checked apron with a pocket in the corner.

"Nobody's dead, but here—here—here're the apples I took from you orchard," I finally said. "This is not all of them, for some I can't get. I et 'em!" I reached her the two apples.

"Well, child, who sent you here with 'em?" "Grandma" Collins asked.

"Mom," I said.

"Where is your mother?"

"Standing down there by that old mowing machine under the butternut trees."

"You are an honest boy," she said.

She took the apples. She wiped a tear from the corner of her eye with the corner of her apron. She walked back in the house with the apples in her hand. I cried harder and walked from her porch toward the gate. My eyes were so full of warm water I stumbled on the roots of the giant fir trees at the gate. I nearly pitched headlong into the gate. It was the hardest thing I have ever had to do in my life. I walked down the road. I didn't speak to Mom. I passed her. She followed me up the road to the house.

I thought I would whip the person who told on me. But I never found out. The children who went to school with me never told. That was their secret. I thought about letting the bull get them—teasing the bull with a red handkerchief— then when the bull came toward us, I'd climb a tree. But the bull would get Sis. She hadn't told on me. I didn't know the right one to get.

I forgot about the hard whipping Mom gave me when "Grandma" Collins told us all the apples we could find in the orchard belonged to us. I would kick among the dead leaves, even after the snow had fallen, and dig mellow apples from the leaves. They were the best apples I ever tasted. If a rabbit had nibbled a little bit on the apples, it was a good one. I learned that the rabbits could find good apples. They would eat only the best. I could tell when a rabbit had bitten one by the marks of his two big front teeth.

When Christmas came, "Grandma" Collins met us where the path came down the hill to the barn. She gave us a big bushel basket heaped with red mellow apples. I took my share, but they were not as good as the apples in her orchard I found under the leaves and the snow. She gave each of us a sack filled with candy. She gave me an extra present. I opened it when we passed her barn. It was a pair of gloves lined with rabbit fur. In the package was a note that "Grandma" Collins had written me. "Jesse, here is a little present for you to use on your bare hands when you are groveling under the leaves and snow for apples. You confessed stealing apples from me and brought two apples back that you had stolen. You will laugh about this someday, but I shall never forget it, for it was the making of a man of you."

Our crops that year did exceedingly well for the amount of time we had to get the ground ready. We raised a large crib of corn. The potatoes yielded abundantly. We had to rush the corn over the last time and lay it by so we could enter school on the twenty-fifth of July. But we always hurried the corn over the last time to get to school the first day. Our road had to be mown out to keep us from getting wet by the dewy weeds. It took my father several days to mow three miles of country path with a scythe.

We started off to school early in the morning to get there in time. On our way it wasn't anything strange to meet a fox on the road. They liked to travel our path, it seemed. Squirrels would ramble through the heavy-leafed branches over our heads and bark. Pheasants would wallow in a sandhole in our path, and quails would call from the weed fields. Usually when we got home on winter evenings the stars would be shining. And usually I would have to stay in for fighting, and Mary and Sophia would be afraid to go home without me. It

(32)

happened that I was never the teacher's pet. We had only one teacher, and he taught all the grades from the first to the eighth.

In the autumn months, when we went to the country schoolhouse three miles away, during the heavy autumn rains when the creeks were swollen, I would have to carry my sisters across the streams. Sophia, my eldest sister, was delicate. She didn't look like a girl used to the hardships of hill life. But she was one of the best students in the school. Mary, my second sister, was brown-skinned and could walk and climb like a boy. She was tireless when it came to pinches of life that called for endurance.

It is a sad reflection but a true one when I say that at the age of eleven I knew as much about nouns, adjectives, and adverbs as I know today. Those parts of speech appealed to me. I loved grammar and argued with my teachers over the way words were used in sentences. I nearly memorized my grammar book.

Following Mr. Clarke's resignation, a young woman of twenty-one, Nora Riggs, came to teach Plum Grove. She roomed and boarded with "Grandma" Collins. I met her on the path her first day at school. I'd done my chores early, fed the hogs, carried in stove wood, went to the pasture and brought the cow to the milk gap for my mother to milk. I hurried to get to Plum Grove early and play before school began. I was playing ball now. When I reached Collins' hill, where our path wound like *S*'s to the top, I looked ahead of me and I saw the new teacher. I ran up the hill and caught up with her. She was almost out of breath climbing this hill. I told her who I was, and she told me she was Miss Riggs, my new teacher. I thought Miss Riggs was so pretty and so nicely dressed, I liked her from the start. And I walked all the way to school with her.

Morning after morning I walked to school with her. I remember once when we walked up Collins' hill, we were passing the mouth of the old coal mine when I said: "Miss Riggs, I'm going to college someday."

"Where do you plan, Jesse, to go to college?"

"Harvard," I told her. "I've read about it. It's the greatest school in America. It's the greatest and the oldest!"

I had read an article about Harvard in a newspaper, and my greatest ambition now was to study there.

Miss Riggs never had a problem in the three months she taught at Plum Grove. The large boys tried to carry her books for her. Each vied with the other to win the favors of this attractive woman. As a young boy I was infatuated with her. I remember my conversations with her were about college. She was the first teacher I had who had been to college. I went so far to ask her what she had to eat at college and if they ate in a big dining room. And after I found out Eastern Kentucky Teachers' College, where she had spent three years, had five hundred students, I asked her how they could cook for so many people. "If you ever had soup beans cooked for that many people how do they get a pot big enough to hold them?" I asked. I remembered the little pot at home my mother cooked soup beans in for us. "Well, I don't know how they cooked them in the kitchen," she said. "I have never gone back into the kitchen. But I imagine they cooked them in a vat." I had never before heard the word "vat." I didn't want to ask Miss Riggs what the word "vat" meant. So when I got to Plum Grove I looked the word up in a little dictionary.

At the end of this year, Miss Riggs didn't reapply to teach Plum Grove. She returned to Eastern Kentucky Teachers' College for her senior year. She didn't finish this year. She married Ross Scott from her home village, Flatwoods, Kentucky, and this ended her teaching career. I went to school at Plum Grove to Miss Elta Cooper. She was a high-school graduate and had normal-school training to teach her how to teach.

She was a small woman, and a very bright one, who kept good discipline at Plum Grove. I remember how she bragged on me in school, how fast I learned, and how hard I played. I was no longer one of the hounds chasing the fox, but I was the fox all of the hounds chased. This was an honor to be the fox.

Miss Elta could discipline us. She was small but she had the ways of a born teacher. We were young and rugged farm boys who hunted in the woods day and night and fished in the Little Sandy River. In autumns in hunting season often we stayed out all night and had never been to bed when we went to school or to the fields or timber woods, as I often did, to work.

When World War I was over, Miss Elta Cooper's fiancé, Earl Kotcamp, came home safely from the war and they were married. Later I taught her son in Greenup High School. The only time she ever had to discipline me, Aaron Howard, Ed Howard, Glenn Hilton, and I left the Plum Grove school on our way home and went away shouting: "Hurrah for Earl Kotcamp and Miss Elta." We had heard they would be married if he got back from World War I. She kept us after school and talked to us about our manners. She was an excellent teacher.

But after Miss Elta, we had for our teacher a very timid young woman by the name of Claris Brown. She had never been to high school but had finished the grades, had taken a teacher's examination, and passed. My father was no longer a school trustee. He had been defeated, in a heated election, by one vote.

Plum Grove school had changed. They were building fires again and chasing each other with lighted torches. There were fights on the schoolground, and students had to part the students, for Miss Claris couldn't. This was no school now for a young eighteen-year-old girl. People began talking. Uglybird Skinner said: "We've got no school. My boys, Mentor and Estill, ain't larning a thing but meanness. My girl, Chattie, as sharp as a honed razor, was about to fergit all she larned and would have if she hadn't walked out and come home."

But the climax came when Jasper Higgins and Coy Yellowlee were sent to get a bucket of water. It took two boys on hot summer days to carry water to thirsting students upon the hill. We had a cistern at the corner of the schoolhouse, but no one would drink the water, since there was the big Plum Grove Cemetery behind the schoolhouse. People said water seeped into it from the graves. Miss Elta Cooper's father and mother owned the farm down in Shacklerun Valley. From the school windows on the east side pupils could sit and watch two boys go a half-mile down the hill into the valley and draw the water fresh and cold from Cooper's well. By the time they walked back up the hill, each taking his turn carrying the large bucket of water, it would be warm. But this didn't matter. They drank the water and asked for more, and two fresh boys went running down to the well after more water.

When Jasper and Coy returned with the water, we were hot and thirsty. As we were lined up for water, Jasper walked up to Miss Claris, who had just emptied her drinking cup, and Jasper mumbled and stammered and then he finally whispered something to her.

"Don't drink that water," she screamed.

"But the bucket is dry," Melvin Spriggs said. "We're ready for more."

When Miss Brown shouted these words, Coy Yellowlee shot out of the front and only door of the Plum Grove school like a bullet. Miss Brown went to the door gagging like she was sick. Then Jasper Higgins became scared, and he ran out too, and off the hill.

Word filtered among us students what had happened. On the way back from Cooper's well, Jasper and Coy had taken the big bucket of water back under the willows that grew by Shacklerun stream, and Coy had urinated in the bucket. And all of us, including the teacher, had drunk of this water. And remembering their reactions it was good that Coy was out of sight and now Jasper was too. We would have done something drastic to Coy, who never returned to Plum Grove. Jasper returned, but we held it against him for not telling us in time about the water.

Now things began to change at Plum Grove. Claris Brown was no longer our teacher. She couldn't discipline us.

"We have to have a man teacher to control the place," Old Annis Beeler said.

And parents were mad over the "water-bucket incident," which spread over the district in twenty-four hours. Coy had to leave the district and go away and live with his relatives in another part of the state. All the boys at Plum Grove were going "to work him over," first by making him drink the kind of medicine he had given us.

Everett Hilton, not a large man and by no means a small one, had finished high school, had taken a teacher's examination, and topped all of the teachers in Greenup County with his grades. He was elected teacher at Plum Grove. He was a popular choice to save the school. He hadn't been at Plum Grove two weeks until he'd spanked or switched a score. Everett Hilton soon had discipline at Plum Grove. And now, even though he was my cousin, I could no longer call him "Everett" as I had always done. I had to call him "Mr. Hilton." He demanded all his pupils call him "Mr. Hilton."

When he watched us play baseball, an idea occurred to him. He organized Plum Grove boys into a regular baseball team. He scheduled Greenup High School team for us. We played with larger Greenup High School in extra innings. In the sixteenth inning we broke the tie and beat Greenup High School 16 to 9. Our Big Aaron Howard pitched the sixteen innings. Everett had an old truck on which he took us here and there, and once we beat a small-town team of regulars. "Baseball is wonderful," Everett told us. "It keeps you out of meanness."

Then he went on to say schools should have baseball leagues to work with youth. Today we have them.

On Friday afternoons we chose sides and had matches, and Everett invited citizens from the community in to watch us participate. We had spelling matches. We had arithmetic matches. And we were so good in grammar, fifth-, sixth-, seventh-, and eighth-grade students participating in diagramming sentences. We took papers, magazines, and always sought to work the puzzle problem in the old *Pathfinder*. We had a debating team, where we debated evenings at Plum Grove, and pupils brought their parents to hear our debates. In the four years Everett Hilton taught at Plum Grove, one-fourth of his pupils went on to Greenup High School. They had come from the Plum Grove hills and walked five miles to Greenup High School. There never was such reawakening in education as there was at Plum Grove. Many of these youth went on and became teachers.

"I owe it all to Calvin Clarke, a great teacher," Everett once said.

Everett Hilton left Plum Grove and went to the University of Kentucky, where he worked his way through college and through the graduate school with a paper route. He taught school, became a school administrator. Then he went into the state Department of Education. After much experience, he headed Vocational Education for Kentucky.

The last year I went to school to Everett Hilton, I went two months. I went back and took examinations. And Everett said: "Jesse, I don't see how you pass. You're a good guesser."

I was working almost full time now. Much as Pa believed in school, he had to take me out and hire me out on a farm for twenty-five cents a day. And while I set strawberry plants, while I dug potatoes or cut corn or helped saw the timber and bark crossties, I wondered how my classmates were getting along at school. My father and his big horse, Fred, worked for two dollars a day; my mother worked for twenty-five cents a day. We had to have money, since our crops had failed two seasons. I had wanted so much to model myself on my cousin Everett Hilton. Now the dream was lost. I had no hopes of ever going to Greenup High School, much less Harvard.

Chapter 2

IT WAS THE SUMMER I WAS thirteen years old. After the first crops were laid by on our own land, part of the summer was left. I would go and find a job. I needed the money. I went four miles over the bony ridge to the little town of Greenup. The town was in the process of being overhauled. There were electric wires being put upon poles. The alleys and the main streets of the town were being paved. The contractors were crying for help. They wanted farm boys, I heard. Well, this was the place to get work.

I began to work for John Pancake. My work was taking a pick and tearing old stones out of the street. They were buried under the dirt that had been smeared in July with oil to hold down the dust. The work paid well, I thought, thirty cents an hour. I worked ten hours a day and on Saturday until noon. That was really hard work, and the walk back home made my legs stiff at night and my hands hurt. One day we were working under an elm shade. Three husky farm boys "white-eyed" on the job and asked the boss for their money. An old man seventy years old working beside me said: "Look at that, won't you. Them big strong devils won't work when they can get it. That's whatsa matter with our country today —jist sich fellers as them. They need their blocks knocked off. Then they'd have a little sense maybe."

It was on the following day some extravagant man bought a green watermelon and gave each one of us a piece. A boy standing on the street said to me: "Hit me on the nose. I dare you." He put his finger on his nose. I hadn't finished the melon, but I let the piece I was eating cover his whole face. "You are fired!" shouted the boss. He was standing behind a tree. Then the old man that had talked about the men that "white-eyed" the day before said: "What is this world a-coming to, anyway? They didn't act thataway when I was a shaver a-kicking up my heels." In two hours I was working for the concrete gang. They didn't know I had been fired from the other gang. I told that boss the other fellow had sent me there—said he was working too many men as it was. "W'y hell! I can't work any more men. Oh, let me see. I can use you over there dumping sacks of cement into the mixer. How is your flesh? Can it stand cement against it in July? You know that damn cement is hard on the skin when you sweat. It takes off the hide."

"I can stand it if the other men have stood it," I told him. I got the job.

September came, and the wires had been tied to the tall poles. "Them are live wires," said an old man. "Touch one, and your soul will be blasted into eternity. Funny how smart people are getting to be. This world can't last much longer." The main street was a white walk of smooth concrete, and the yellow elm leaves were skipping along on it. The concrete mixer was moved around in front of Greenup High School. When I saw that schoolhouse I had many thoughts. I would go home and get my sister, and we would come to this place to school. It was a beautiful place, a bluish-gray brick building with a spire shooting above the tops of the elm trees. I saw the children going there, and they were all well dressed. I wanted to go there. I told the boss to pay me off. Our streets were finished.

Everett Hilton, my cousin, had been one of the few from Plum Grove who finished the eighth grade and then went to Greenup High School. Others who finished, married and lived on the land. They didn't dream of high school and college. But my cousin Everett had only five miles to walk to school, five miles home, ten miles a day. When my Uncle Martin Hilton moved to another farm, which was eight miles away from Greenup High School, Everett walked eight miles there and eight miles home.

While Everett was going to Greenup High School, my father bragged on him more than once.

"Look what your cousin is doing," he'd say. Then I began to try to imitate my first cousin Everett Hilton. I had dreams that I might go to Greenup High School someday.

The next Monday morning Sophia and I walked under the tall door when the bell sounded. I remember hearing a red-headed girl say, "I get mixed up when I talk to the teacher about the bell. You know, when I sleep late of a morning and have to talk to her about it. I don't know how to say that 'ring, rang, and rung.' I get them all mixed up. Oh, what is the use of all this schooling anyway? I'll clerk in the old man's store someday anyway!" I thought that was funny. She was afraid of three little words.

The students did not take to us very well. I remember a boy saying, "That Stuart girl is right good-looking if she had good clothes to wear." One day a skinny boy asked me what I knew about the price of eggs. I asked him what he knew about the length of mattock handles. The students standing near all laughed. That was a great place, I thought. I saw many boys wearing fine clothes I envied. I wanted a long red sweater like Burl Mavis wore and a necktie like the one I had seen around Fred Mansfield's neck. I wanted many things I could not get. When I ate my lunch that I brought wrapped in a newspaper, I always got away from the other boys. I went around by the old flour mills. I didn't want them to see biscuits with meat and mustard between, and the cornbread.

Schoolwork was not hard for me. And I would hear the boys by the houses along the streets tell their mothers that the work was terribly hard at school. Some spoke of the teachers being unfair. That was funny too. We walked eight miles each day and helped to do the work at home. When we had an arithmetic test Burl Mavis sat beside me and called me Stuart. At other times he told me to get the hayseed out of my hair. The greatest enjoyment I could have was to work a problem when the rest of the class had failed. I did this a few times. One day Miss Hamilton said: "There is a Patrick Henry in this room. Now, you just wait and see. To whom do you think I refer?"

"Me," shouted one or two of the boys.

"No," said she, "there he is."

She pointed to me. After that the students would pass me and giggle: "Patrick Henry, how about 'Give me liberty or give me death'?" they would say. That year I made three B plus's and one A. My sister made four A's. I thought I'd like to be a teacher in a big school like that. A teacher—there was something to be!

One teacher I really admired was Miss Lena Wells Lykins. She not only ran the Greenup Independent School System as well as it had ever been supervised, but being a tremendously energetic woman, she taught a full schedule. There were less than a hundred pupils in Greenup High School at this time. It was the first and oldest high school in Greenup County, where the early settlers from New England settled and established schools. Miss Lykins had a faculty of three teacher and one assistant. And she was our math teacher. My sister and I took algebra with her. While Sophia made A grades in algebra, I was puzzled by this strange subject. I

(43)

couldn't understand how such subjects had ever been created in this world. To me it was the solving of problems with letters instead of figures. I was so confused by the subject I went to the school's largest dictionary to find its real definition. I counted twenty-three kinds of algebra which confused me more than ever. I had always been very good in arithmetic. I certainly couldn't understand algebra. One day, due to my algebra, which I was failing, I got up, walked out of the school, and went home.

When Sophia went back to school next day, Miss Lykins asked her about me. "I think he's quit school over algebra," she told Miss Lykins.

That afternoon Miss Lykins walked home with Sophia.

"Quit Greenup High School because you can't get a subject, huh?" she said with a big smile. Miss Lykins met my mother and father, my two younger sisters, and my brother. We felt as much at home with her as if she were a part of our family. "Jesse, are you going to be a quitter? Are you going to let one subject keep you from finishing high school? You're not going through life like this! I've walked five miles out here to get you back in school. I hear other teachers bragging on you! Now, I have to get back to Greenup tonight. I'm going to a dance. And I want you to take a lantern and light me back over the hills and ridges and down the hollow to Greenup. I'm afraid I can't find my way back over that winding, crooked trail."

My parents invited her to spend the night. But she said she wanted to get back. I took a lantern and lighted her back over the crooked, winding path, across our pasture valley, through our orchard to the ridge path, out the long ridge, down a steep mountainside to Academy Branch, where we could see the streetlights in Greenup. This was one of the important walks of my life. All along the way, Miss Lykins sold me on the value of an education.

"If I fail you in algebra, you won't be the first one I have

failed," she said. "Algebra is an exacting science. You get it
or you don't. And you're not getting it, but stay with the
class, and perhaps next year it will be as easy for you as
walking over this mountain."

I asked an old man about how old the schoolhouse was. I
had noticed that the steps were wearing thin. "I don't know,"
he said. "My Grandpa Jake Filson went around there. It is
mighty old, son. I just can't tell you. But I know things have
changed mightily since I was a boy and went there." I
learned later that it was one of the oldest schools on the Ohio
River.

The last day of school Miss Lykins met us in her office and
gave us our report cards. She said: "The school year is over
now. I hope you have enjoyed it. Here are your report cards.
You've done well. Come back." We didn't need any encouraging.

That summer I went back to the farm. It was not the same
place. I wanted to think about the town over the bony ridge
—Greenup. I could see the happy, well-dressed girls going
along talking about nothing in particular. There was that
flashy red sweater Burl Mavis wore, and Fred Mansfield's
pretty necktie I could see. Lord, that was lots to live for, and
the world was big.

My father worked away now. I was the boss on the farm.
I planted the corn. I planted the potatoes. I sowed the cane
hay. I prepared the land for tobacco. It was a big job for me.
My mother, my sister Mary, and my brother James worked
in the fields with me. I did the plowing, and I selected the
grounds for certain grains. And since I was boss, my orders
were to clean the corn and tobacco well the first time—get
every weed. "Don't leave a weed in any row. Clean the
stumps well. I like to see the fields clean. The corn isn't
smothered then."

"There is a hurricane of weeds in that piece up in the

hollow. We must get to it soon, son," my mother would say. My father would say: "That boy of mine is tearing that place all to pieces. I'd put him against any man in the country. He's worked them mules down lean." Uncle Rank Larks would say, "Mitch Stuart, with a family to work like yourn, you ought to be independent rich." When we sat down at the table at home it was: "Now, children, eat something that will stick to the ribs. Don't mince around over that sweet stuff too much. You'll be hungry before night comes."

I wanted to get the corn laid by as soon as possible this summer. I had heard of a military camp where boys got their way paid there and back and all expenses while they were there. I put in my application. I was fifteen, and the first boy in the county to try it.

That summer was a hot one. But we had plenty of rain and plenty of weeds. The corn shot up out of the earth. It was a fine season. The beans covered the corn, and the pumpkins lay over the fields. It was all over, and the season was a glorious one. Mom would pickle her beans now, can the peaches and berries, and later make apple butter and wild-grape jelly. There are so many things for a woman to do on a farm about this time of year. And my mother was called over the country for sickness. She would get out of bed at midnight and go. It did not matter, rain or shine—when a child was sick, she would go. But even with all this work she found time to work on her quilts. She would go out and find a wildflower she liked. Then she would make the same kind of flower with quilt pieces. She loved to do it. She would sit far into the night looking at the beauty in a new design she was creating.

After the season was done with, I took the mules to the pasture and gave them their freedom. Their manes and tails could grow out now and their hoofs grow long. I did not care. I was ready to leave for a place below Louisville, Kentucky. I wanted the trip. I had never been fifty miles away from home before, and this was three hundred. And I collected the mattocks, spades, and plows and hoes and put them in the shed. The season was over.

The trip to Camp Knox by day coach was the trip of my life. I took the longest way possible on government money. I went to North Vernon, Indiana; then I turned directly south to Louisville. At Camp Knox I found that a fifteen-year-old farm boy, six feet tall and weighing one hundred and thirty pounds, was out of place. "Did you bring a bottle along, Gawky?" said a gentleman from a north Ohio town. "I don't know whether you would call it a bottle or not," I said, "we'll see." I pulled a blank pistol from my pocket which I had brought for curiosity. He made his way rapidly through the crowd. When the other boys saw the gun was a fake, they laughed. But Camp Knox was a torture for me. I was put in the awkward squad for throwing my rifle to a captain when he asked for one. I was kept there three days for that offense. I was given a cold mud bath for throwing a bucket of water on the corporal in charge of the barracks. I was placed on K.P. for coming to reveille with my shoes unlaced and leggings left in the barracks. I did not conform very well to military rules and regulations. Then the fellows tossed me up and let me fall back on a blanket. I went through the blanket to the ground. I was sore for weeks. They only laughed about it. That was why I threw water on the corporal. He had a hand in it. I actually cried when I was put on the awkward squad for speaking at attention. But it did no good. The army is no place for tears. But I excelled in doing exercises and shooting. I loved to do them. I learned them all, and the counts they were done in.

I also liked the marching. Loved to hear an army band putting pep into the soldiers' steps. Loved to see the officers and their wives out looking us over at the reviewing stand. But one of the things I didn't like was bayonet practice. I didn't think I could stick anybody with a bayonet unless I was awfully mad at him. One day out there I met a captain who said, "What's your name?"

I said, "Stuart, sir."

"What company you from?"

"Company I, sir."

A short time afterward, at bayonet practice, this captain had charge. He had a memory like an elephant. He singled me out. He said, "Stuart, I would like you to have enough sand in your craw that, if I was to stick out my arm and tell you to whack it off with a bayonet, you would do it."

And I said, "Sir, stick it out." That evening I was pulling weeds, splitting kindling with a dull ax; two men were over me with rifles and real ammunition.

When I reached home again I was glad to see the hills. I had learned enough about the army to make me join the navy during the war. I went out and looked over the corn. And I said; "My, how this corn has grown! It is as big as it will ever be. The cane hay is ready to cut. The potatoes are ready to dig, and it will soon be time to start off to school again." I was glad to get back home and tell my brother and sisters stories about Camp Knox and Louisville. I had been in Louisville only twice, and that was passing through both times. But I had big tales to tell about everything but K.P. and the awkward squad. I never mentioned them. Another part of my education. Maybe they didn't love me, but they taught me.

Autumn came again. The oak trees in northeast Kentucky were shedding their leaves. The flying leaves were of many colors. The crows began to go in pilfering trains over the country. And wild geese went southward with many a honking cry. It was beautiful back there, and the best place in the world after all. The corn was getting ready to cut now. The brown fields of heavy corn looked rich. It was the victory of hard labor.

My sophomore year in Greenup High School was a happy time in my life. When I went back to Greenup I felt just about the equal of Burl Mavis. "I would be better than Burl," I let myself think, "if I only had some clothes." I had an idea —two of them. I could buy my own books, my sister's books, and buy myself some clothes. I would ask my father's permission to make crossties from the timber on the farm to sell. I would hunt the fur-bearing animals in those surrounding hills with old Black-Boy. I could make money. I was too tall now to wear knee pants.

I started making crossties in our barn lot. I could make them well, I found out. I would cut down a black oak tree. Then I would measure eight and a half feet. I would hack that place with the ax, trim the branches from the tree, and measure another length, and so on. Then I would measure the thickness of the crosstie on the body of the tree—hack little lines to score by. Then I would smooth down the sides with a broad ax. My brother would help me to saw the ties apart. I would bark them, and they would be ready for market. On a bet one day I made twenty-two crossties and got them ready for the wagon. Many people doubt that, but it is an actual fact. If you know anything about timber, you'll know that is a day's work. I ate my father's timber up so rapidly that he stopped me. But I had fifty dollars now. I went to Ironton, Ohio, and bought myself a long suit of clothes. It was a gray tweed suit and cost me eighteen dollars. I bought shirts, ties, and socks. I gave my sister some money and bought our books.

There came a frost and hit the corn. The blades turned white and began to fall. "Save that feed, son. The cattle will need it this winter. You will have to miss school long enough to cut that knob piece of corn."

"I'll cut it all on Saturday," I said. That Saturday I dressed well to keep the blades from cutting my face and hands. I "railroaded" the corn from daylight until four o'clock that afternoon. I cut it twelve hills square on a steep slope. I tied one middle band around the shocks and two outward bands to make it stand well. My father would not believe that I had cut fifty-four shocks until he counted them. He opened his eyes wider when I went back that night and cut twenty-four by moonlight. "Go to the store and get anything you want. My credit is good and nothing I've got is too good for a boy that will work like you." The corn was out of danger now. The frostbitten blades were safe for the cattle. It is a great thing to have a strong body. I have thought that often.

I would take Black-Boy and go alone into the woods at night for miles and miles. I would trust Black-Boy quicker than I would any person I knew. Black-Boy was a powerful cur. He had hound blood in him. A little hound blood gives a dog a good nose. He had strong front legs, a heavy pair of shoulders, a thin body near his hips. He was built for speed, power, and endurance. He was as vicious as he was powerful. I was not afraid to go anywhere with Black-Boy. I knew the kind of affection he had for me in a time of danger. Though he was nine years old now and his face was getting gray, his teeth were still good. On a night's hunt I would take a lantern, a coffee sack, a mattock, and a couple of books. I would go off in a silent dark hollow and tie the lantern to a tree. I would sit at the base of the tree and study plane geometry and read English—especially the poetry of Robert Burns. I would get interested, and Black-Boy would tree. If he barked fast, I knew I must hurry. If he barked slowly, I took my time. When I got to him, sometimes he would be fighting an opossum. I would put it in the coffee sack and move on to another patch of woods. He would run and bark in an old field. I knew what that was. It was a skunk. I hated to handle them, but there was the money. A skunk hide would bring from one to seven dollars.

This would go on some nights all night long. I have caught as many as eleven opossums with Black-Boy in one night.

That was on a night when he didn't find a skunk. The scent of a skunk always hurt his nose. He could not smell as well afterward. For miles and miles around my home I knew where every persimmon tree of any importance was. I knew where the papaw patches were. I went to those places for opossums. Black-Boy went just as strong at three o'clock in the morning as he did when we started, if he didn't run across a skunk. And one night I remember getting four skunks and one opossum. I made money that night. I hunted over those hills night after night during the autumn season.

I sold the opossums. I sold them to the Negroes for the meat, and I got the hides back. One shipment of fur I recall getting forty-three dollars for. And there was the fun of hunting. I would take Black-Boy when game began to get scarce in the black oak hills and go into the old fields near the town of Greenup. There I found plenty of game. I sat down to figure it out. Fur-bearing creatures are no fools. They learn the fields that are molested less by man and dogs. After I had hunted a valley out, I would tell the boys where I had been getting the game. They were always silly enough to follow where I had gone.

This was the year that I began to try writing poetry. It was because of the wind I heard in the dead leaves and the loneliness of sounds at night. This was my first year to study literature. I had the course under a southern woman, Mrs. Robert Hatton. She was one of the finest teachers I ever had. I knew more grammar when I entered Greenup High School than many pupils who leave high school today, even though I'd had approximately twenty-two months of elementary education in one-room Plum Grove rural school. Grammar came easy to me. I also had the urge to write themes when I entered Greenup High School.

My getting a teacher like Mrs. Hatton was one of the finest things that could have ever happened to me in my youth. Mrs. Hatton was born Hattie McFarland somewhere in Missouri. She was a graduate of the University of Missouri, and she was one of the best-qualified teachers for that day to step inside a high school. She had a major in English, and in music and journalism as well. And she had something else as important as her educational qualifications. She had a deep love for all the pupils she taught. To her, they were her sons and daughters. She was an inspirational teacher.

Mrs. Hatton was tall and slender and she walked slowly. Her voice was soft, and she talked very gently. Her husband, Dr. R. E. Hatton, who was superintendent of the Greenup city schools, walked fast, talked fast, and did everything on the run. They had one son, Robert, six-feet-four, who finished Marshall University at seventeen and in his last two years played college football. I was very fond of the Hatton family.

Where I came to know and love Mrs. Hatton was in the English classroom. Here learning was love, and we never finished a class assignment on time because we discussed so many things. And we accumulated so much work ahead that we held a few extra sessions to complete these assignments. Mrs. Hatton had an English schedule like this: Two days of the week were for grammar; one day for written work; a day for assignments from our literature books; then, one day was given to memory work. There were no more schooldays in the week, but she added more work. We had Literary Current Events, for Mrs. Hatton said there were two kinds of English, written and spoken; and since we spoke more than we wrote, we should be able to stand on our feet and address a group. Since she required us to speak before the class, she said we should give the best current events of the day from the best magazines and papers. In addition to this, we had to read twelve novels each semester and make book reports on these. We had to learn how to outline a novel and a short story. I received under Mrs. Hatton the best English courses I have ever had in my life.

The part of my English class assignments I liked best was "Theme Day." Mrs. Hatton called this period "Creative

Writing." She had her ideas about this, too. We were given freedom in this class to write about any subject we chose. She said the things we knew the most about we could write about with the most enthusiasm, and therefore, she concluded, we could do our best writing on these subjects.

Quickly I learned by experience that this was true. And she let us choose our favorite medium of creative expression —poem, short story, one-act play, and had one of us been ambitious enough, a novel. She never gave us topics unless one of our class asked her for a subject.

I didn't know about as many things then as high-school youth know about today. But I knew another kind of world, all about snakes, terrapins, and toads, lizards, possums, minks, foxes, rabbits, groundhogs. I knew the flora and fauna that covered the landscape. There was hardly a tree in the forest I couldn't identify. I knew and could identify most birds. I knew the predatory birds and animals and those they preyed upon. I knew the habits of wild animals, birds, and reptiles —how they nested or lived in the ground or in hollow trees and whether they gave birth to living species. For instance, the blacksnake, lizards, turtles, and terrapins laid eggs. The poisonous copperheads gave birth to their young. I grew up observing wildlife and living with it. Then, I knew about our domestic animals, for I worked horses and mules, and I fed cattle and milked cows. I wrote about these things.

One of the themes I wrote was about finding a hen's nest in a papaw grove with twenty-two eggs in it. When my mother requested that I remove the eggs from the nest, I left one. The hen went to setting on this one egg and hatched a young rooster. She took him to the hills, scratched for his food, and raised him. He grew up a fighting rooster. He killed our roosters, then went to our neighbors' homes and killed their roosters. Their hens followed him to our home, and we had trouble with people who accused us of stealing their chickens. And I closed this theme with the tragic fate of my rooster. One night a cowardly little screech owl flew in to the white oak tree where he roosted with a number of hens. While my rooster, Nest Egg, was asleep, the owl pecked him to death. Mrs. Hatton gave me an A for this one. She laughed until she wiped tears from her eyes. "It's the best theme that has ever been written in one of my classes," she said. I titled this theme "Nest Egg."

When I went to college, I took "Nest Egg" and other themes I'd written for Mrs. Hatton. Since I entered college with $29.30 in my pocket, I worked a half-day and went to school a half-day but carried a full schedule. Although I never stopped writing themes and poems, I also submitted in my college English classes themes I had written for Mrs. Hatton in high school. And to my amazement, they made A's in college. I submitted "Nest Egg" first, always to the different English teachers I had in college. After graduating from Lincoln Memorial, I went to two more schools. And I submitted "Nest Egg." This theme made twenty-seven A's in all. Twenty years after I had finished high school, I submitted "Nest Egg" to the *Atlantic Monthly*. "Nest Egg" was accepted. Then I knew twenty-seven schoolteachers had been right. "Nest Egg" has since been reprinted in a collection of my stories, and it has been reprinted in a college textbook and high-school literary anthologies. This was written when I was sixteen and a sophomore in Greenup High School.

We had a few pupils who claimed they couldn't write a theme. Mrs. Hatton asked these to write her a letter and tell her why they couldn't write a theme. And several of these letters were read in class, for they were excellent themes. She never had to ask me to write her a letter and tell her why I couldn't write a theme. Since there was no division for the eight grades in Plum Grove, where I had done my first writing, every pupil listened when I read a theme. And many a time, I had everybody in the school laughing. I had already learned that I could create myself an audience by putting words into sentences, sentences into paragraphs, and paragraphs into a theme or story. Now, in Greenup High School, under Mrs. Hatton, I had a different kind of audience, a more critical and a more appreciative one. I found only one fault with "Theme Day." I didn't get to read enough. To say I took only one piece of writing each day to Mrs. Hatton's class, as my classmates will remember, would be an understatement. I have taken as many as twenty-four pieces of creative writing, theses, articles, and poems at one time. If my classmates didn't have their written work, I'd read for all who didn't have, if Mrs. Hatton would permit me. I wasn't exactly bashful.

Mrs. Hatton gave me a volume of Robert Burns's poetry. She read poetry well. She stressed Robert Burns because she loved his verse. I would read his poetry every spare minute I had. I carried his poems wherever I went. I thought I had never heard words more beautiful than those in "Flow Gently, Sweet Afton." It was sung in school once or twice each week. The sentiment of that song choked me, for I loved it deeply. And there was "Highland Mary," "John Anderson My Jo," and "The Cotter's Saturday Night." I feasted on the poetry of Robert Burns. It seemed as if something big in life had taken hold of me. I wanted to write poetry like Robert Burns. He was a Scottish plowboy. I read all that in his life. Now I knew it didn't always take the boys that wore sweaters like Burl Mavis to do things. And my prayer then was to write poetry that would endure like the poetry of Robert Burns.

Until I finished Greenup High School, Robert Hatton, Mrs. Hatton's husband, remained our superintendent and our teacher. I took general science under him. I made an A. He said I had "horse sense." He could teach any subject in the high school. He taught a course in bookkeeping, an elective subject which I took because he taught it. This course gave me trouble. He taught a course in Bible, which we read and discussed from cover to cover. We memorized some of the books of the Bible. Here I found poetry, short stories, and great writing. Then came the subject plane geometry. Here was a subject that gave me plenty of trouble. I finished with a grade D minus. "You finished, Buster, by the skin of your teeth," he said. He called all the boys "Busters" and the girls "Tootsies." "I just hated to fail you."

"Yes, but, Mr. Hatton, I'm not taking that grade," I said. "I won't have it."

"Why, Buster, I stretched a point to give this low grade to you," he said.

"But I don't know any plane geometry," I said. "I don't deserve D minus. I'm taking it over next year. I'm going to learn it." And I had a reason for telling him this. I was taking algebra over and making A's.

Mr. Hatton was a father to all pupils in Greenup High School. Here was a teacher who taught beyond his subject matter. He lectured to us on honesty, manners, morals. He lectured to us about going to college and amounting to something in life. In later years in my teaching I borrowed so many things as teacher and school administrator from this great teacher. He changed our lives by creating in us ambitions and creating in us a sense of purpose. The little Greenup Independent School System had paid high for this man in that day and time. He received the best salary ever paid a superintendent, but he was worth all they paid him and more. He made Greenup High School a first-rate, quality school for that day and time.

I would go home at night and tell my mother that I wanted to do something in life. I told her my plans at the milk gap every evening after spring came on and the cows were turned out on the grass. The second year of high school had taken hold of me tremendously. My mother would be surprised at the things I said to her. She would say: "You know, sometimes I have felt like I would just like to get out and go and go and go. I have felt that these hills could not hold me. And if I had been a man I would have gone. But a mother tied down with a family cannot go. I want to stay and take care of my children. They are all I have that I care anything about. I want to see them well-raised young men and women. And when they go out into the world, I want people to say, 'There is a respectable family of children—the children of Martha Stuart. She tried her best to raise them right and she did.' "

We would talk on at the milk gap. I would try to milk a cow. She would kick the bucket out of my hand. I would want to hit the cow with a stick. "You mustn't hit one of the cows. They feed you half you eat. The way you like milk and then hit a cow! Here, put my apron on, and you can milk that cow. My cows are not used to menfolks." I put the apron on. The cow stood perfectly still. Then I set the bucket on the ground and zigzagged two streams of white milk into the zinc two-gallon water bucket.

It was lonesome to hear the whippoorwills calling and walk over the new-plowed fields in April. When I came in from school I would pull off my shoes and slip into the silence of the evening woods. I would steal quietly. I would watch the young rabbits play in the pasture. I would hear the crows ca-caw in the pine trees. I would take a paper and pencil and go to the pine grove over from the house and write my themes. Mrs. Hatton would say: "There is a flavor of the soil and a picture of the sky and the trees in your themes."

The time had come to sow lettuce and tobacco beds. It was the time to take the mules and go into the fields and plow all day long. James was big enough now to keep the stalks and sprouts cut ahead of the plow. But he was only six, and when night came he would be very tired.

When the red worms came to the top of the ground around the hog pen, it was time to go fishing. We would dig redworm bait and then go to the branch and seine minnows with a coffee sack for bait. "Them crawdads ain't very good bait. I can't have any luck with them," Uncle Rank Larks would always say. James and I would go to the W-Hollow creek. I would teach him how to fish before we went to Little Sandy. I would take a minnow hook. I would catch a fly with my hand—put it on the hook and drop it with a little plop into the water. The minnows would fight over it before one could swallow it. Finally the bottle cork would go under the water, and I'd flip the string tied to the end of a short pole. A silver-colored minnow would gape and wiggle in the wind. "Stand back here so a minnow can't see you. It is always better. Go silently and never shake the brush along the bank. It will be better, you'll learn later. But this doesn't have anything to do with fishing in Little Sandy—only you must learn to keep quiet when you fish and wait a long, long time for a bite sometimes. But keep at it. Change your bait when they don't bite. Different kinds of fish have different tastes. And whatever you do, don't drink water out of these streams. They are dangerous to human flesh." James learned to catch minnows first. He later learned to fish.

But against what I warned him about the treacherous streams, one hot June day he drank from a stream. Typhoid fever lasted for five weeks and one leg was left lame. "The water was clear as the sky," he said, "and it looked good to drink." Do not be deceived by the crystal clearness of high hill water. It is sometimes full of a thousand germs that will put you flat on your back. You will want to die. Your bones ache and your flesh is hot. I have been that way twice because I drank of that beautiful liquid—cool to the parched lips and fine to the taste, yet treacherous as a copperhead.

Once I drank of blue mountain water under the shade of beech trees. I went above and found a dead horse in the stream and two spotted hound dogs pulling carrion from his flanks. I wanted to vomit, but I could not. The buzzards sat upon a dead oak limb in the sun and waited for their share. The buzzards are worth thousands of dollars and save many lives by cleaning the carrion off the land.

During the second summer of my high-school career after the crops were planted, I took a supply of Tennyson's poetry and the songs of Robert Burns and went to live at Carter Caves, free to hunt and swim and just lie back. I went with Tillman Cartwell. We took a small tent and lived in a place called Horseshoe Bottom. That was a drowsy place there.

I would sit at the mouth of a cool cave and read Tennyson for hours. When I left there, I left my books in this cave. I never went back for them. I wrote and told Farmer Rankins, whose land we were on, he could have them for the many good meals I had eaten with him. I directed him in the letter to the cave. "Upon a shelf of rocks, when you first go in at the entrance," I said, "you'll find them, away from the dripping water."

When the last food we had was eaten, we started the twenty-mile walk to the railroad station. We were on our way back to Greenup. Tillman Cartwell would enter school that year as a freshman. He would get along fine.

Back to school again. The pigskin was flying in the air. I had always thought I would play when I put on some more weight. The big fellows had graduated off the team. I was getting to be one of the big fellows there now. Tillman encouraged me: "Get in there, Stuart. You can make the team. You're tough as Spikey. He made it his first year out."

I was introduced to Rawl Briswell. He was the bully of the town and the school's bad boy. It wasn't anything uncommon to see a boy with blood running out of his nose. Ask what was wrong, and someone would say, "W'y, Rawl Briswell hit him." Rawl was six-feet-two and weighed nearly two hundred pounds. The boys in school were afraid of Rawl. He knew it too. He would slap them around any way he pleased. If they didn't like it, he would slap them again. Nothing was said, for there was nothing to say, only that Rawl Briswell did it. There was nothing to do about it. This was his fourth year in school, and he would have one more year to finish. He stayed only to play football and fight. "John Briswell's boy don't go to that school for any good. He just goes there to bully the boys around. It's a bad streak running through his blood."

Tillman Cartwell told me one day that he had heard Rawl talking about me coming in from the country and getting cocky. He told Tillman he was going to take some of it, if not all of it, out of me with his fists. He said he thought he would do it before the day was over. Tillman warned me to watch him. I knew that he was foul in a football game. He would spit his opponent's eyes full of tobacco spittle. The next time he would slug him under the chin with his fist. I have seen boys carried from the field when Rawl hit them. The referee was not wise enough to catch Rawl in the middle of the line. Often he would yell he had been slugged to hide his own foul play.

We were all in the room—a crowd of boys and girls. Rawl came in. He said: "Fee fo fum." I never knew any more until I arose perhaps five minutes afterward. Rawl was laughing and chewing his tobacco in the schoolhouse. I never said anything. There was nothing for me to say. I was weak. My eyes were blacked, and my right eye was closed. I felt ashamed. That was the first time any fellow had ever done me like that. I wanted to sneak out and never come back to the school. That night, going home, I got mad. I thought I ought to conceal a pistol on me and walk up and shoot Rawl.

I told my father about the way it had happened. He said, "You are big enough to take care of yourself. No man would ever do me thataway." But I wouldn't kill Rawl. It was weeks before the black rings left from under my eyes. I could hear people in the town saying: "There goes that boy John Griswell's boy hit. They said he shore beefed him. Hit him right under the eye, and the next thing that Stuart boy knowed, they's a-pouring water on him. I tell you, John's got a bad boy. He'll go to the pen if he don't mind out—that boy will." Then flashes of madness would return to me, and I would want to kill Rawl Briswell. At last I made up my mind to hit him and hit him hard. "Always get a man the first lick. That does the work. Hit him hard too. Stand on your toes and throw your weight behind your fist. Hit him hard the first time. That's the way your Uncle Rank always did."

When I went home that night I got a coffee sack out of the corn crib. I went up in the gap and filled the bottom of it with seventy pounds of sand. I took it inside the smokehouse and fastened it to the pole where we had kept the middlings hanging. Then I took a brush and drew the nearest likeness of Rawl's face I could. I made a long mouth like he had, with corners that dropped. That afternoon I practiced hitting that face with my fists. I would try it with a left and then a right. I was trying to get where I could swing the sack over the pole with my fist. This was in the spring of the year. I did it day after day, week after week. My father would come watch but wouldn't say anything.

One day a crowd of us were in the same schoolroom where I got hit by Rawl. Rawl was in the room. He started to say "Fee fo fum—" but before he had said his battle song completely I drove a left into the flesh of Rawl Briswell's face he'd long remember. As he was sinking to the floor, I followed it with a right to his left jaw. The girls in the room began to scream. The boys closed the windows and held the door—so that there would be no excitement. Rawl came to himself in a room filled with students who were wishing that the two licks had been fatal ones. "Did you hear about that Stuart boy beefing that Briswell boy? I took the wad of tobacco out of his mouth, and that was the whitest boy I've ever seen. He hit him hard enough to kill."

When Rawl came back to school with his eyes blacked, the

teachers never said a word. They were glad it had been done, but they hadn't wanted the trouble of blacking his eyes themselves. It was a greater task than teaching the school. I know I didn't want to do it at the cost of the lick he struck me. When he passed me in the schoolhouse one day he gritted his teeth and said: "I'll get you yet."

I just said, "Rawl, you won't get any boy your size. You won't get me. I'll whip you so quick you won't know that you are whipped." I determined to do it.

The last of the third year passed. I went back to the farm. One more year and I would finish school now. The summer before my senior year in high school I farmed another heavy crop. The new land on our farm was productive. During crop time I sat for the teachers' examination and got a second-class certificate. That was good enough when only twenty-two passed out of forty-four, and I had only twelve credits in high school. After the crops were laid by, I went out and taught in a country school. I told about that in my book *The Thread That Runs So True.* Sixty-eight dollars a month beat making crossties and opossum hunting. It was easy-made money. I paddled a few girls for cursing and chewing tobacco behind the schoolhouse. The old women talked about that young man teacher putting young girls across his lap and using a book on them. "I don't think that is right to paddle a girl. He ought to take a willow switch and tickle her legs. I am afraid my man John will go around there to him if he paddles Susie again." I had a great time with the hill children. I knew them. I was one. They didn't know it, and I didn't tell them. I let the little children play all the time they didn't have to recite. I turned them loose. It did them good. I knew I would not be teaching there long. When I left there I gave the kids a bucket of mixed candy. It was their treat. When I said goodbye, several of them cried and said: "We'll never see you again, Mr. Stuart." Well, they were right. I never went back.

When I returned to Greenup High School I had confidence in myself. I had nearly one hundred dollars now. I bought two new suits of clothes. I stepped out. I was a senior in high school now. I was invited to parties by the friends of Burl Mavis. When a substitute teacher was needed in mathematics or history, I filled the place. And time after time I served for days as a substitute teacher in the grades, making up my high-school work at night. I played football that year and did some punting—something I liked very much to do. I was elected president of the Y.M.C.A. and of the Hi-Y club. I tied for the highest honors in my class. Burl Mavis had dropped from school now. He flunked his final exams when he was a junior. He went back to work in the store. The redheaded girl who had trouble saying "ring, rang, and rung" was married by this time. At least the wedding bells ring, rang, rung for her.

Before I knew it my high-school days were just about over. I had walked the eight miles per day with ease, but during my senior year I stayed one-third of my time in Greenup. I was a welcome member of many families. Now what was there for me to do? I was out of school. Must I go back to the farm? I remembered that on a snowy day in April, 1918, I had broken a path for myself through the snow. I would not stop in my father's broken path. I had said that I would not live among the hills forever and die among them and go back to the dust of the hills like my brothers had. My father would live his life among them. He would give all of himself to the hills, and in the end, the hills would take him back and protect his bones against the elements. And briers and trees would soon cover his grave, and the dead leaves from the trees would hide the print of his grave. Now must I follow my father? I loved him. "Son, I'm in debt for part of this land yet. I'd like for you to go ahead with the work this summer. You know I am not able to hire help, and James is too small to plow."

I thought it over. I told him I would stay for a while. But

all the time I thought of the vows I had made to my mother at the milk gap. One day we took the mules to Greenup. It was the last time they were to see our farm. It was the last time I would follow them in the plow. We traded them for a team of horses. "Horses can stand up on this land now. It is pretty well worn, and there are not many roots in it." My father talked on. "Horses are not so dangerous either. They're not half so bad at kicking as mules. I got a little afraid of that Barnie mule when I went to put hay in his manger by lantern light at night. Mules are bad to kick." But a mule hates to leave a place where he has given the best of his strength to get ready the land for corn and tobacco each spring. We had fought for a home of our own. Why not keep one for the mules? The mules moved on, older and with less strength maybe, to a new home, and the land that they had given their strength to help get in shape went to the horses. "Ain't it funny that a horse in the hills gets a quarter a day for his work and the man gets seventy-five? The horse does more than the man. Ain't it a queer thing?" Uncle Rank Larks asked it that way.

I worked hard with Dad in the fields that fall. We played hard together. But things to me were not what they once were. I dreamed of something beyond the hills. I wanted to go and go and go. I had to do something more.

One night I was sitting in the chip yard talking to my father. I told him fifty acres of land was not a big enough place for me. He sat silently and gazed at a bunch of hollyhocks in the moonlight.

I said, "Dad,"—the moon had come out, and it was the spring of the year; I think a few hollyhocks were budding to bloom—"I would like to go to college." He said, "Jesse, you can't go." Then I turned to him and I said, "Dad, I'm going to amount to something." He looked at me strangely and he said, "Jesse, who told you that?"

I couldn't answer. I had dreams beyond the Greenup

County hills. I took the team in and put it in the barn. I knew my mother would weep when I told her what I was going to do. I went to the house, packed my clothes, packed the themes I had written for Mrs. Hatton, walked downstairs with my suitcase, and I met Mom. Mom said, "Where you going, Jesse?" I said, "I'm leaving home." My mother laughed as she had never laughed before. "Why," she said, "I think it's wonderful, Jesse. Go ahead. Chickens come home to roost. You'll be back." I went up W-Hollow. My dad came around the ridge. I missed him. Good that I missed him, too, for I would never have gotten past him. I arrived in Greenup, Kentucky. Where was I going, with only a few dollars in my pockets? The street carnival was there. The man that took up the tickets at the Merry Mix Up lost his job. I asked for it and got it. I started out with the street carnival, came down back of Cincinnati, played the towns in east Kentucky. Boys and girls would come in and want to spend their money and ride on the Merry Mix Up. They were about my age. I would let them ride. Then they would stand around when they had spent their money and want to ride some more. I would still let them ride some more. Then, if the boy would get off and take up tickets in my place and let me ride around with his girl, we would ride some more. I had fun and then I lost my job.

I read in a newspaper where a man, who became president of a steel company, had hired in as a standby laborer. I said if he could do it, I could do it. The closest steel mill was Auchland, Kentucky—the American Rolling Mills. I went there and got a job as a standby laborer. I worked four days on the outside; then they took me inside. Being a good worker—I'm not bragging when I say that—I went in and started swinging a sledgehammer in a blacksmith's shop. Then one night the men in the shop got drunk. I didn't drink. The boss got out somewhere and started cooking a turtle. He came in and asked me if I would have a piece of this boiled turtle. And I told him no. I stayed with some razor-blade steel and kept thirty thousand dollars worth of it from burning. The next day I was promoted to a blacksmith at the American Rolling Mills. Now I paid up my bills in town and was a few dollars ahead.

But something happened. The leaves turned color again; September had come. What is it about September with teachers and school people, when the leaves turn color and you see the children going down the dusty road to the little school, walking down the leaf-strewn city streets to the high school? You see the football in the air, and the young teacher uneasy in the schoolyard, and the new boy being sized up, and the books under the arms . . . something gets under our skins.

Chapter 3

I SHIPPED MY TRUNK TO BEREA
College, Berea, Kentucky. I followed on the highway. I had
thirty dollars in my pocket. I carried a dollar suitcase in my
hand. It was pasteboard. I got it at a dry-goods store in Ashland, Kentucky. I had a couple of changes of clothes in the
suitcase and some sandwiches. I had my books in the trunk,
a sweater, an old worn-out overcoat, two quilts, and a pillow.
I had no real suit of clothes at this time. I had a blue coat that
I combined with a pair of blue sailor pants for a suit.

It was fun thumbing my way across Kentucky. The open
air of the shaggy eastern Kentucky hills blew on my face. It
tasted clean. I loved to breathe it. It was different from the
filthy air at the steel mills. It was an air slightly tinged with
the smell of autumn leaves. The leaves had begun to color
now. The white clouds floated over the high blue skies. The
buzzards sailed in circles over the old pasture fields. The
crows flapped their wings and cawed on trees by the road-
side. This reminded me of the freedom I had once known.
It was great to be out again and feel the wind and sun on one's
face. Life was great.

It took me two days to reach Berea. I was not an artist at thumbing my way. I slept in a haystack the first night. It was out in a small meadow by a creek somewhere east of More-head, Kentucky. I felt fresh the next morning after I washed my face in the stream and cleaned my teeth. I went back to the highway, and at a little country store I breakfasted on a couple of eggs and a cup of coffee. I took the eggs raw and the coffee hot. Then I stepped out on the highway.

I never knew it, but what I needed then was a couple of signs on my pasteboard suitcase and a freshman cap on my head. Or a sweater with a big G or a big F across the front would do. Just something for identification to show that I was a schoolboy. But it was hard for me to get a ride. I was too brown to pass for a schoolboy. I looked like a man used to work. I looked like a farmer tanned in a hay field.

At five o'clock that afternoon I was at the depot at Berea, Kentucky. My trunk was there. I went up on the campus. It was the first college campus I had ever been on and the first college I had ever seen. It was a great place to me. Now the next problem I had was getting in. (Sure, I had wanted to go to Harvard. But I didn't think about that now.) My only desire was to stay at Berea. A thought came to me: "I will see Will Sears. He is a senior in Berea now. He passed through the hills of Kentucky three years before and sold me a Bible. He was selling Bibles, he told my mother and me, to pay his way through school. She bought a Bible, and so did I. I think Will can help me. He is from Tennessee. I'll look him up."

The first boy I met on the campus had only one arm. "Hello, Buddy. Say, can you tell me where Will Sears rooms?"

"Will Sears? I don't know Will Sears. How is he classified, do you know?"

"He's a senior this year if he hasn't flunked any courses," I said.

"Well, I'm only in the fifth grade. I don't know any college seniors. You meant he was a college senior, didn't you?"

"Yes."

"No, I don't know him."

"Well, this is none of my business, but how old are you?"

"I'll surprise you, I guess. But I'm coming twenty-seven this October."

"How did you lose that arm?"

"I don't guess it's none of your damn business nohow." He moved on.

I went up to the Y.M.C.A. building. It was a little house set over under some oak trees. I went in and called for Will Sears. "Will is down in Georgia selling Bibles this year. He hasn't come yet. We're looking for him most any day now. Is there anything I can do for you?"

"Yes. I want to get into Berea College. Can you help me to do that?"

"Have you ever sent in your applications?"

"Yes. I've tried three times. Three times I've been rejected. Now, I want to talk to the president of Berea."

"Maybe the reason you didn't get in was because you don't live in the mountains."

"I live far enough back in the hills that the hoot owls holler in the daytime. They mistake daytime for night; the hollow is dark and deep. The sun never shines on our house except for a couple of hours in the afternoon. They always write and tell me the college is crowded."

"Wash some of the dust and sweat off your face and put on a clean shirt and we'll go over and see the dean. The president isn't here. He's on a business trip up east. Get him a towel and some soap, Charlie."

After a general clean-up we walked out across the campus toward the dean's house. Squirrels played under the oaks. A lazy wind dragged through the dying leaves. Boys and girls laughed and talked to each other on the byways. They were all happy, it seemed. "College is a great place, and tomorrow

I may be one of the group," I thought. I knew I would never go back to the steel mills. I might never go back to the farm.

"Dean, here is a boy that wants to enter Berea College."

"Stuart is my name."

"I'm glad to know you, Mr. Stuart. Where are you from? Sit down there in the rocker—or on the sofa. Just any place."

"I'm from Greenup, Kentucky."

"Why is it you want to come to Berea College, Mr. Stuart?"

"The first reason is, it is a place where a man can work his way when he doesn't have money and just has to pay a little when he does have money. The second reason is, it is a good school."

"Mr. Stuart, do you place Berea College above all other schools?"

"No, sir, I do not. I put Harvard, Vanderbilt University, and the University of Virginia above Berea College."

"Well, Mr. Stuart, why don't you attend one of your favorite schools?"

"I don't have the money. And I prefer Berea College to any of the other small schools."

"Well, Mr. Stuart, to make a long story short, we have one hundred and five students on our waiting list, and we can't use you until next year, and maybe not then. But I'll tell you a place where you can go. I have a very dear friend teaching there. He was at Berea for twenty years and now he is dean of Lincoln Memorial in Harrogate, Tennessee. If you go there, you tell him I sent you. His name is Charles D. Lewis. Make the best of life. I'm sorry we can't keep you here. Good-bye."

He closed the door in a kindly way. I went back to the little plank Y.M.C.A. house under the trees. I got my old paper suitcase with the end mashed out of it where I had sat on it waiting for rides along the highway for the past two days. I started out of the door.

"Have any luck?" said the boy who had taken me to the dean's home.

"Not a bit."

"Too bad. You're not leaving, are you?"

"Yes, I'm going to Harrogate, Tennessee, tonight."

"You are going to Lincoln Memorial then, I suppose."

"I had never heard of Lincoln Memorial before. Yes, I'm going to try."

"You've got three hours yet before the train runs. You can just wait and go to chapel with us."

The chapel was a big place to me. The college students got the finest seating section in the auditorium. On one side of the college auditorium were the academy students, on the other side were the foundation-school students. Up in the balcony were the normal-school students. The auditorium was crowded. It was hot inside. The bugs flew in at the windows and swarmed around the lights. The orchestra played "My Old Kentucky Home." A violin string broke, and the temperamental music director flew into a rage. No one laughed. They all took it seriously. A man spoke a few words in high tenor praise of Berea College. A woman from Ireland got up and said: "I'm glad Berea is my alma mater. It is known all over the world—in Ireland as well as over this great land of America." The children in the foundation shouted in applause. The college students, normal students, and students of the academy clapped their hands. A man led in prayer, and we were dismissed.

When I went out of the chapel door, I was tapped on the shoulder. I looked around. Here was the one-armed boy, the first I met on the Berea campus. "Say, I thought I'd ask you how you expect a fellow to know Will Sears when they's twenty-six hundred students here. Found him yet?"

The train left Berea at 10:30. I rode in the smoking car and talked to three boys that had been sent away from Berea for smoking. "Hell, they can a man up there fur purt' nigh anything. Old Baldy even gets out at night and crawls around on his hands and knees looking for cigarette butts. He finds 'em too, under the boys' windows at Hanley Hall. Then he goes up and smells in the rooms. He's got a nose like a hound dog. He shore does get the boys. We throwed a cigar down on his head that had fire on it. He come up from on his hands and knees a-whooping and a-hollering. I say he did." The boys laughed then.

The train rattled on into the night. The wind, filled with small cinders, blew alongside the moving train. At a distance from Berea College I could see from the train window long blue lines of hills in the moonlight. The corn was cut in the fields and I could see the shocks of corn in the moonlight. I could also see the moonlight on the coloring leaves and on the old pasture fields as the train moved on into the night.

Morning came and I got off at Harrogate. There wasn't any depot at Harrogate. It was a wide-open country place.

"Where is Lincoln Memorial?" a girl asked me.

"I don't know. I'm hunting for Lincoln Memorial too."

"Right this way. This way. Bring your baggage and get in for Lincoln Memorial." A freckle-faced boy stood next to a Ford truck. We all piled in. The girls, two of them, rode in the front seat, and the boys stood up in the truck bed. It was only one mile to the school. We were soon there.

"Say, Jim, a body would have to use a microscope to find Lincoln Memorial after he gets here. Where is the place, anyway?"

"You see this tall grass around here, don't you? Lincoln is hidden in the grass. You'll soon find her when we get all this grass cut and all that mountain of corn you see over there in the valley cut. We've got forty acres of hay to rake and God knows how many potatoes to dig. We've got to build some new hen houses over on the chicken farm, paint the dairy barn, and lay three miles of water pipes. You'll find out where Lincoln Memorial is when we get all this done."

We formed a line at the auditorium-gymnasium down under some locust trees on the campus. I was on the end of the line. I didn't have any money, and I didn't want other students to hear me tell Charles D. Lewis that I had none.

It was eleven o'clock before I reached the dean. I handed him my registration card. "Are you able to pay all your expenses here?"

"I'm able to pay ten dollars for this quarter, and that is all. I want work. I figure I can work a half-day and go to school the other half."

"I know, but that is very little money for you to expect to start your first year's work on. Can't you get any from home?"

"No, sir, this is all I can get." I didn't want to tell him I had run away from home.

"Where are you from, Stuart?"

"Northeast Kentucky."

"I'm from Kentucky too. I grew up in the mountains of Kentucky—back where the hoot owls holler in the daytime." He laughed.

"I'm from that land too, where the hoot owls holler in the daytime."

He laughed again. "Does anybody here know you? I have never gotten an application from you. When did you decide to come here?"

"No one here knows me. I have never sent you an application, either. I never decided to come here until ten o'clock last night. I made an attempt to get into Berea College last evening. The dean sent me here. He said he knew you well. He said that I was to tell you to enroll me as a student here and give me a job." The dean had never told me that at Berea. But anyway, maybe it helped to get me enrolled as a freshman at Lincoln Memorial.

"What kind of work have you done?"

"I have done farmwork, taught school, cut timber, worked

for contractors, dug ditches, spread concrete. I can do mostly anything. By trade I'm a blacksmith."

"We don't have any blacksmith work around here. We'll find a place for you on the farm. Wait a minute until I call Anthony."

That afternoon I went to work in a hay field with seven men. The tractor windrowed the timothy and clover hay across the long field. Each boy took a pitchfork and stacked the hay in what Anthony called "doodles." The field was long, and the hot September sun came down and burned where our shirts fitted tight across our shoulders. The smell of clover hay and the flying dust from the tractor wheels filled our nostrils. There was a spigot out in the middle of the field. The other boys kept going for water. Once I saw them all get together, and I heard one say, "Let's work that damn Yankee to death. What do you say?"

"It suits me."

"Me, too."

"Now, let's move a little faster with our windrows. Then we'll make him follow."

They hurried their work along faster and faster. I increased my pace and stayed with their lead men. They went for water too often. I soon took the lead. I could stand the heat better. I was hardened, too, by the work at the mills. I was not playing around like the students usually did under a boss from their own midst.

The boys got together again and talked. I could not understand what was said, for the tractor was straining up the west slope of the hay field. When we had started back to work, a tall, sweaty, long-faced boy came over to the outside windrow I was working on and said: "Say, feller, there's a boy over here by the name of Claymore Jones. And this boy Claymore takes fits. Old Claymore is a good feller. He's all right when he gets over one or before he takes one. If he takes one, you just get outen his way. I just thought I'd come over and tell you about Claymore, for he usually makes for a stranger when one of them fits comes on him." And the boy went back.

It was getting near quitting time. I thought it was a made-up piece of work. I knew what I was going to do when Claymore took his fit. I was going to sober him with a pitchfork. It was a sure cure for frame-up fits.

I heard a noise. It was first like dogs a-barking, then like a mad, bellowing bull—spittle was flying from Claymore's mouth as if he was having a fit. He came right toward me. His hands were spread, and he was clawing the wind. I stepped back. He thought I had started to run. The fellows were laughing. I hit Claymore with a nice swing of the pitchfork. The steel part of the fork hit him alongside the short ribs. He fell to the ground. The boys came over. "No prongs went in me," he told the boys, "but the lick has shortened my breath." I walked off the field. No one followed me. They remained with Claymore.

Lincoln Memorial stands at the foothills of the Cumberlands. The scenery of the place is the finest I have ever seen. It is not surpassed by any place in all the eastern United States, I have been told. Grant-Lee Hall is located on a spur of a Cumberland foothill. On the south slope is an apple orchard. On the east slope, which runs down into Democrat Hollow, grow many tall elm trees; on the west slope, a blue stream of water runs and sinks into an underground cavern that takes the waters from Democrat Hollow too. North of the Hall is a water tank. It is painted gray with blue letters standing for Lincoln Memorial. North of the water tank are the wooded mountain slopes, and at the edges of these woods are fields of pasture daisies. They looked like blooming fields of white cotton.

At Lincoln Memorial dining hall, ten students ate at each table. The tables, of poplar and pine planks, were made by students at the woodworking shop under the supervision of

Anthony. They never used cloths on the tables. When we went in for dinner, breakfast, or lunch, we gathered in our regular places. The matron tapped the bell at the faculty table, said the same blessing at every meal, and after the blessing was said, we sat down, and the first ones that got the food were often the only ones fed. I almost starved my first two months at Lincoln Memorial. But I got used to it. I learned to slip a little bread into my pockets and reach and grab like the other students did at the tables. Three hundred students ate in this dining room. Many of us boys worked. We ate heartily. We were always hungry.

There were approximately seven boys to three girls in Lincoln Memorial. The matron of the hall managed to get at least one girl to every table to make the boys behave. If a table was filled with only boys, they threw bread, they stuck their forks into the soft pine wood—they nearly wrecked the table —threw pepper into each other's eyes; and a girl at a table made a difference. She was the hostess and passed the food. It stopped the boys from hogging over the food and kept me from putting bread into my pockets. But I soon learned to find a table where there were more girls than boys. Girls ate less. I found a table where there were seven girls and three boys. Then I began to get enough to eat.

One night at a table in the dining hall, I heard a girl cry out, "Let loose of my leg, you damned old fool, Paul Sykes." Everybody laughed. Paul Sykes had reached under the table and pinched Primrose Halton's leg. The boys stuck their forks into the soft pine tables and laughed and threw biscuits.

My classwork was stiff, and the work I did in the fields helped to make it stiffer. I attended classes during the forenoon. In the afternoons I worked for four hours. On Saturdays I worked all day. At noon, morning, or night, when a student wanted off in the kitchen, I asked to do the work and make something extra. I wrote themes and history term papers as a sideline. I wrote themes for my roommate, and in return he helped me to understand algebra. I wrote a term paper on Mary Stuart, Queen of Scots, that served its purpose in both English and history classes. It made two B's for me and six A's for other students. Once a student handed in one of Woodrow Wilson's speeches, copied word for word, for a term paper. It came back filled with corrections. "You will have to rewrite this paper. You don't have the right angle on your subject matter. Your English is terrible." The student flunked the course. I studied all day on Sundays. I tried to make good. I tried to make what the teachers called "good."

My teachers were a varied lot. I particularly remember Henry Dickinson, a real live wire. He taught psychology, and I had a class with him both summers I spent at L.M.U. When he taught our class, this six-foot four-inch man, who played tennis and baseball when not teaching psychology, would jump up from a standing position on the floor to the top of a table, and there he would flap his arms as a rooster flaps his wings before he crows. He also crowed like a rooster and cackled like a hen. He said he did this to get our attention and our reactions. Well, he got mine, all right! I was all in favor of this lively, energetic man. He put himself unselfishly into his teaching. I was so much for him that I memorized all the important parts of the dry-as-dust textbook.

Professor Dickinson was criticized by many because of his actions, but he was never criticized by me. He got my response in laughter and in liking his course—under this man I made a standing-up A, best in his psychology class. In his class I never thought about grades! I thought about what he was saying. And I never missed one of his lectures. I went out of my way to take Henry Dickinson's classes.

Not so many years later, while he was still young, cancer mowed down this powerful athlete and wonderful teacher.

Science was a required subject at Lincoln Memorial. I had to take biology and have a passing grade before I could graduate. Professor Frank C. Grannis was head of the Science

Department. My problem in biology was I couldn't cut up a living frog to watch its heart beat after it had been dissected. I couldn't cut open a living blacksnake to check for protozoa in its stomach.

Two girls in our class did my dissecting for me. They planned to be doctors, but they never made it. Professor Grannis laughed at my feelings. Then there was a student, Henry Willis, who called me a "softie" and a "bleeding heart."

"I won't cut up a frog, and I won't cut open a blacksnake," I told him. "But if you will go outside this science laboratory, I will cut you up for good. I've had enough of you."

But in a course I detested I made a B or a C. I don't remember. I don't care. I'll never forget the inhuman feeling for life in Professor Grannis' biology class. There were those who said he was a fine teacher. Maybe so. But I never said it. I thought he was a mediocre teacher without any feeling for life. When I took protozoology under him to complete enough hours for my required science, I used timothy hay and warm water to produce protozoa. When I produced life, even when it was in microcosm, I was delighted. I was creating something. I made no bones about not liking the man. But I am grateful to Lucille Jordan, who helped me to get through biology, a dreaded course. She cut up frogs for me. The two languages at Lincoln Memorial, German and French, were taught and controlled by two of the best-educated teachers on the campus. As far as I know, Dr. Lucia Danforth was the only teacher at Lincoln Memorial in my time there with a Ph.D. She was not my teacher. I studied German but the reason I mention her is because everyone who studied German became involved in a continuous feud between Dr. Danforth and the German teacher Madame Eppinger. This feud spread beyond languages. The German and French languages at Lincoln Memorial could have been called Germany and France. There was a borderline between these worlds, strong feelings in a world of the mind, and no one dared to cross into the other's world. There was no Alsace Lorraine. Though not a French native Dr. Danforth spent more time in France than many French nationals. She lived and breathed France in Tennessee. Her literature, music, and art were all French. She had but little to do with me, because I chose German. The reason for my choice was the teacher. Madame Eppinger was delightful and friendly. She was born and educated in Dresden.

Madame Eppinger's German classes were never as large as Dr. Danforth's French classes. Word got around that German was a more difficult language than French. Maybe this was why Dr. Danforth's French classes were filled to capacity.

Madame Eppinger often deviated from her subject matter. She would tell us about the Germany she knew from childhood. She told us about their system of education and about the good beer in Germany. "France, with her sweet wine," she'd say in her broken English. "Wine makes the head woozy!"

She told us how the Germans liked to eat and to drink their beer. She taught us Germany as well as the language. She taught us the world she knew in Germany before World War I. Madame Eppinger never lived to see the devastation of Germany in World War II.

We loved to hear her talk, and loved to be invited to her home on the campus. She cooked German dishes. I was always hungry, and her food, I thought then, was the best. She made me want to visit Germany and France to make my own comparisons of the countries and of the "the sweet wine" that made the head "woozy" and the German beer. While Madame Eppinger entertained us at her home, Dr. Danforth was entertaining her French students in a home which she had built and where she lived alone.

When Dr. Danforth and Madame Eppinger met on the

campus, I don't know whether they even spoke to one another. I believe their feud reached the no-speaking point. With these two women teaching German and French, our Spanish teacher became an unknown, and the Spanish language virtually died on our campus. Besides, our handsome male Spanish teacher went behind the campus shrubbery, half-hidden from students who were passing by, and used these bushes for an outdoor toilet.

The two women's strong personalities had an influence on our campus literary efforts. The Madame Eppinger creative-writing students in spring, summer, and autumn met under one big eucalyptus tree. Here we read our poems, stories, one-act plays, and articles to each other and received comments from members of our group. Under another tree about fifty feet away, Dr. Danforth's larger group would be reading their work and making comments. Here was that invisible dream world of Germany under our tree and Dr. Danforth's perfect France under the other. Since we students at Lincoln Memorial had to create most of our entertainment, as our school was in the country in a small village, about all we could do was work and think.

Twenty years later, on one of my returns to Lincoln Memorial, I was led in the direction of our two literary trees.

"Look up there won't you!"

"I can't believe it," I said.

But it was true. The large tree where Dr. Danforth's literary influence had reached high proportions was dead. I knew I was looking at it. But their competitive influence had not died and would not die. It would go on and on, as big waves go out when a stone is thrown into the water. The waves get smaller and smaller, but they continue to go on and on.

One of the people I remember most fondly wasn't a faculty member at all. She was the school nurse. She was everything to L.M.U. students—pretty, thirtyish, unmarried Ida Shipley. I would like to know how many lonely mountain boys like myself and girls who weren't able to go home or go any place on weekends and vacations she took in her T-Model runabout Ford to visit a mountain town and to see a movie on a Sunday afternoon. She broke the monotony of continuous school study and hard labor for me many times. I would like to know how many young men in Lincoln Memorial were secretly in love with this nurse because of her thoughtfulness, her kindness, and her attractiveness.

Once, after eating lunch in the L.M.U. dining room and after drying the pots and pans that Parker Sears had washed, I was still hungry. I'd not had enough lunch. Knowing where the canned food was stored in the L.M.U. kitchen, I waited until everyone was gone and I got myself a can of pork-and-beans and a slice of bread. I got a can opener and on my way back to Grant-Lee Hall, a quarter of a mile away, I stopped in the old L.M.U. gym to eat my pork-and-beans cold. I never had better-tasting food. I finished the pork-and-beans and sopped the can with my bread.

That afternoon I became sick. My roommate, Mason Gardner, summoned our nurse. I became so sick that I lost consciousness. But I remembered Ida Shipley's words: "Jesse, if something happens to you, tell us who to notify." Miss Shipley and Mason Gardner thought I was a goner. And I would have been if I hadn't vomited up that can of stolen pork-and-beans, which left a green stain on the floor of our room that wouldn't come out with a week of scrubbing. Not until Gardner and I later used a sander on our floor to remove it.

I had ptomaine poison from eating stolen food from a can. And I still remember my half-thoughts, blurred, when I was so sick—how could my poor parents get my dead body from L.M.U.? And what would they think of their son, of whom they were so proud because he was in college, getting poisoned on a can of pork-and-beans he had stolen.

It took me a week to recover. Miss Shipley said I came closer to dying than any student she had ever attended at

L.M.U. We didn't have a hospital or a college physician at L.M.U. All I had was our Miss Shipley, who doctored me days and nights. It was embarrassing for me to tell Miss Shipley I had stolen a can of pork-and-beans from the dining room and had eaten the whole can in the gym. I told her I was hungry, and she understood. In fact, she laughed and I loved her more than ever.

"Stuart, would you like to add some honor points to your record at L.M.U.?" Gardner, my roommate, asked me.

"Sure, I would," I told him. "How can I do it?"

"Leave it to me to find out," he said. "Word soon gets out when we get a high grader around here where it seems to be an honor to flunk a student. You told me about losing that A in Geology. To make it up, take Education under Professor Woodward. It's a real crip course!"

I had seen handsome W. S. Woodward, tall and straight as a ramrod with a Gary Cooper face, only much older, smoking his cigar. There was always a trail of aromatic smoke trailing this professor.

I did as my roommate suggested. I registered for this "crip course." All we did was follow the dry-as-dust textbook which Professor Woodward called "the Bible of Education." We never discussed a school problem. We never deviated from the text which had none of the problems I'd encountered as a young teenage teacher in a one-room school.

At the end of the course and after we had taken our final examination and I was the last student in the classroom, Professor Woodward asked me to come up to his desk.

"Stuart, I know you just took this course for credit," he said. "I am sure you're never going to be a teacher. You're not of the right temperament for a teacher. I've been debating whether to give you a B plus or an A minus. Now, you fall right into this category."

"I hope the A minus, Sir," I said.

"Well, I'll tell you what I'll do," he spoke pleasantly and

smiled. "If you'll go buy me a twenty-five-cent cigar [he told me his brand] that will make the difference between B plus and A minus. A minus your grade will be! I disagree with Woodrow Wilson's Vice President—let's see, what was his name—ah, shucks, I can't think of it at the moment [neither one of us could think of his name]. Well, forget his name and let's not overtax our minds trying to remember, but what we need in these flourishing times is a good twenty-five-cent cigar."

"Say, Professor Woodward, I have a better idea," I said. "When you give me this A minus, it will go on my record as A if ever a transcript of my grades goes out. Why don't you let me get you two twenty-five-cent cigars and you give me a standing-up A without any trimmings!"

"A smart young man," he said. "It's a fine idea!"

"When do you want these cigars?"

"As soon as you can get them!"

I left the classroom in a hurry. I didn't have a penny in my pocket. I looked up Gardner, my roommate, and asked to borrow fifty cents. He let me have the money. I went straight to a store in Cumberland Gap, Tennessee, and bought the two cigars. Professor Woodward got his cigars and I got my A.

At the end of the first quarter I stood fourth on the honor roll at Lincoln Memorial. My grades were not high. But good grades were hard to make at Lincoln Memorial. I had worked for all I got. I was in line for a scholarship if it took grades to get one.

My work got harder all the time in the fields. One of the boys I raked hay with the first day I went to Lincoln Memorial told Anthony that I had taken a fit and hit Claymore with a pitchfork. I never knew it then. I learned this later. But I noticed that Anthony would never get near me. He always put me to work in a place by myself. The first work I did was dig potatoes, then help to fill the silo, cut corn, and rake leaves. After the leaves had fallen from the trees and the corn was all cut, I helped to lay the water line from the mountaintop to Harrogate, Tennessee. It was zero weather, and a water pipe often broke loose at the joints, and we were wet from head to foot. We had to dig the ditch for the pipes. Often we had to go many feet down through the frozen earth and the hard clay soil and the rock. It was half a winter's work for fifty boys working one-half day all week and all day on Saturday.

When the water line was laid, I went to work at a stone crusher. At this stone crusher we dynamited the limestone rocks out of a small cedar-covered hill, beat them with sledge-hammers and crowbars, and then we wheeled them in Irish buggies to a crusher. We put them in the crusher, crushed the stone into a fine powder to fertilize the Lincoln Memorial farm and put on the walkways over the campus. We used different burrs in the crusher and crushed a coarser limestone and sold it to the State Highway Commission of Tennessee as ballast to use on their highways.

I had written and told my mother, in the meantime, that I was in Lincoln Memorial, at Harrogate, Tennessee. She told the neighbor women about it. She told Brother Tobbie. Brother Tobbie told her to bring me home. "Write and make that boy of yourn come home. That college will send him right to hell. He was a right pert boy before he left here. Get him back. Just write and tell 'em you'll git the law after 'em. Hoss that boy right back here. This world don't need no eddicated people. What this world needs is more people with salvation."

Many of the neighbors talked it over. I had run away from the hills. I had left my home. There was not much to me. I was a runaway. I wasn't anything. Mom told them that I was in college. She told them she was proud of me. They could not understand why she was proud of me. I had run away.

I would never return. When Mom wrote to me, she would always tell me what these neighbors had been saying and how she would defend me. Her letters, poorly as they were written, read like the best parts of a good novel. She could express herself in words that I could understand.

One fellow on the campus of Lincoln Memorial was called Ron East. Ron was a leader among the students. He was a young minister and wrote poetry. He was six feet three inches tall and was a powerful athlete. He was elected to more offices of organizations than he could fill. We exchanged poetry with each other that we had written. We went onto the mountaintops and walked at night. On Sunday afternoons we went out on the mountains and across the old fields. Ron would preach at the little mountain churches and I would go with him. Autumn in the mountains of eastern Tennessee is beautiful. No place else is it quite so splendid. I thought Ron East was the finest man I'd met in Lincoln Memorial. He was working his way in Lincoln Memorial too. He dried dishes.

When December came, I wanted to go home. I was homesick. It had been a long time since I'd seen my people. Seasons had come and gone. I wondered about home. I wondered how they were getting along without my help. I would go home this Christmas. But I did not have the money —how could I? It was all I could do to stay in Lincoln Memorial. I had thumbed part of my way to Lincoln Memorial. I could thumb all my way back.

The Christmas holidays came. When I saw the students leaving Lincoln Memorial for their homes, I could hardly stand it to see them go. I wanted to go too. But it would be hard to thumb rides on the highways. A cold December rain was falling, and muddy water ran across the highways and in little ditches by the highways. But that was not going to stand in my way. I was going to try it anyway.

I went to see if Ron had any money. "I have one dollar,

Stuart. It is every cent of money I have. You are welcome to it."

"I don't have a cent. I hate to take the last penny you have. But I'll need a dollar on a trip like this, three hundred and twenty miles, and the rain still pouring down."

"Yes, you'll need a dollar, all right, and then some. I've done a lot of thumbing. I have gone that far on a dollar, but I'd hate to do it at a time like this. Try it if you like."

I took the dollar from Ron, and the old paper suitcase, and through the cold gray December rain I went on the highway. Around me were mountains with their tops hidden by the clouds. Sheets of fog lay in the valleys. The sides of the mountains were drab-colored. The trees that had worn many-colored robes when I first came to Harrogate, Tennessee, were now barren, and the wind and rain beat through their bare branches. The huge rock ribs in the side of the mountain looked like scaly monsters getting soaked in the rain. But the holly bushes were green, and the pines and the mountain ivy.

I caught seven rides before I made the first twenty miles. One of the rides was in a jolt wagon for three miles. The other rides were in feed trucks and coal trucks. But I didn't care what I rode in, or how wet I got. I was going home— going home! All the touring cars that passed me were loaded. And those that were not loaded would not stop.

It was getting late now, and I had started at nine o'clock that morning. I had covered only twenty-seven miles. Darkness came early on that short, gray December day. I was standing by the highway, and a quarter-ton Ford truck rolled up by me and stopped. "Which way you going, buddy?" His voice was rough. He spoke broken English.

"Going north."

"Get in out of the rain and let's go." I wanted to put my arm around him. A ride at last! We went moving slowly northward.

We passed two fruit trucks going north. Each had "Florida Fruit" in big black letters written on the yellow side. We reached Corbin, Kentucky. We asked a fellow on the street which was the highway leading north. He pointed it out to us. We took this road, and soon again we met two large fruit trucks going south. They were exactly the same kind of trucks, and I remarked to my friend that the driver of one of the trucks was fat and had a light moustache like the fellow we had overtaken less than an hour ago. "The mountains are getting higher. This shouldn't be true, and us going north."

"Now, you are young and restless and excited. I am an old man. I have had lots of experience. I know what I am doing. You leave it to me."

When we had two blowouts at one time and had to stop, we were at Four Miles, Kentucky. We were within twenty miles of Lincoln Memorial. "I thought we were coming south all the time. I could tell by the mountains getting higher."

"You never thought anything of the kind. I should not have picked you up. I was talking to you and made this mistake. Now we are in a mess." He went around to the back of the truck and got us a couple of apples apiece. "Well, let's drive her back up the road a piece and park. I have blankets in this box here in the back of the truck. We can take them out and wrap up together. The rain can't go through them. I have an old oilcloth I can spread over the blankets. It would be fine if we could find a barn someplace." We drove up the highway on two flats. We stopped by a little plank house by the side of the road. We parked the truck. We got out, and investigated the house.

We found that chickens had once roosted in this house, but now there were none. The manure had dried on the shaky floor. He held the toy flashlight while I took a board and raked the dry manure off the planks. We knew that the wet blankets would dampen the dry manure, and the heat of our blankets against the manure, after our bodies had warmed them, would create a terrible smell, and the manure would stick to the blankets. I was a little afraid of a light in a hen house. I thought somebody might be living close and shoot into the building. We got the blankets from the box in the back of the truck. They were damp. There were four of them. We put the wettest blanket on the floor. We put a dry one on top of that to be against our bodies. We put a dry blanket over our bodies, and on top of that dry blanket we put another wet one. I pulled off my coat and shoes. My friend pulled off his coat, pants, and shoes. We rolled up close together.

"You know, I got a girl about your age, and four boys older. But me and my wife, we separated, and she ruined me. I had some money, but she sued me and got it all. Now I am an old man ready to die. I am very tired too. And I don't have anything but this old truck and these blankets and five dollars. And I've got to go back to Michigan on that."

"Where have you been in the South? And what is your name?"

"My name is Frederick Menkovitch. I have been down in Florida. I have been following the boom. I am a carpenter by trade. I made good money for two years. Then I turned around and invested it in land. The price of land dropped to the bottom. The bottom fell out of the price, I mean, and I was left without anything. So I am on my way back home." We went to sleep.

That night, at above twelve o'clock, Menkovitch woke me up with threats and curses. "I'll kill ye. Ye damn right I will. By God, I'll do it!" I got out of the bed and broke off a piece of a rail the chickens had once roosted on. If one of us had to die, it would be he unless he shot me with a gun. The skies had cleared now. The stars had come out into the blue December sky. And the moonlight and the starlight shone through the broad hen-house window, screened over with chicken wire. Menkovitch dozed off to sleep again. His curses

TO TEACH, TO LOVE

got softer and softer, even down to a whisper. But I did not
go back to bed. I stayed up the rest of the night, wrapped in
a blanket with a piece of the chicken roost in my hand.

At daybreak, a farmer walked into the hen house and introduced himself as Tillman. I told him who I was. Menkovitch
told Tillman his name. "Boys, this is my hen house, and if I'd
a-knowed you fellows was up here, I'd a-come up here and
got you and tuck you down to the house and give you a better
bed. I am a man of the Lord, and this is a shame for me to
let two fellows sleep in my hen house. Come on down to the
house and git you some breakfast."

We followed Mr. Tillman down the path that led from the
highway to his house. We went into the mountain home. It
was very much like the home I was from. "Here, meet the
better part of my life. This is Mr. Stuart. This is Mr. Menkovitch, Mrs. Tillman."

"I didn't quite get the last name."

"My name is Menkovitch, Mrs. Tillman."

"Wash your faces. Here is hot water in the teakettle. Here
is a bar of soap, and over there is a clean towel. Breakfast will
be ready for you when you are ready for it. I ain't getting
anything extra. I didn't know I was going to have company.
I guess you can stand for one meal what we have to live on
all the time."

We sat down at a table filled with food. We had coffee,
black and strong. The steam rose from the pot and the coffee-
cups up over the table. We had hot fluffy biscuits. They were
white as cotton inside. We had apples, berries, peaches, cherries, and pear preserves. We had butter, ham, and brown
gravy. We had sorghum and a dish of honey, white in the
comb, stacked upon a plate. I never sat down to a breakfast
like it. "Martha, I guess Mr. Stuart is used to more than this
to eat. He told me up there in the hen house a while ago
that he was from Lincoln Memorial." My mouth was too
full to answer. This food tasted good. It was all I had had

since the morning before but a couple of apples.

I had one dollar, but I did not intend to spend it. "Now, boys, reach and help yourselves. Just feel like you was eating at home. You know you are welcome here."

"Have some ham, Mr. Menkovitch, and some gravy."

"No, madam, I don't eat meat on Friday. It is against my religion. I am a Catholic."

Mrs. Tillman acted like she had been hit above the eye with a brick. Mr. Tillman sat silent.

Then Menkovitch said: "They tell me the Kentucky mountaineers are ignorant. They tell me they don't have any roads, and I believe it. Look at all this desolate country, and only the one road in it. It is one poor place. They tell me that Georgia niggers made that road up there on the hill, and they did it under the whip. Kentucky is one poor place." Mrs. Tillman hit Menkovitch on the temple with a heavy cup filled with coffee. He fell from the chair. "Now, say some more about us, will you?"

He got up on his knees first; then he arose and went out. He went up the hill to the truck. I offered to pay for the breakfast. Mrs. Tillman refused money. "Son, I wish you didn't have to travel with an old tramp like he is. I believe he is a crazy man."

We fixed the two punctures. It was eleven o'clock. We loaded the blankets in the truck box and were on our way again. The skies grew dark, and the rain began to fall again. Before we reached the top of the mountain, we had another blowout. The rain beat down against the drab Cumberland Mountain earth. The wind blew through the naked trees. It was the day before Christmas. I wanted to be home for Christmas.

As we were fixing the flat tire, a Ford rolled up and stopped. "Do you need any help?" said the driver.

"Yes, an inner tube if you have one. An old one if you can spare it."

"Here is one that may do you some good." He pitched it out, and I caught it for Menkovitch.

"Are you loaded too much for an extra passenger?"

"No. How far are you going?"

"I'm going to east Kentucky. I must go as far north as Lexington and then turn directly east."

"I'm going to Cincinnati. Get in and go with us."

I took my suitcase and changed cars. "You're not going to leave me, are you, buddy? I need you. I have helped you this far."

"Good-bye, Menkovitch." I left him fixing a flat tire on Cumberland Mountain on Christmas Eve.

It was six o'clock before we reached Lexington. A tractor had to pull us through three water holes on the highway where small streams had flooded the low places. The water was touching the bridge over the Kentucky River. It was a terrible journey. We were tired when we reached Lexington. I wondered how I would go on. I still had the one-dollar bill that Ron East had let me have at Lincoln Memorial.

I bought a ticket from Lexington, Kentucky, to Winchester, Kentucky, and that took sixty-seven cents. I had thirty-three cents left. I intended to ride that far on the train and then hide in the toilet the rest of the way. I could not catch a ride on the highway on a wet December night on Christmas Eve. I went back in the toilet, and the conductor found me hiding after we had passed Winchester. "I'll kick your damn tail. I'll stop the train; I'll throw you off—you scum of creation!"

I explained where I was trying to go. I told the circumstances I was trying to make the trip under.

"That don't matter a damn to me. I'll put you off here. My troubles ain't your troubles. I am hired to work for this company and not to let bums ride in the toilet. That's a penitentiary offense. I'll road you if you talk back, too."

Allie Young, a boy from Morehead, Kentucky, was riding

in the smoker. He heard the racket. He came out. "Don't you put him off this train. I got the money to pay his fare first. But why don't you let him ride on into Ashland? If you don't, I'll get my old man to get a hold of you, and you'll wish you'd let him ride."

"I don't care for your old man. Who is he, anyway?"

"He controls the governor, and the governor controls this state. The state controls the railroads; therefore, my dad controls you."

"He'll pay or get off."

All the time the train was carrying me on. I had ridden at least thirty-five miles since the quarrel started. I thought if we could keep up quarreling, I could ride on. There were only a few stops between Winchester and Ashland for the night train.

"Here's your damn money. How much do you want?"

"Here's my thirty-three cents." I pitched it in against Allie Young's will.

"I want three dollars and sixty-four cents."

The debt was paid.

"Young, I'll send you that money as soon as I get home."

I rode that night without food. I drank water to keep from feeling weak. At Ashland, Kentucky, I waited on Christmas morning from four until seven for daylight so that I could catch a ride to Greenup and then walk out the old ridge path home. I caught two rides. They put me back in my old home town.

It seemed a long time since I had been to Greenup. Seasons had passed, and some of the fields I noticed had grown up in sprouts. I was on the path that led me home. I was glad to go. Home again, going home, old friends, pine trees, oak trees, hound dogs, plenty to eat, lonesome water to drink— home again! Lord, I could hardly wait. Just four miles, and home again! It was more like a dream than a reality. Winter oak trees and the gray December skies. Wind in the barren oak trees had a whipping sound. Wind in the pine tops had a lonesome sound. The church bells of Greenup sounded out across the desolate country. I remembered how they used to sound when I first went out this path into the big life in Greenup High School. That high school was only a little life now, I thought. But the bells kept pealing softly over the land, and the rustling of the dead leaves—all this seemed to say:

> *Hie away to Greenup,*
> *Hie away to prayer;*
> *Hie away to Greenup,*
> *I shall soon be there.*

I would soon be home. There was the shack in sight now. I would not make any noise. I would slip up through the chip yard and go to the kitchen window and see what Mom was doing. I would surprise her. "I don't believe he's coming home. Now, put that chicken in the box carefully. Put in a couple of backs. He always liked backs of chicken."

"Yes, and I'm right here to eat them." There was a family reunion in our kitchen. James showed me his twenty-two rifle he had got for Christmas. Glennis brought me her doll. Mary showed me her new dress. Pa showed me his leather coat.

"How do you like college? Tell me something about it."

"How are you paying your expenses, and how do you like Tennessee?"

"How did you come home? Why didn't you come sooner?"

I could not answer the questions. There was not one word said about me running away from home. It was all forgotten.

"Now, you let Jesse alone. I want to take him out and show him the corn and the stock. I guess it's his Pa's right to talk to him a little while."

"Now, hurry back. Dinner is nearly on the table."

"You see, Jesse, this is a right good crop of corn. We just got this crib full this year. It was a good season. We missed you a powerful lot last summer. God only knows what a time we had without you. I plowed at night when I come in from work on the railroad. I worked in the moonlight. I worked by lantern light."

"I think you have done mighty well. This is a fine crib of corn. And look here what a stack of Irish potatoes! How did the sweet potatoes do?"

"Not so good. The damn crawdads cut the plants down faster than we could set them out. You see, your Ma worked awful hard, and Mary and James worked out in the fields like grown-up people. Them kids are workers, let me tell you. I hate to see your Ma go out to the fields, but, Jesse, if I was worth a million dollars, she'd go out just the same. W'y, when the trees begin to leaf out, she's gone. She just lets the house go. She won't stay inside at all. And she knows every kind of a weed that grows. Did you see all them flowers she's got out there at the house? They're a perfect damn nuisance. But I help her with them just because she likes them. Anything she wants, I try to get it for her. Your Ma's worked mighty hard, Jesse, and I have too. We're both getting along in years, and hard work is getting us."

I could see deeper lines across my father's face. I could tell that he was going down the hill. He would never go up again, either. Age would not let him. Hard work had gotten him. I knew it. Hard work in the hills and exposure to bad weather had put marks across his face.

"Say, this is a nice pine here in the yard."

"Yes, me and your Ma, we had a little racket about that pine. I wanted to cut it down. She wanted to leave it standing. You know it is a pretty shore sign if you leave a pine standing in the yard or set a pine tree in the yard when it gets big enough to shade a grave, it's a sign of death in the family. But she would let it stand. I told her about it."

"I heard you bought fifty more acres of black oak hill land?"

"You heard the truth. I bought all that hill over yonder running back with Wilburn's line."

"What do you need with that? Work yourself to death to pay for one fifty-acre farm and build a house on it, then go and buy another farm. You'll kill yourself paying for it."

"I am older than you. I know what I am doing. I need that land. I love land. I can't get enough of it. I'm going to get all of this in grass. I'm going to raise tobacco. I'm going to quit working on the railroad section. I'm going to die on this farm. I like it here. And let me tell you, I've made every penny I paid on this land by the sweat of my brow. I work for all I get. You know, Jess, your Pa is an honest man."

"Sit down over there at your old place. We are so glad to have you with us. Guess who was asking about you the other day? I saw her in Greenup, and it was Maria Sheen. She is a pretty girl if I ever seen one in my life. But she wears her dresses a little short, don't you think? Now, reach and help yourself. Remember you are at home. Don't be bashful."

"I guess he gets so many good things to eat at Lincoln Memorial, he can't stand the old home grub any more."

"If I'd see a table like this at Lincoln Memorial, I'd run off and hide."

"Now, you don't mean that, Jesse."

"Yes, I mean it too. I fill my pockets full of bread, for often I don't get enough. Good night! Look what a table of food —spareribs, ham, gravy, sweet and sour milk, roasted goose, chicken, blackberries, strawberries, cherries, apples, huckleberry preserves, wild-grape jelly, honey, biscuit and cornbread, pickled beans, pickled corn and kraut, pie, cake, and quail meat extra. What more could I want?"

"This ain't 'food' here, son. This is old country grub. Take this from your Pa."

"And just think, you put up this food from the fields. Mom,

you are more industrious than a honeybee. You certainly can turn out the work."

"But I only canned twenty-five gallons of blackberries this year. The people from town got our field of berries. Mitch got mad about it, and I said let them have the berries. They needed them."

"How many peaches did you can?"

"I canned thirty gallons of peaches. I would have canned more, but Mitch grumbled about me using too much sugar, and I had to quit."

"Yes, that is the way. Lay everything on Mitch. If I went away from this place, I'd like to know what you'd do. When one of the kids does something good, you say: 'Yes, he takes after me!' That's what you said when you found out Jesse was in college. When James took the gun and slipped off to the woods, well, he takes after me. Jesse, that's the way things go around here."

"Pa, how is old Black-Boy? I forgot to ask."

"That dog is the best dog in these hills. I went out Wednesday night and got four possums and three polecats. Then I had to tie him to bring him in. He'd a-hunted polecats and treed possums the rest of the night. But I had to get a little sleep, for I work hard out on the road."

"And don't you know Black-Boy killed a copperhead just before it got under the floor? It was the biggest copperhead old Black-Boy ever killed. It bit Black-Boy in the head, and we had to give him snakeroot and whiskey in sweet milk. His head swelled up as big as two heads, but he got all right. The snake might have bit me when I crawled under the floor to get the eggs."

"Jess, the leaves are damp, and old Black-Boy is in good trim. Let's go out and knock down some cottontails. I'll beat you a-shootin'." We walked out by the barn and into the second-growth black oak timber. Pa gave me the old, old Columbia single barrel. He took a double barrel he borrowed from a neighbor.

Black-Boy jumped a rabbit. It came toward me. I shot and missed. I shot again. The rabbit went on. My father shot. The rabbit rolled over and over. My father got it on the run. He laughed and laughed. "I think books hurt the flesh. You ought to come back to the hills. You ain't a good shot like you used to be. Here you have missed two good shots."

"I think it is the fault of the gun. Surely I can beat this." But another rabbit and another miss. My father got it. A third rabbit, and my father got it. He killed five rabbits, and I killed one. He laughed as we started home. "Boy, your old Pap can put it over on you. And I ain't no shot at all. Nothing like Pap used to be."

I used to come into these same woods and get more rabbits and birds than any fellow in the crowd. I do believe books hurt the flesh. I don't care about hunting and killing as I used to do. I am thinking about Lincoln Memorial and the things I learned there. I am thinking about red-hot steel, smoke and steel, and dead men. I am thinking about merry-go-rounds and gay crowds. I want something different. I was happy here until I went away to school. I was dissatisfied because I was so ignorant when I measured my ways with other people's! And I want to know more and more and more. I can't learn enough facts to suit myself and my teachers. What good do they do? They make me dissatisfied. They help me to know that these quiet things I left are the best after all. There is something good about the old country life that is passing. It is the real sweetness of living down against the soil. And that life will never come again.

We went around through the pasture and by the crab-apple trees and pine grove home. We went out behind the corn crib to skin the rabbits. My father had a nail driven in a back log of the crib to hang the rabbits on when he skinned them. He cut the flesh through under the leader of the hind leg and hung it over the nail. Then he jerked off the skin and threw it to Black-Boy. Black-Boy knew what his share was—the skins, heads, guts, livers, lights, and paws. He always cleaned up the scraps and never had enough. My father put the cleaned rabbits in a crock and put salty water over them and let them set one night. Then he hung them up in the smoke-house to let them freeze. Then they were ready to be cooked.

"I want you to finish college and come back here and run for county school superintendent. I'd rather you'd have that as anything in the country. Wouldn't you like to have it?"

"I don't care about that. I don't know what I want."

"Well, I was talking to Ike and Brady and Uncle Rank Larks, and we aim to run you anyhow. They say you are the man for it. And I think it is a big thing. You can keep that job and stay right out here on the farm."

"Mom, I've been here eight days now. I must get back to Lincoln Memorial. I am ready to go back."

"Do you have money to go back on?"

"No, I do not."

"We'll rake up some money someway for you. I have seven dollars I've saved selling eggs and cream from the cows. You can have that. Mitch can give you five dollars. That will be enough, won't it?"

"Yes, that is enough, but I hate to take if off you."

"You go on and take it, child."

I went back the ridge road I came. I patched the old suit-case while I was at home. I pasted Lincoln Memorial stickers on the sides to let people know I was a college student. But Lincoln Memorial and so many people were not like Kentucky hills and so many sprouts. I didn't want to tell people about it, but I loved the Kentucky hills and the trees on them, especially this December, more than I had ever loved them.

Back to Lincoln Memorial. I was glad to get back early. I thought one of the students who worked in the dining hall might possibly drop out, and I would be there to ask for the job. I registered for the second quarter. I was going in debt sixty dollars. I must work hard to keep the debt down. I was not making extra money to buy clothes. I would have to make arrangements some way to buy clothes. I did not have a suit. And all the clothes I had were patched. The elbows were out of my coat and sweater, the seats were thin in my pants. I bet a boy my old overcoat that I could cut fifty shocks of the heaviest corn the university farm had grown, twelve hills square, and do it in ten hours. I bet him the coat against a new pair of shoes. I lost, I cut forty-seven, and the ten hours were up. I lost my old overcoat.

I was sent to the rock quarry. I went there every day. It was the hardest work at Lincoln Memorial. Before graduating from L.M.U., I had done almost every kind of labor on our campus, from cutting and shucking corn, mowing grass, putting silage in silos for our dairy herd, to laying bricks, doing plumbing, laying a water line, blasting limestone rock from a quarry and crushing the stone into ballast and to cleaning out manholes.

I really had two groups of bosses. I had the faculty members, under whom I studied to become a college graduate. My greatest ambition at this time was to be a college graduate.

Then, since I was a full-time work student, without help from home or a scholarship, I had a labor boss and bosses, from whom I had to take orders. I found it was better for me if I got along with them. I had to work to defray my expenses.

One of my most unpleasant and difficult jobs started one night when Mason Gardner woke me.

"Stuart, I'm dying," he said. "It's my stomach! Get the liniment out of my medicine kit and rub my stomach!"

Gardner had a medicine kit. And he used liniment for most of his ailments. He also had a sewing kit which he used to sew on buttons and to patch his and my clothes. He taught me to sew on buttons and to patch. We had to do this. Nearly all of L.M.U.'s young men students did, since we couldn't afford to have our clothes mended.

I did as Gardner requested. "You helped me when I had ptomaine poison from eating that can of pork-and-beans," I said.

Gardner was groaning. He pulled his pajamas off. And I poured the liniment from the bottle onto his stomach. I was rubbing it on and pressing down when he let out a strange shriek. He jumped up from his cot, ran across the room naked, out at the door, and down the hall. I knew he was on his way to the men's room. I went back to bed but left the lights on.

"Stuart, something is wrong here," Gardner said excitedly. "The men's room is jammed. They couldn't wait. They used the floor—and the place is a mess!"

"What caused it, do you think?"

"That canned beef we had for supper," he said.

Now I began laughing. Mason Gardner was a two-hundred-pounder, and he loved to eat. We ate at the same table, and Gardner had got his second helping and the last piece of meat on the plate—a piece I had wanted, but Gardner got it because the dish passed him before it got to me.

"I think it will be your time next," Gardner said. "You got one piece of that meat. And when you get the pain, it won't be a laughing matter."

I was still laughing. I couldn't help shaking with laughter, not because Gardner had the pain, but the way he got the last piece of meat on the plate when I had wanted it. I was laughing because I hadn't got it.

Gardner got back into his pajamas and was ready to lie down on his cot, when suddenly he dashed out of the room again. I was still laughing when he returned. The situation was a funny one. I heard men running outside down the corridor, hollering for someone to get out of the way. They were running fast.

At about two in the morning, I, who had felt neglected because I got only one piece of corned beef, rolled from my cot and was on my way. I'd never had a pain in my stomach like this one. It was like torrents of spring. I wasn't laughing now. Gardner was right! The men's room, our only one on the second floor in Grant-Lee Hall, was a mess. We couldn't get outside! We didn't have time! Gardner was back with me.

"We're poisoned, Stuart," he said. "I'll never eat meat from a can again!"

On all three floors of Grant-Lee Hall the situation was the same. All the students who ate in the dining room, ninety percent of our student body, had been caught in this dilemma. The only ones who could possibly escape were vegetarians, and we had none at L.M.U. All night long everyone on our floor was up and down.

When the commodes failed to flush, I knew what was wrong. Being a full-time work student at L.M.U., I had helped with plumbing in girls' and boys' dormitories. I knew I would be in for some work. And it wouldn't be nice work.

That morning, when I went to breakfast, very few students and teachers were there. They were in bed—and a few girls had been taken to the hospital in Middlesboro. The story was the same. It had happened in all the dormitories. We had been poisoned on canned beef. I heard threats of suing the company that sold L.M.U. the canned beef. I didn't eat much breakfast. Gardner hadn't come with me. I left him in bed. I had to be there to dry pots and pans. But Ed Shipley came running in.

"Let someone else dry the pans, Stuart," he said. "This is an emergency. The girl cooks can dry the pans this morning. We need you to help unstop the manholes and start this sewerage system again. It was flooded last night. It's not working. We're in a mess. We've got work to be done."

"We can't give you double pay for this," he said. "Student labor has to be the same! Twenty cents an hour. But I can give you double time, which is same as double pay. I need you! You're experienced! And many men are not able to work."

"Can you furnish me old clothes and boots?" I said.

"Sure can," he said. "Come on! Let's hurry!"

Not many students would do this. I was one of six. I hurried to the toolshed, got into old clothes and boots. I went down into one manhole, which certainly wasn't a pleasant place to work. I went down into another and another. I worked until afternoon, cut classes, to help clean out the manholes and get the sewerage system working again. And I got double time and maybe triple time. I knew I could make up my class cuts, for this was an emergency, and I was none too good to clean out manholes on a college campus for a college education! To be a college graduate was my dream! And I was one of the solid workers and one of the versatile workers on our labor force.

One day at noon in front of the dining room I heard a sophomore say: "It's time we's a knockin' a little of the cockiness out of these freshmen." A freshman knocked him down. A sophomore hit that freshman and knocked him down. A free-for-all started. The freshmen outnumbered the upperclassmen. The whole two hundred boys were in a fight. Fists were skinned and noses were bleeding. "Don't use sticks! Don't choke! And no fair gouging!" One could hear these cries. "Who in the hell's a-gouging?"

The boys trampled the shrubbery under. The deputy sheriff was called. He couldn't stop the fight. The faculty members were called. They couldn't do anything about it. The dean was called, and he had to let them fight. They fought until they gave out and all agreed to stop. The fight lasted over an hour. From this date on, it was dangerous for boys to go about unless they were in groups. Freshmen waylaid the upperclassmen. Upperclassmen waylaid the freshmen.

"We must be like other colleges," Professor Dixon said.

"We can't let a thing like this go on. We must have better sportsmanship between the lower- and upperclassmen!"

Professor Dixon pulled the neatly folded handkerchief from the pocket near his coat lapel and carefully ran it over his mouth and his shoebrush moustache as he looked us over with his black beady eyes. We upperclassmen sat on one side of the auditorium while the lowerclassmen sat on the other. Not one of us dared cross the broad aisle. The feeling between our groups was high.

Only an hour before, Dean Lewis had called a special chapel at Lincoln Memorial. He gave a long talk, pleading for "harmony between the upper- and lowerclassmen." Then he prayed for "divine guidance in this time of trouble," since all he and his faculty members had done toward ironing out our differences had been fruitless.

After the big fight, Dean Lewis met with his faculty and decided to do something about it. That night a meeting was called in Democrat Hollow in an apple orchard, where we were supplied with wieners, buns, and marshmallows. A bonfire was built for us, and someone brought a brand-new hatchet. After we ate, only a few men from each side testified how well they liked their fellow students on the other side. Then we sang songs together, but the singing was very weak, and after the singing we buried the hatchet.

But only a few of the more peaceful mountain boys from each side participated in this affair. On that very night strong upperclassmen stood back under the apple trees whose autumn leaves glowed in the soft bright firelight. They whispered to each other while the singing went on and looked beyond the bonfire at another group of larger boys and more of them, known as lowerclassmen. We could hear their voices and a few cuss words as they looked and pointed at us. We knew the trouble was not at an end, that we would meet sometime somewhere and fight it out, even if on this night we had buried the hatchet.

"Now, back East we had good sportsmanship at all the colleges and universities," Professor Dixon said, as he put his handkerchief back. "And I don't see any reason why we can't have it here. Of course, this is my first experience in a mountain college. But I think we can initiate a few games between the upper- and lowerclassmen that will promote a spirit of friendly rivalry."

Then Professor Dixon looked us over. Not a man on either side smiled. One could hear a person breathe.

"I have a little game in mind," Professor Dixon said, "that we used to do back East. And it's fun. We'll put a flag in the top of a big tree and let forty-five of you upperclassmen defend the flag and let fifty lowerclassmen try to take it from the tree."

"Why let them have fifty men and us only forty-five?" Big Dick Donley, president of the senior class, asked.

"But you see, Mr. Donley," Professor Dixon persuaded, "the lowerclassmen have an uphill fight. They have to climb the tree to get the flag, and you can put as many men around the tree as you want to guard the tree and as many men up in the tree as you think are necessary to keep the freshmen down! They have the odds against them!"

When we left the auditorium, our side went out together. We followed Big Dick. The freshmen followed Bullie.

"Now, you can call your men off to themselves and plan your strategy," Professor Dixon told Big Dick.

Big Dick arranged for himself and eleven more of his most active men to go up into the tree. He selected twelve more men, the heavy powerful men, to guard the trunk of the tree, and the remaining twenty-one to meet Bullie and his gang as they came uphill toward the tree. Big Dick called us his "assault troops," and he put me with this group. When he selected me, I shook like a leaf, for I knew what was coming. I'd seen too many fights between the lower- and upperclassmen already. I'd seen Big Dick hit Stanley Graff, knock him clean through a window, taking out sashes and windowpanes, when we were working in the shoe shop.

But this freshman came around the house and back in at the door for some more. He was tough. They were all tough.

Professor Dixon led the way, and Big Dick followed him, and we followed Big Dick. The men to follow Big Dick up the tree, mostly our basketball squad, were up near Dick. And the tree guards, which were mostly the linemen on our Bulldogs, followed the tree climbers. And we "assault troops" followed the tree guards.

I don't know what Bullie said to his men or how he arranged them. They followed us, hollering like a pack of wolves. When Professor Dixon showed us the tree, we looked to the top and saw our flag, a big white cloth, flying from the topmost twig above the copper-colored leaves.

It was a big elm tree, the biggest and prettiest tree on the campus, where many of us had sat with our sweethearts on Sunday afternoons. Those students who had been more interested in the course of "love" than any other subject in our happy years at Lincoln had an affection for this tree. But now it was just another tree.

Big Dick put his powerful arms around its trunk and went up its stalwart body like a cat until he reached the first limbs. Then the climbing was easier. Behind Big Dick were Big Nick Darter, Amos Smelcher, Tim Evans, Johnnie Dowling, Enic Pratt, Charlie Fugate, like ants following each other up the tree. While down below us at the foot of the hill was Bullie Sneed in front of his men, waiting until the signal was given to battle us. Our tree guards gathered around the tree trunk and waited, while we, the assault men, grouped together, each one trembling like a leaf in the wind, and waiting for the signal to meet Bullie and his fifty men. There were twenty-one of us. We knew we wouldn't be able to stop Bullie and all his men, but we could slow them.

"All right, let's go," Professor Dixon commanded.

"Let's meet 'em with full force, fellows," Ickie Porter shouted, running downhill to meet Bullie.

When we met Bullie and his men we hit body to body, head on and every way that men could hit. I was never hit harder in line practice in football.

Men were knocked down, and they groaned when others fell upon them or over them. Fists flew and men kicked. We knew it was a fight to a finish. As I went around and around with some freshman, I looked below me and saw some big man had Ickie down sitting on him, resting as he fanned his hot face. And then as we whirled around in a tussle, I saw Bullie, with a pack of big men, shoving our men aside and making toward our guards.

"Take 'em, men," Bullie screamed as they fought their way to the tree. "Knock 'em out! Knock their teeth down their throats!"

And I saw our men upend Bullie's men as they approached, but not for long. Bullie and his men would reach up and get one of our guards by the hand or pants leg or sleeve and jerk him down the hill over the slick grass, stripping his clothes as they went.

"Fight 'em, men," Big Dick yelled as he observed the fight from the treetop. "Stand your ground! They're closin' in!"

"Stand, hell," someone shouted.

We were a battered lot. Many of us hardly had on enough clothes to hide our nakedness. Noses were bleeding, teeth were knocked loose, hands were hurt, and men were lying senseless upon the grass, but the fight went on.

Finally I got my man down, and he was willing to lie down for a while. He had had enough. I went to rescue Ickie, for three of Bullie's men were sitting on him, resting while he groaned beneath the load. When I approached, one of the men jumped up, grabbed me at the neck, stripped my shirt clean, and slung me twenty feet or more down the hill, where I whirled and spun before I finally hit headfirst on the grass.

"Hold that tree, men," Big Dick shouted as he directed the fight from his safe perch.

Now Bullie and several of his men had places up in the elm. And our men had dropped down to kick them, but they caught their feet and legs and were trying to pull them from the tree. One of their men was holding to Big Nick Darter's legs and swinging like he was on a grapevine swing while Big Nick held to the limb above with all his strength.

Girls could no longer be held in their dormitories. They broke out and came to see the fight. The upperclass girls were on our side, yelling for us, while the others were yelling for the lowerclassmen. Faculty members came too, and though they preached sportsmanship to us, they started yelling for one side or the other. Someone called the town marshal and his deputies and the county sheriff and his deputies. It was one of the woman teachers or maybe the president who got scared again. And they came, but they couldn't do anything with the ninety-five men who were determined to fight to the finish.

In twenty minutes there wasn't a lower limb left. A few limbs remained in the top, where Big Dick was still safe, for he was guarded by three men below him. But Bullie must have had twelve men left. We wondered how long it would be before they got Big Dick and our flag. Bullie was the highest of all his men, but one of our men stepped down and put a foot on each of Bullie's shoulders and jumped up and down. Though Bullie hugged the tree like a bear, he couldn't take this. He dropped down without a limb to catch him, but he fell on a soft pile of men.

"Stop the fight, Sheriff," some faculty member yelled.

"Here goes my football team!" Coach Powers yelled. "Who planned a thing like this, anyway?"

"My basketball team," Coach Charlie Andrews yelled. "Sheriff, can't you do something?"

But the sheriff couldn't climb that tree where the fight was raging. There wasn't any more fighting on the ground, for no one there was able to fight.

The fight was up among the last limbs, where the elm top rocked in the wind. Every time a man started up, Big Dick kicked him down. He kicked Bullie's men until they fell out or had to come down. Just one man stayed. He wouldn't leave. That was Stanley Graff. He would reach up to get Big Dick by the leg. But Big Dick would kick at his hand, and he'd jerk it back, while everybody yelled like at a basketball overtime period when the score was tied.

Big Dick got mad at Stanley's tactics. He dropped down a step to put his feet on Stanley's shoulders to shove him from the tree. But Stanley got him by the legs and started swinging, and since Big Dick was so heavy and the top limb was so small, with Stanley's extra weight the limb slivered, and down they came, bringing all the treetop but the one twig that held our flag.

"There goes my track team," Coach Speed Mullins yelled as Big Dick dropped through the air, still clinging to the elm limb and with Stanley Graff holding to his legs.

Then the crowds rushed in to help care for their wounded. I wasn't hurt like many of the others, but I had escaped only in my undershirt, shorts, socks, and shoes. Since Lincoln Memorial didn't have an ambulance, they rushed the college truck to the scene. I saw them carry Big Nick Darter, our best baseball player, and the two lowerclassmen that had swung on his legs to the truck. They were knocked cuckoo.

Then they picked up Bullie Sneed and carried him to the truck. He yelled, cussed, kicked with one leg, and screamed, and his words sounded funny, for he had lost his front teeth and one leg was broken. Next they carried Big Dick and Stanley, who were knocked cold as icicles, and laid them side by side in the truck bed. The driver gunned the truck and was away, rushing them to Natesboro General Hospital, across the mountain. The rest of us could nurse our own bruises.

"Come on, pal," Ickie Porter said to me. "You've got on more clothes than I have. Look," Ickie said, stopping to point back at our flag. "It's safe now! Not anybody on this campus that can climb that tree now."

Ickie was right, for there wasn't a limb left except the topmost twig, where our flag waved. And there wasn't a piece of bark left on it big as a matchbox.

Chapter 4

DURING MY FIRST YEAR AT
Lincoln Memorial, I took this sonnet to an English teacher
in the college.

Muddy waters, how I have loved your crying
Night and day—forever past my open door
Down through the reckless channel breaks along the shore
Where winter wind in ankle-sedge is sighing,
And the infant moon circles low above the hill.
I have gone down at midnight, sat beside you
In woven reeds when winter winds whistled through
Your lonesome bank-side trees—Your pulsing will
Was surging your body down one lost way.
Like some deep singer in the void you fling
Futility to the wind and flow and sing
New songs, perhaps, for new youth molding clay
While I return to where my candle flame
Burns low, and the world will never know my name.

"I don't like your sonnet at all. Get away from sedge and
muddy waters and the night wind. Write high, beautiful
things like Shakespeare, Keats, Browning, and Longfellow.

Don't waste your time on such low, vile things." She was well-intentioned, I guess, but what terrible advice. I was writing what came naturally as well as I could write it.

The teacher who said this was Miss Kathryn Howard. On another occasion I brought up the name of Robert Burns. She literally froze where she was standing in front of the class. "Mr. Stuart, don't praise that immoral man in my presence! His immoral life among women defiles all his verse. I cannot separate the author and his work."

This led to an argument in the class. The book of Burns's collected poems that Mrs. Hatton had given me I'd read at the plow, with the street carnival, at the steel mill—I'd worn out one book and bought another. I couldn't do without Burns. He was always with me.

I told Mr. Kroll, an English teacher I really respected and thought great, what Miss Howard had said about Burns. "She's not got any sense," he said. "Pay no attention to her. Burns was a great poet, and he loved women. And a real man should love women. I know that I do. What would this world be without women for men to love? Pay no attention to that old juiceless cow!"

Then rumors began spreading that Miss Howard and Professor Wells were dating, that they were head-over-heels in love.

If I ever had a sourdough professor at Lincoln Memorial University, it was H. G. Wells. I took a course in education under this short, medium-sized bachelor who was perhaps in his early fifties. We students in his class wondered if there was anything on earth he liked well enough to praise.

He would ask a few questions pertaining to the lesson. Then he would engage in a stream of consciousness about clothes, automobiles, radio. He was against the men's and women's fashions of the day. He let us know that all men, young and old, should wear hats.

If there was anything he hated most, it was radio, which

was beginning to flower with a number of popular programs.

"Don't ever waste your time listening to a radio," he told us. "Always wear your hat." I sinned on both counts.

Professor Wells and Miss Howard were a perfect couple, I thought. There wasn't any rumor yet that there would be a wedding until Professor Wells bought a new automobile, the first one he had ever owned. One of my classmates, a student in his education class, taught him how to drive.

"He might get killed in that car," Elmer said. "The old professor is a wild and reckless driver."

Then we saw Miss Howard riding over the campus with him. He brushed the hedge, ran over flowerbeds, and barely missed trees that lined our roads.

Very few students had cars at L.M.U. Usually when students went five miles over the mountain to Middlesboro to see a show, they rode the train or hitchhiked. When boys occasionally went sixty-five miles to faraway Knoxville, they hitchhiked. Two of my classmates were hitchhiking back from Knoxville when Professor Wells whizzed up, stepped on the brakes, and slid to a stop. He offered Fields and Smith a ride back to L.M.U. Gladly they accepted, got in the rear seat behind Professor Wells and Miss Howard. That was when the highway from Cumberland Gap to Knoxville was one curve tied onto another.

Professor Wells got up speed, cut corners until Fields and Smith got so sick, Fields asked him to stop the car. Both rushed out to vomit. They were that sick. Fields told me later half of his sickness was caused by fright. Said he was never as scared in his life. He said Miss Howard was hugged over close to Professor Wells and enjoyed his fast driving.

And now both teachers began to change. Professor Wells walked over the campus bareheaded. He even retracted what he said about the automobile and radio. He said he loved his car and it got him to his destinations in nothing flat. Said he wondered how he'd ever done without one. He said the radio was the greatest invention of the time, that he had just purchased one and had it in his bachelor's quarters. He said the most beautiful love song of the time was "My Blue Heaven."

Miss Howard came to me and said: "Mr. Stuart, I owe you an apology about Robert Burns. I have put aside my prejudices and read his collected poems. He has written some of the finest love lyrics in the English language."

"Scottish language and dialect," I corrected her.

My grade went up in Miss Howard's class. My grade went up in Professor Wells's class. He was no longer a "sourdough" professor. He was real. He was genuine. He was in love. Miss Howard had turned from a petty to an inspirational teacher. These two married and were foolishly in love with each other the rest of their lives. They were never great teachers, but they were unforgettable.

The English teacher who interested me most on the Lincoln Memorial faculty was a big ruddy-complexioned man. His name was Harry Harrison Kroll. He looked a little out of place among the members of the English faculty. He looked to me like some of the men I had known at the steel mills. Yet, at the same time, he didn't look like them, for he had more color in his face than any of the steel-mill men, and this color made him look more like a farmer. Several students in my class thought he might have been a prizefighter. Many wondered if he were all brawn and didn't have anything in his head. The majority thought he looked out of place at the head of the English Department.

I liked Mr. Kroll's looks. And after I attended one of his classes that first year, I went back to the registrar's office to see if I could take another course under him. I was impressed with this man who made the teaching of English a living thing. And one day when he inquired in our English course if anybody would be interested in creative writing, my hand was the first one up. But almost every hand in the room went up. He didn't have any trouble getting together a class. The idea of writing seemed wonderful and romantic to most of the mountaineers in this school.

Mr. Kroll was born in Indiana, and his people were Dunkards. The family moved South in a covered wagon. All of his early life is in his book, *I Was a Share Cropper*. That's what he was in his youth. He picked cotton on meager wages along with other members of his family, and for a long time the family lived in a covered wagon.

Mr. Kroll was a graduate of Peabody College. Peabody College gave him a chance as a special student. He had roamed all over the South working in the cotton fields, then as an itinerant photographer. On one of his sojourns in Louisiana, he met a pretty teacher in a one-room school. He married her, and she changed his life to books.

He read books, took a "teacher's examination," passed, and became a one-room schoolteacher. His wife had also written children's stories. Harry Kroll stayed in the South. He taught one-room schools in Mississippi, Tennessee, and Kentucky. Knowing Mr. Kroll's temperament, I don't know how he ever disciplined youth. He would never inflict even modest punishment. I remember he used to chase his own boys with a fly swatter as they ran to get away from him, laughing all the time. He'd say: "Old boys! Why didn't Nettie and I have girls? I've always wanted a daughter." He had three sons, Harry, Tarry, and Larry. The first and second were born before he came to Lincoln Memorial, and the youngest was born while he was there. We called them Big Short Story, Middle-sized Short Story, and Baby Short Story.

When Mr. Kroll entered Peabody College, he had never seen the inside of a high school. He had never finished the eighth grade, so he told me. He said he got his eighth-grade diploma, his high-school diploma, and his B.A. and M.A. at Peabody College at the same time. Before he passed an examination for a teacher's certificate, he had had less than a year of formal education. He once told me with a laugh: "Abraham Lincoln enjoyed a long formal education in comparison to mine. I was picking cotton and carrying water to the hands when I was six." Yet, this intelligent, talented man could read and understand more books faster than most of his contemporaries.

Mr. Kroll was ambitious to write himself and was selling little stories to small magazines to supplement his meager twelve-hundred-dollar salary. Now he found himself surrounded by forty ambitious students ranging in age from sixteen to sixty-five. He let us write anything we wanted to write—poems, short stories, farm articles, plays, essays, letters, diaries, articles on religion (there was a young minister in the class), and any other form of writing that came to mind. I can't remember anybody's being very modest in Mr. Kroll's creative-writing class. Since everybody was eager to read his own creative efforts, an hour in this earthly paradise was too short a time. But Mr. Kroll solved this problem. He took time from his own classroom work and his own writing and met with this class in a vacant classroom at night. Often in the warm days of spring we sat out at night and read by a streetlight. It didn't matter to us.

I remember when Mr. Kroll told me that poetry was my field and for me to "go after it." He told me to bring two or more poems to the class, and I went with sixty poems and felt a little hurt when I didn't get to read all of them. Creative writing, under this teacher, was like many a religious revival I had seen sweep my own mountain vicinity. Mr. Kroll told us if we had just a little talent and worked hard enough at it, we could become writers. I did hundreds of poems, and scores of articles on my hill people that people called "stories." I never bothered what they called them, just so long as they read them.

One of these pieces, after many revisions, I later sold to the *Atlantic Monthly* as a short story. I sold one to *Harper's*, one to the *American Mercury,* two to the *New Republic,* and two to *Esquire.* But I didn't know then that they were short stories. And Mr. Kroll didn't encourage me along the short-story line. He told me my field was poetry, and I believed him while I was going through this fervor of creative writing that had swept the campus at Lincoln Memorial. Even one of the long poems I read in this class, many years later, sold to the *Yale Review.*

We filled the college paper with our creative efforts. We swept into the wastepaper basket all the idle college gossip and chatter that the average college student loves so well, and filled the paper with articles on writing, authors, current literature, poetry, and short stories. Even this wasn't enough. Mr. Kroll finally persuaded the school to finance a small magazine for our creative work. He did the line drawings, as he later illustrated his own books, but he didn't take any of our space for his own writing. He remained in the background and let us have the show. For he had other things in mind.

But despite all my creative spirit, and I was certainly one of the most spirited, I found myself a back number in the class, on the bottom. The only way I could get a poem published was to have myself nominated for editor of the paper, and after being turned down by a vote of the student body time after time, I was finally selected by the faculty. And the first thing I did was to publish one of my poems on the front page, and I used my name, not a "pen name," and ordered sixty extra copies of the paper at the school's expense and sent them out to my friends to show what I was doing. I carefully marked the poem on each copy. And it did me more good to see my first poem in print and to see my name signed to a poem than it has in later years to make the best magazines in America, England, and Ireland. The publication of that poem gave me more of a boost than having my first book accepted.

While I was manuevering to become an editor of the paper so I could get a poem published, other pupils in Harry Harrison Kroll's creative-writing class—it became the best-known class on the campus—started selling articles to farm journals, small magazines, and a few large magazines.

There wasn't any let-up of spirit among its members. As time passed, they grew more and more ambitious, the fervor fanned into flame, for the little checks were something to the needy students. Seeing their names in magazines made them as proud as I had been to see my name in the college paper.

But what I wanted to hear most of all for just one time was that I was one of the more promising young writers of Harry Harrison Kroll's creative-writing class. These words would have been sweet music to my ears; but so far as I know they were never spoken. As we walked over the campus, I often heard this student or that one spoken of as "the creative genius." I heard it so much that I went to the dictionary to get the different shades of meaning of the word "genius." Everyone was speaking of the fine poetry Louella Mason was writing. And they spoke in "glowing terms" of her short stories. Often I wished she were out of the class so someone else would have a chance.

We didn't know what Mr. Kroll was doing though we could see his lights burning past midnight, but we soon found out. While he was head of the English Department at L.M.U. he wrote his first novel. He had sold his first short story for two dollars to a small farm journal at the age of twenty-nine, and now in his early thirties he had his first novel, *The Mountainy Singer,* accepted.

After this acceptance he walked proudly in the wind, and we rejoiced with him, for when our teacher did the things he told us we could, we knew he was a writer all right. Besides, he was the first teacher in the English Department of this school ever to write a novel while he was teaching at Lincoln Memorial. Our faith in this man was unbounded. When any student in one of the other English classes made uncomplimentary remarks about Mr. Kroll, he would have one of us to fight. And we had some rugged men among us who wanted to be writers instead of football players.

When *The Mountainy Singer* was published, something happened that we students couldn't prevent. The faculty was up in arms, not just the English faculty, but the majority of the teachers of the school, especially the women. The woman who started most of the talk was a Ph.D.—we called her Doc —who had never married and was well past her fifties. She said there was entirely too much kissing in this book and that it was "just plain sexy." (It *was* sexy for those days, tame for these.) Men on the campus said it made them love their wives more when they read it. One male faculty member tore his copy of the book in two and laid both ends in the fire. But before Mr. Kroll was thrown out of the school because of "his lascivious writing," he had another novel, *The Cabin in the Cotton,* accepted, and sold it to the movies. Then we knew Harry Harrison Kroll, our teacher, must be right and everybody who opposed him was wrong.

Never have I seen a group of students so loyal to a teacher, or fight so hard for him to stay. When he was ousted anyway by the powers that were, many of us shed tears. He had to go. But when they started to fire him, he almost got the chancellor fired. It was a battle royal, and Kroll fought to the end but lost. We fought for him, but who were we? We were pupils the school didn't have to have, for we didn't help it any with our finances. Nearly every one of us worked for the biggest part or all of his expenses.

There was an expression that went among us after Mr. Kroll had gone: "You can see what too much creative writing can do for you! It can cause you to lose your job! Look what happened to Mr. Kroll! It's hard to believe that creative writing is as explosive as a stick of dynamite, but it is. It's dangerous!" L.M.U. was not the same without Harry Harrison

Kroll, for where on this earth would we have another former baseball pitcher for our teacher who would get up and leave his class and tell us we could stay in classroom if we wanted to but he was going to watch the college baseball game? And where could we get another teacher who would inspire us to fill the college paper and magazine with our efforts?

The majority of Mr. Kroll's Lincoln Memorial students kept in touch with him by visits and letters throughout the years. None of us could ever forget him.

Harry Kroll was one of two inspirational teachers I had at Lincoln Memorial. The other was Earl Hobson Smith. They were friends before Mr. Kroll was fired and stayed in touch until Mr. Kroll's death.

I studied speech and drama with Professor Smith.

He came to Lincoln Memorial in the spring of 1926 as a journalist to finish the term of a teacher who had resigned to accept another position. He was a trained journalist with dual majors in his M.A. degree, in drama and speech. He came to L.M.U. to teach two months and remained forty-three years. He has the longest tenure of any teacher who has ever taught at Lincoln Memorial. Since Lincoln Memorial is a small school and has always had small graduating classes, he holds in his memory all of the graduates for forty-three years. He has taught each graduate in one or more subjects. There are not many teachers who have done this. He is now Mr. Lincoln Memorial University.

Recently, while speaking at a banquet of the Knoxville, Tennessee, Teachers League, I looked down from the podium at the table where he sat. His hair had not changed much in the forty-three years since he taught me speech, drama, and English. He was a young man in 1926 and his hair was blond. Now it was a silver shock. If I speak within a hundred-mile radius of Lincoln Memorial, my teacher and friend Earl Hobson Smith will be there with a pad and pencil and grade me on my speech. He is always a teacher with his students.

In the autumn of 1926 I enrolled in this young man's speech class at Lincoln Memorial University. The first speech I ever gave in his class was about "How I Became a Blacksmith in the Steel Mills." Professor Smith spoke of my five-minute speech (I extended my allotted time) as concrete. He said that in a speech the speaker had to have something to say and say it well.

I wondered as he sat at that table watching me and listening (he had driven sixty miles from Harrogate to Knoxville to hear and grade my speech) what was going through his mind. If he were thinking of another day and time. I wondered if he remembered when I told him I took speech because he taught it, that I would never be a public speaker. "Everybody is always a public speaker," he quickly told me then.

Now, after more than five thousand appearances in forty-four of our fifty states, after speaking all over Egypt, Greece, Lebanon, Iran, West Pakistan, East Pakistan, the Philippines, Taiwan, and Korea, I wondered if he sat there thinking about how right he had been when he told me at nineteen I would have need to be trained to stand before and address a public gathering.

After Mr. Kroll was fired, another teacher came to take his place. He was a short man with pink rosy cheeks who wore a black bow tie that worked up and down with his Adam's apple. He had a soft voice and he rolled his R's when he spoke which was quite different speech from the mountaineers'. When DeWitt Davis made his first chapel talk, Harry Kroll's creative-writing class was there. Not a student cut chapel. Not one of us had lost his creative-writing fervor. Each nurtured his own ambition to be a writer. But when Davis stammered on the stage over the word "ousted," rolling and rolling it and finally pronouncing this word "oosted," we were a little shocked. Though we were not always accurate on pronunciation, we could certainly handle such a simple word as this one. Everybody in chapel laughed, too. We were off to a bad start.

"Now, I'll tell you what I'll do," he said the morning he met our creative-writing class. "I'm going to do something that has never been done before in this school. I'm going to sponsor a writing contest. I'm going down in my pocket to give a prize of twenty-five dollars each for the best poem, best short story, and best essay. And," he went on, "there'll be a second prize of ten dollars and a third prize of five dollars. Each contestant will be allowed to have one entry in each event. That'll make enough papers, since there are about forty of you. How many of you plan to compete in this contest?" he asked thoughtfully as his blue eyes scanned us from behind celluloid-rimmed glasses. "Will you hold up your hands, please?"

I thought about how rich our new teacher must be!

Every right hand and a few lefts went up.

"Wonderful," Professor Davis said. "You certainly have the right spirit!"

"Professor Davis, who will be the judges in this contest?" I asked.

"No one from this school," he said. "I think it best to go outside and get judges from the English Departments of our larger southern institutions."

"Amen," someone said in the corner of the room. We laughed, but uneasily.

Then Professor Davis went over a list of probable judges, saying this one had written such-and-such and that one had done so-and-so in the field of letters. I hadn't heard of many of them, but I thought maybe my education was still sadly neglected. But I was glad he was going out and getting judges away from school, for I was afraid if it were left up to our own judges, some of the contestants would whisper to one of the local teachers the title of his story, essay, or poem. I was glad that our battle would be decided among strangers who didn't know any of us. And I heartily approved of this contest, as much as I disliked this man because he had taken Harry Kroll's place. Thoughts were going through my head. What if I can win first place in poetry? Besides the honor, I shall have enough money to buy a suit of clothes!

One day in class when Professor Davis returned the papers we'd read the week before, several of my poems and a couple of articles were tattooed with red pencil marks. My face must have flushed until it was the color of these marks. Harry Kroll had taught us to get the thought first and that "any damned pedagogue can punctuate it afterward." However, Mr. Kroll did teach us "the ever-changing fundamentals of the Mother Tongue."

"Stuart," Professor Davis said, as he saw my temper rising. "I know your former teacher was a popular one, and I doubt that I can fill his shoes, but I do know when a thing is well written. And," he talked on slowly, softly, cautiously, "I never heard of your teacher until I came here."

"But you will hear of him," I said. "And you will hear plenty about him! I've just had a letter from him, and he tells me his third novel's been accepted!"

The gulf widened between Professor Davis and me. If I met him on the campus, he begrudgingly spoke to me, and I barely grunted. But there was one thing I wanted more than anything else in life right now. I wanted to take a first place in the contest and take some of the money he had offered in this contest, which came, I had found out, from his meager college teacher's salary.

But Louella Mason would walk away with the prizes. That's what nearly everybody in the creative-writing class thought. And faculty members at the school said so too. She was the creative genius. And big things were expected of her.

Yet that didn't keep the rest of us from trying. Often I gave up hopes for a first place after I figured that 120 papers would be in the contest and only nine could win. I would be contented with a second place. Dollars looked as big to me as wagon wheels, and ten dollars was not to be dreamed about. And if I couldn't get a second place, I'd be glad to get a third. That would put me in the upper nine places.

I never worked harder than I did on this creative-writing contest. It was close to my graduation from college, and I was out for track that spring too. While I ran cross-country and the two-mile, I would think about a new idea to add to the essay or a change for the story. I went over them and over them and lost many hours of study and work in the kitchen and at the rock crusher. I went over the story and essay repeatedly and was never contented with them. I took four sonnets I'd written at the steel mills before I entered college and went over them, tying them into a sequence. I was actually afraid to submit just one poem and lose the poetry contest after Mr. Kroll had told me that poetry was my field and for me "to go after it." I was after it.

And I was after the prize. I was after the twenty-five dollars from Professor Davis' pocketbook too. And I worked furiously, neglecting everything else, right up to the deadline when the papers had to be submitted.

After waiting for more than two weeks, we walked nervously to the classroom one morning to hear the announcement of the winners. Our names had never been used in the contest; we had been asked to devise some numeral or sequence of letters or both for the pieces we submitted. Not even Professor DeWitt Davis knew the authors of any of the essays, poems, or stories submitted. When he walked in and dropped in his chair, he took an envelope from his inside coat pocket. There wasn't a whisper or a sigh as Professor Davis opened the sealed envelope and took out the paper that told the winners.

"Well, here they are, students," Professor Davis said. "First place in poetry goes to 2224-X!"

"That's mine!" I shouted. My classmates looked curiously at each other.

That was the happiest moment of my life. I had won first place in poetry and twenty-five dollars. That means I'll write Harry Harrison Kroll today, I thought. It means the new suit of clothes.

And then I thought about how everyone had said Louella would not only take the short story but her imagist-styled poetry would also win first place. Charles Clampton got second in poetry, and John Hughes got third.

"2225-X gets first place in the short story," Professor Davis mumbled his words, his face coloring.

"That's mine too!" I shouted.

But my words were drowned by the pandemonium breaking loose among the contestants.

"What about that?" I heard one of the girls say to Louella. "I never thought. . . ."

Professor Davis had to call for order in the classroom so he could read the second-place winner of the story contest.

"If you don't get quiet," Professor Davis shouted, "I'll have to postpone these other announcements!"

"Second-place winner in the short story," he spoke cautiously when the noise had partially subsided, "is . . . let me see . . . 2226-X!"

"That's mine too," I said. "But that's not a short story, that's my essay. . . ."

"Give 'em all to him!" one of my classmates shouted behind me.

"How can an essay be a short story, Professor Davis?" Bert Estes asked.

While Professor Davis called for order, he looked thoughtfully as if he were trying to solve the problem of how an essay had been mistaken for a short story.

"Tell you what we'll do on this," he concluded finally. "We'll put this to a vote of the class."

"No we won't, either," I said, my temper rising. "This was the judges' decision, and it will stand."

"Mr. Stuart, I'm still running this class," Professor Davis said. "My word is final here."

And he went ahead with the voting, which was done by secret ballot. When the votes were collected and counted, I received one vote to keep the second place in the short story.

I didn't wait to see who won the third place in the story contest and the three places in the essay. But I later learned Weston Hartwell got third place in the story and Humbar Keaton, one next to me in low grades for creative writing, had won first place in the essay, and that Mercy Story and Tom Reynolds, two unknowns in our class, won second and third places respectively.

Much has happened since that time. In the Depression, when I was selling hens' eggs for seven cents a dozen to buy postage stamps to send out stories and poems, I missed a five-thousand-dollar prize for a nonfiction book by one vote after waiting for months for a decision. And once when the Book-of-the-Month Club gave ten thousand dollars to four needy authors, I was number five on the list! How I needed that twenty-five hundred dollars! When my first novel was accepted, my publishers announced four publication dates, since the Book-of-the-Month Club was interested. Two judges were for my novel, two were for another book, and the fifth judge finally decided against me. I lost these things, but the combined loss did not hurt me half as much as losing second place in this story contest. It was the way I had lost that hurt.

I left the classroom with tears in my eyes. It wasn't soft sentimental crying, either, for I was mad. I wanted to fight the teacher for his going against the judges' decision and putting it to a vote, and I wanted to fight my classmates, one at a time, who voted against me. But I couldn't do this. There wasn't anything I could do but dry my tears, cool my temper, and forget.

As I walked across the campus, I thought again about Harry Kroll, a great teacher, who had lost his second teaching position because of unrestrained love in his new novel.

I worked in the kitchen my second year in college. My job was to dry the pots and put each pot, skillet, lid, fork, knife, big spoon, and meat cleaver in its place. It took me a month to learn the work. Spence Fillis was headwaiter. He was thirty years old. He was a short, stocky, strong man. His word was law among the students. They were afraid of him. He tried to tell the dining-room matron what to do. He sparked one of his cooks. Spence fired the students when he got ready. He was the big boy of the dining room.

This job paid my board and room rent. I worked on the campus on Saturdays for my tuition. I was faring fine. My grades were good during my second year. It was the golden year in college for me. My poetry was accepted by many small poetry magazines.

My job in the dining room had gone from bad to worse. Spence had become unbearable to work with. He told me one day that I was fired. I told him that I would not leave the place until he gave his reasons for canning me. I asked the matron if I was canned. She said I was not. She and Fillis stood face to face and quarreled. The next day Fillis told me I was fired. "I'm not leaving here until I get good and ready, Spence Fillis. I've taken all I care to take off you."

"You are a goddamn liar. You are going now."

He drew a chair across his shoulder to hit me. I beat him to the first lick. I hit him under the ear. The fight had started. It was after the noonday meal on Sunday. All the students had gone. The matron of the dining room was there, and the cooks. Fillis was strong. I would not let him get hold of me.

He lost his head. He ran into my licks. He swore viciously
and he was a lay preacher. His arms were shorter than mine.
He could not reach me. I kept him off at arm's length. I
pounded him. We stopped. He pulled off his glasses. Then he
grabbed a bread knife. He hit me across the guts the first lick.
It was turned broadside. He hit me across the heart. The back
part of the blade hit me. I hit him with every ounce of weight
there was in my body. I stood on my toes and tore my shirt
across the shoulder. I hit him under the eye. He hit the table
and knocked all the dishes off it. He twisted down to the
floor. The matron he had been fussing with brought a poker
up this time. "A man fighting a boy! You ought to be
ashamed." But Spence was on the floor. The matron called
for the dean. He wasn't there. She called for the business
manager. He wasn't at home. She called for the sheriff. He
came, but he need not have come. The fight was over. My
hands were burst open and my wrists sprained. Fillis' face
was bruised. His eyes were black.

The fight was discussed on Monday morning on the Lincoln Memorial campus. I was watched until then. I packed
my trunk. I knew it would be a trip home. I was called to the
office. "We are going to let you decide whether Fillis can stay
on and finish his work here or not." C. P. Williams, the
school's business manager, did the talking. "It is left up to
you. He is a preacher. He swore time after time and tried to
cut you with a knife, the matron said. He has six weeks to
stay. Do you want him to finish or not?"

"Let him stay. He won't bother me."

"Don't let this go to your head. But Fillis was a hard man
to fight. He chased his own brother out of Lincoln Memorial.
I tell you, he was a mean fellow when he first came here. He
ran eight of the boys away from the dairy barn. He was the
boss down there, and he ran them away one night. He came
in with an ax. He ran them off like they were children."

"Why didn't you fire him out then?"

"He's the best worker we have at Lincoln Memorial. He's the first man that ever made expenses at the dairy barn. He is the first man that ever made the dining room pay. That is why we held him."

My labor boss was no longer Ed Shipley. He was replaced by J. D. Walker. J. D. was deputy sheriff of Claiborne County, Tennessee. He was interested in politics on county, state, and national levels. If and when trouble came up on the Lincoln Memorial University campus, he was on hand to quell it. This seldom happened.

"Boys, would you rather take the Presidential election day off to vote, or would you rather work?" he asked us one morning as the election day approached. "We want our man to be President of the United States."

We didn't question our labor boss, J. D. We agreed to go cast a vote and get a day's work. But I had never voted, and since Tennessee at this time had a poll tax for voters, I didn't have money to pay my poll tax. J. D. saw to it that those who were not registered were registered as bona-fide voters, and our poll taxes were paid if we couldn't pay. All of this was done in a hurry.

"Leave all this to me," J. D. said. "I'll take care of it. You just do the voting. Remember Herbert Hoover on election day! We don't want Al Smith. He's not the man of our party."

I'll never forget that election day when I cast my first vote for a President of the United States of America.

Sheriff J. D. Walker filled our biggest Lincoln Memorial-owned truck with work students. We filled the truck, until there was hardly standing space. We were crowded against the truckbed railings. Three men sat in the cab with J. D., and two stood on each runningboard hanging on to the door when the door windows had been let down. We were on our way to Cumberland Gap to vote. Here, J. D. got us in line and told us to hurry it up. I figured I'd get back on the campus and get some schoolwork done. I'd have most of this day off.

By the time our long line had filed through the voting precinct in Cumberland Gap, it was after ten o'clock.

"Hurry up, boys, and let's reload," J. D. said. "We have more work to do! We've got to go to Arthur."

Arthur was another voting place in Claiborne County. J. D. drove the lumbering truck over a dusty road, a truck loaded with young voters—and clouds of dust moved up and filled our mouths and nostrils.

At Arthur, J. D. knew the officials at the voting booths.

"We have to be back at the college dining room at twelve," he said. "So, rush them in—we don't have too much time."

Again we lined up—and one by one we voted and went back to the truck. When we had finished at Arthur, we had only fifteen minutes to get to the dining room. We were allowed thirty minutes to eat lunch at L.M.U. Yet we were told to eat our food slowly and to chew it well.

When we got to the dining room, Spence Fillis, student dining-room boss, met us at the door. "You're ten minutes late, and you can't get in."

"Mr. Fillis, I'm deputy sheriff of Claiborne County," J. D. said. "My authority is higher than yours. And I say they will come in, or we'll break the door down."

"Yes, yes, Mr. Walker," Spence said. "They can come in."

And in we went, all hungry, for we had found voting harder than doing campus labor. When we had finished our lunch, J. D. was waiting by the door.

"Go back to the truck," he told each of us. "We've got more voting to do."

We loaded into the truck again. This time J. D. drove the truck to Sewanee. It was very close to Harrogate, where L.M.U. was located. Here we formed in a long line and voted again. Due to interruptions, we voted more slowly here. There were voters who wanted to go in and vote and who didn't want to wait until we had finished. J. D. and some of the officials had some sharp words. We didn't get finished at 4:30.

"It's too late to make another precinct," J. D. said. "I had another one in mind!"

"Boss, it's quitting time," Roy, a classmate, said. "We've really worked today. This has been harder than campus work."

Many of us had to be on campus too, for we had jobs to do. Many of us worked in the dining room. Many had cows to milk, cattle and chickens to feed, and dormitories to sweep, furnaces to fire. Lincoln Memorial couldn't operate without us. Deputy Sheriff J. D. Walker knew this, so he rushed us through clouds of dust back onto the campus.

When I cast my first vote for a President, I, like all others, had voted three times. No wonder Mr. Hoover carried Claiborne County, Tennessee, by a fantastic majority. I was scared after we had done this. I looked for an investigation afterward. But there was never a protest or a word said about it. It passed over like a bright autumn wind blowing over the multicolored hills in Claiborne County, Tennessee.

My friend Ron East had gone to his home in Georgia. His mother was sick. While he was there a telegram was sent to him telling him to stay. He was expelled from Lincoln Memorial. "You are not allowed back on the campus," the telegram stated. But Ron East came back without money. He thumbed his way. He stayed in the woods in a cabin. I didn't have money to buy food for him, and I stole it out of the college storeroom. No one knew Ron East was there. He kept it a secret. I took the telegram he had received down on the campus and showed it to the students. "Ron East, you are expelled from Lincoln Memorial. You are not allowed back on campus." The boys would ask me why he was expelled. I told them what Ron told me. "I made a speech down in the chapel one day. I told them too much about this place. They didn't want to hear it. I told it to them anyway."

The students rose in revolt. "We are going to have Ron East back. We'll wreck the damn school if we don't. Ron East was right when he said Lincoln Memorial was a crude place. We are going to have Ron East back." Before trouble started, a telegram came from the chancellor, who was raising money in the North, reinstating Ron East.

When I was carrying food to East in the woods, there was a tree down in a dark hollow I met him by. I gave him the news on the campus, and I carried letters from him to his girl. She sent letters back by me. I met him in this secluded spot where I knew no one would be near. Clara Good sent him a message in one of the letters that Spence Fillis had insulted his sister. "I'll whip that Spence Fillis if it is the last thing I ever do in my life."

"No use to whip him now. I gave him enough. See this bandage on my hand. Well, under that bandage is a fractured bone. And it hurts. That was done the last lick I gave Fillis. He got a good whipping. He'll not bother your sister anymore."

Once Clayton Jarvis said, "Things are going to be popping around the school soon. Mind what I tell you. There's been a strange man on this campus for three days now. Just walks around and looks things over. Don't know just who it'll be this time. But a lot of the teachers will have to go. It's getting about time; we're due for a house-cleaning here."

The house-cleaning came. Dean Charles D. Lewis, the man who took me in, had to go. "Why does Dean Lewis have to leave here? He's one of the best men I've ever known."

"Don't ask me, Bert. There's a Higher Power over this school, the chancellor. When the Higher Power cracks his whip, boy, they clean house around here and never give a reason." Many teachers were forced to resign. I was too young to understand academic politics.

It hurt me to see these teachers go. I had had classes under many of them. Dean Lewis had taken me into the school and had given me a chance when I didn't have money.

Charles D. Lewis, dean of Lincoln Memorial University, was acting president.

I studied geology under this delightful man. He had been my friend to permit me to enter L.M.U. I wasn't nearly as interested in geology as I was in the man who taught it.

I gave this course everything I had—to show Dean Lewis he had not made a mistake permitting me to enroll, the hitchhiker trying to find a school that would take him.

Geology came the first period after lunch. I had only time to eat, then dry the pots and pans Parker Sears had washed, pots and pans used to cook food for three hundred hungry students. But it crowded me to make Dean Lewis' geology class on time. I had to rush. And the first and second six weeks in this semester I had made A grades. I spent extra hours on this subject, which didn't especially appeal to me.

It was in the third six weeks I ruined myself. I arrived in class after eating a big meal. I was hungry after working all morning, in the cold wind, digging on the water line being laid from Cudjo's Cave in Cumberland Gap. After a full meal and the warmth of the dining room and working in the kitchen, I became sleepy. In Dean Lewis' class I went to sleep, pitched forward out of my chair face down on a concrete floor, which really shook me up. For a few minutes I was addled while the dean was working over me wondering whether he should call a doctor. I was slow to come to my senses. He was embarrassed to have one of his students go to sleep in his class during his lecture and fall out of a chair. From an A grade I was dropped to C minus for the semester. I let the man down who had made it possible for me to enter Lincoln Memorial University. What had happened to me in Dean Lewis' class made news all over the campus, and in the end hurt Dean Lewis' teaching reputation more than the fall had hurt my head. I still feel badly about it.

My third year at Lincoln Memorial was my hardest year. I carried the mail from the post office, worked in the dining room, edited the six-page college paper (*The Blue and the Gray;* I was proud of that paper), and carried a heavier schedule of work than the college was supposed to allow. I was called to the president's office. He said: "Mr. Stuart, by a mistake in the office you have been allowed to carry three hours too many this year. To improve the standing of this institution, we must deduct these hours."

"I cannot graduate then. I'll have to stay another quarter. I hoped to get out this year."

I left his office. I was called to the office a week later. The president said: "Mr. Stuart, we have decided to give you three honorary hours in English for your good work on the college paper." The three hours deducted were B grade, the three honorary hours were grade A. I made three honor points in the deal, but honestly it was something I could never understand.

At Lincoln Memorial I wrote about five hundred poems. They were experiments in verse, every form. I still wanted to write verse. The urge was a part of me. It would not leave. I wanted to put thoughts into words. Words were living things. In verse they took on a living force that would be felt.

It hurt me to leave owing the college money. I hadn't done what I had expected to do. I expected to work all of my way, and leave not owing the college a penny. I owed them one hundred dollars and fifty cents. The most money I'd got from home was two one-dollar bills my mother once sent me. But school was all over now. I had finished in three years and two summers. I had bought my own books and clothes, such as they were. I had made something like a B average. I never stopped to count it up. I graduated. I was the first of my father's people to finish college.

In my own mind I tried to sum up my education at Lincoln Memorial. I was once told I was one of the better-prepared students to enter Lincoln Memorial. This I could believe. I had better training in the four years I had spent at Greenup High School than I had in the three years and two summers I had spent at Lincoln Memorial.

All but one of my teachers in Greenup High School had been outstanding.

In Lincoln Memorial University I had had only two great inspirational teachers, Harry Harrison Kroll and Earl Hobson Smith.

Still, Lincoln Memorial University had been a second home to me. It had been my second mother. And I wanted to be a graduate that would honor L.M.U., since no other school would have me. I wanted to make L.M.U. proud of me —this small school, without money or prestige, that had taken me in off the road where I was a hitchhiker. Lincoln Memorial had given me a chance. I had tried other, better-known colleges that had refused me entrance. It was Lincoln Memorial that had accepted me and had given me a chance. I would be eternally grateful. I had realized my dream. I was a college graduate!

I took the old suitcase and put more signs on it. I was ready to travel. I said good-bye to the teachers and the students. I said farewell to Ron East. He smiled and wished me well. It was the road again. My first ride took me somewhere in Kentucky. Darkness overtook me among the mountains. I couldn't get another ride. A heavy black cloud arose, and a storm came. I remember the lightning flashes and how I ran by their light down the highway until I saw a church house upon the bank among what looked like a thousand white tombstones. I had slept in many church houses before, and I would sleep in this one for the night.

My mother was proud to see me when I came back from school. All of the family were happy, though Pa was still a little sore I'd left him.

That first evening after supper my mother and I slipped away from the house. We went down through the garden.

"Now, here, Jesse, are my beets. They are put in two rows lengthwise of the bed. Don't you remember the way you used to want me to plant them? You always said you could hoe them faster thataway. Here is my early corn. It's that little early sugar corn. It won't amount to much when it comes to ears. But you know it comes in right handy in the middle of the crop, when everything else is scarce."

"Mom, how much sugar corn do you think James and I have eaten raised from this garden?"

"You and James! Well, you know James is small, but he is as big an eater as your Pa. I know you boys have eat enough to fatten a hog off this garden." She laughed. "Say, Jesse, I didn't tell you about Brother Tobbie preaching the other night against education, did I? Well, don't you know he got up and preached a sermon on mothers sending their children away to college where they would be educated right for hell. He looked right at me when he said it. He knowed you was away, you know. Oh, he just made me so mad! I wanted to tell him to go on and preach about the Bible and God Almighty and not things he didn't know about. Yes, he did go over that old story again about the Lord calling him to preach when he was a-cuttin' hay on that piece of ground back of the barn. I got tickled when he said he just fell off the mowing machine like he was shot when the Lord called him."

I stood in silence for a minute. I thought: "What if Brother Tobbie could get up in the chapel at Lincoln Memorial. The boys would hoot at him. They would surely throw rotten eggs at him. If he'd tell that mowing-machine story at Lincoln Memorial, people would say he was crazy." Mom and I went down through some young field corn. We went through between the rusty barbed wires of the pasture fence. She held the wires apart for me to climb through the fence. I spread them apart for her so that the wires would not catch her dress.

The evening dew was settling on the grass. The shade had come over. As the sun sank over the green hills, the shade spread in an uneven line, uneven as the poplar tops on the hilltop were uneven. The thin crabgrass growing in the pasture caught in the eyes of our shoes and between the crosses of our shoestrings. I thought of the days when I went after the cows and pulled the ragweed seed from between my toes. But now my feet were shod, and I was a college graduate. I had come back to the little shack among the hills, and I had got to be something. I was looked up to by all the family.

We turned now and walked around toward the house. We were walking on a white dry path, worn that way by the hooves of the horses when they were taken to the barn from the pasture and from the pasture to the barn. The road wound through a little patch of sumacs and then under the pine trees. "Where the black shoemakes grow, the land won't sprout black-eyed peas. But where the red shoemakes grow, I'll tell you, it's the land to slip a few beans in with your corn and a few pumpkin seeds in around the old stumps. I tell you, that red-shoemake land will certainly grow the corn, pumpkins, and beans."

The cold stars of May glittered in a starry sky over our heads. When we looked through the pine tops at the stars, we were silent. We walked on silently to the house. We slipped in quietly to keep from disturbing those already sleeping. The moonlight came in at my window and shone on a broad strip of my floor.

This is my old room. Over there on the wall plate is where I kept my books, but they are gone now. I burned them. I wish I had them tonight so that I could go over the places I had marked and turned the corners of the pages down. "Don't ever mark a book," teachers used to say. "It is a disgrace. And don't turn the corners down. Keep your books in good condition. See, mine are nearly in mint condition." I want to say, "How would you like to go straight to hell and stay when you get there? My books are my own. They are not things to keep in mint condition, either. They are mine —and sure as pencils leave traces of where they have been, you'll see mine traced and retraced. My books are to be used, and I use them. Not many of them."

I felt the quilts on my bed. They must be the same old quilts. The bed was turned the same old way. Everything in the room was placed just like it was when I left. There was the old battered shotgun without a sight. There was my old fox horn on the wall, the wooden table, and the old dresser Grandpa Stuart gave my father. Everything was still here but the books. They were burned under the wash kettle. Well, it was fine to be back home again. I went to bed. The moonlight streamed in across my bed. I had been sitting up two hours in the room thinking about days and nights I had spent in this room.

May in the Kentucky hills. A boy a-sleeping in the upstairs of a shack. Moonlight in bright floods pours in at his window. He gets up and takes a rag out of a pane so that more can flood in before he goes to sleep. Dew is on the grass and the leaves of the trees. Moonlight on the dew that's on the grass makes a thousand little stars down on the earth. The fields have been plowed for planting again. And on many of them the little green blades of corn are twisting through the earth. The whippoorwills are calling by the edges of these fields and out in the pasture. One will start calling, another will answer. Soon the whole countryside will be made into a mournful song. The frogs croak in the pond. The katydids are noisy, and the beetles drone and drone. Kentucky night and ten thousand stars swarm in the sky over the green hills.

I had taken the road homeward to the low, shaggy greenbrier hills around Greenup. Here was a Silence I could love. Silence under me in the great Earth, the mother of creation, and Silence above me in the starry Heavens. I could love the two great Silences I lived between.

Chapter 5

I STAYED AT HOME THE REST OF the year. I said I would. Dad said, "Jesse, I forgive you for running away from home. Even out on the railroad section where we carry the crossties up the side of the banks and put them on the key rails, the young men take the heavy end of the ties and go in front because I got a boy who has finished college."

Mom said, "Jesse, what are you going to do now."

I said, "I don't know."

She said, "I know what you're going to do. You're going to teach school. The superintendent of the Greenup County schools wants to see you. There's a place waiting for you."

I always listened to my mother. I went to see the superintendent of the Greenup County schools. He said, "Yes, we have a place for you."

I said, "Where is it?" I thought it was the main high school.

He said, "Red Hot High School." It got that name because a steam engine blew up there. The old people still use that name, but we had so many people laugh at the name that we had to change it to Warnock, Kentucky.

I said to Mr. Norton, "How many students at Red Hot High School?"

He said, "Fourteen."

I said, "Who will be the faculty?"

He said, "You'll be the faculty."

I said, "What will I teach at Red Hot High School?"

He said, "algebra, Latin, plane geometry, history, and English."

I said, "Mr. Norton, I can't teach algebra."

He said, "Aw, yes you can. You have a nice transcript of credits in here. We've got your credits. Why can't you teach with an A and a B in algebra?"

You know you can't cheat on any one subject, so I decided then to learn algebra. I said, "Mr. Norton, I'll be your faculty."

My fourteen students at Red Hot High School lived up to their school's name. I entered them in a scholastic contest with a far larger and better-staffed school, and these farm youngsters who had to get to the contest on muleback won that contest. The town youngsters laughed when they saw my hayseed pupils ride up on their mules, but nobody laughed when the contest results were announced. These young people made their teacher proud.

They also made him famous—well, at least in Greenup— for that year I was asked to become principal of Greenup High School. I served for two fine years at this high school which I had attended with my sister Sophia. My brother, James, was a pupil while I served as principal. I asked for a raise from one thousand to twelve hundred dollars and the superintendent fired me. I left Greenup High School mad.

I went back home to W-Hollow restless. I wanted to be a writer, a poet. How could I find the inspiration and enrichment my mind needed without mixing with other young writers, other established writers too?

At Greenup Uncle Rank Larks helped me to rope my

trunk and strap my suitcases for shipment to Nashville, Tennessee. I was going to take a crack at Vanderbilt University. "Jesse, it's a plum shame that you are leavin' here. You know I hate to see you go worse than if you was one of my boys. I've knowed your Ma since she was a little girl wearin' ribbons on her hair. They ain't no better woman than your Ma. They ain't no better man than your Pap. Your Pap's the hardest-workin' man in this county. He grumbles a lot, but he's a good man. You know I hate to see you go."

"Well, Uncle Rank, I don't mind to go, but I can't see my way through. It's going to be a little hard, you know, without money, and work so hard to get."

"You'll be back here again sometime. You know, boys always come back to drink of the lonesome waters they left at home."

"Well, Uncle Rank, the bus is coming. Why don't you go along with me?"

"No, Jesse, the Old Woman is a-makin' apple butter, and I promised her I'd be back to stir it for her by nine o'clock. It's nearly ten now. She'll comb my hair, Jesse."

"Well, here, Uncle Rank, let's shake good-bye for a while."

The old man turned away with tears in his eyes when he saw me go. That is the clannish brotherhood we have among the hill people. It is great to live among people like Uncle Rank Larks.

On my way to Vanderbilt University I thought of such names as Davidson, Wade, Mims, Curry, Warren, and Ransom. They were all well-known teachers and writers. I would rather be with them than be principal of a county high school. I was tired of teaching school anyway. I was tired of everything. If I lived always in Greenup County, I could never get anyplace writing. I needed contact with men who'd seen and knew the world. But I was afraid, for I didn't have the promise of work. I had only one hundred and thirty dollars. It would not go far in Vanderbilt University.

I didn't know anyone in Vanderbilt. But I said to myself: "You're turning to be a damn coward now! Have you got clay feet? Go on and meet things like you have met them before!"

All that I told myself didn't matter. I was afraid and didn't know why. I was a stranger, and I was afraid. When I registered at Vanderbilt University, I told Dr. Mims the circumstances. "It looks as if you've got something big before you, Stuart. I don't see how in the world you can do it and do yourself justice." He was right. But I was not turning back. I was going through with the ordeal. I was going to stay.

As I was walking up Wesley Hall stairway, I saw between me and the murky September light the familiar outline of a tall rugged man sitting at the window. His face was turned toward the smoke-clouded city. I had almost passed him when he glanced around. It was Ron East! "Stuart, what in the world has brought you here!"

"More education . . . my M.A. What brought you here?"

"I'm getting my D.D. this year, preaching and working in the slums."

"Same old Ron East!"

"In flesh and blood but not in spirit. I've been kicked out of three churches since I preached in the mountains. I've seen so much human suffering, Stuart, that I've grown bitter. I've been trying to save human beings on earth instead of preaching to them of a reward in heaven."

Strange the way the paths of destiny cross and recross. Ron East, six-feet-three, a great cross-country runner, a great high-jumper. His heart big as all out-of-doors. He used to work his way at Lincoln Memorial and send his poor parents money to support a big family. He carried baskets of grub that he bought with the money from his own pockets to the mountain people in Poor Valley. Didn't he often go there and preach the funeral for one of the mountain dead, and do all the singing too at the funeral when there was no one to help him? Hadn't I found a friend at Vanderbilt University! Didn't he always tell me on the cross-country runs that the man a step ahead of me was just as likely to fall as I was, and that I should vomit and keep going? Didn't he always lead the pack of us and come in at the end of the five miles hurdling the fences a mule couldn't jump? I always felt as strong as a mountain when with Ron East.

"Why don't you register in the School of Religion, Stuart? You can get by there on the money you have."

"Hell, I can't preach. I don't ever intend to. If I were called on to lead in prayer, I'd sink through the floor."

"That's not the thing, damn it! Others are doing it, and they're not ministerial students. You could too."

"Yes, but do you know what they are when they use religion for a blind like that? They are a bunch of cheats. I don't intend to do it. I'd have to drop two of the courses that I'm taking in the English Department for a couple of courses in the School of Religion."

I spent all my money registering for the first quarter and shipping my trunk and typewriter and bringing myself. I had kept back four dollars when I registered, but at the business office I had to make a note to the university for eight dollars. Well, there was nothing left to buy books with. I'd have to borrow or do without. The first quarter I had mostly to do without. I took examinations and never had time to study for them. I made poor impressions on the faculty members—a graduate student doing no better than the undergraduates of the university! But I couldn't do any better. The university was so much bigger than Lincoln Memorial. Everything was different. My mind was in a muddle. If ever I could get lined out just right, I'd show them I wasn't a fake. But I could never get a chance. I was with many very bright students.

One day I stepped up to Oscar Boswell and said: "I think you had a very good poem in the university magazine, last issue. The poem was about the ghosts of dead leaves following you on the street."

"I'm glad you think it was poetry. I do not." But I knew he did think it was poetry. He was pretending to be modest.

"Well, I try scribbling verse too. I've placed a few poems in one-horse magazines." He only smiled.

He didn't believe me. He thought I was a faker.

I went down the corridor of the hall and up the street. I thought if I were to tell these teachers at Vanderbilt University that I wrote over five hundred poems in three years and did regular classwork and worked my way in Lincoln Memorial, they would not believe me. They would think I was a newspaper crooner—a poem a day keeps the doctor away.

It was just in me to write poetry, and I did not suppress the desire. Poetry took me along. It made me its servant. I couldn't handle poetry. That is funny to say, but I heard Lum Dryasdust say something funnier at Vanderbilt: "I'm reading the sonnets of Shakespeare now. I'm getting inspiration from them to write. I'm reading Edgar Allan Poe's 'Poetic Principles,' about how to construct verse. I'm going to sit down and write poetry when I get my term papers off and have a little time. I want to be a poet. I want to write novels too."

Oh, dear Lum Dryasdust! You are taking poetry along with you. It doesn't have you by the heels and drag you everywhere you go, through the steel mills, through the pasture fields and the cornfields, through the tie-timber woods, at the plow, and everywhere you go. No, you are going to sit down and write poetry when you get ready. All I have to say is, don't tell everybody about it. Poetry puts you down and makes you write. Edgar Allan Poe is not going to tell you to do anything. You have to be your own self. Poetry will tell you to let the term papers go to hell. It will make you lie to your teachers.

For three weeks I went daily to see the university Y.M.C.A. man for work. He found me a job. It was selling tickets for an automobile concern on High Avenue. I sell the book of tickets for a dollar. I get fifty cents of the dollar. But one of the fellows selling these books at Vanderbilt University gets a nickel out of my fifty cents. But forty-five cents isn't half bad. I work me up a sales talk like this: "Hello, mister. Would you be interested in a bargain for your car repairs?"

"No."

"Oh, now wait here just a minute. Look at this! Two car washes absolutely free. That's worth a dollar of any man's money. Now, over on the little blue ticket—look at this! A free rim inspection. Two of them."

"That don't amount to nothing. I can do that myself."

"All right, then. Over to the little green ticket, two green tickets. Look at this. Two free greases with a change of oil each time, that is, you must pay for the oil."

"Oh, yes, I thought there was a catch to this."

"Now, just a minute. You've not seen all of this. Over to the two yellow tickets. Within a radius of five miles, if your car gives out of gas, all you've got to do is call this garage and they bring it to you at the regular price. Now, what do you think of that! Over to the orange tickets. Now, here's the fine thing about this ticket book. Here's the best thing in it. You get two flat tires fixed free here with this book of tickets. Now, you just think about it."

"Say, how much is this book of tickets anyway?"

"Only one dollar."

"Here's your money. I thought it was ten or twelve dollars the way you was showing me through it."

"I didn't want you to miss a bargain like that."

I had faith in the bargain at first. And I wanted the forty-five cents. But once I went and stood in front of this garage, and the manager chased me away. "I'm selling your own products. I'm helping you, and I'm helping myself."

"But hell, you'll ruin our trade."

"Well, what did you put out any such thing for? My heavens, put out a bargain and then be afraid to let one of your agents sell it in front of your garage."

"Don't argue with me. You go now. Don't you know you are going to ruin us, standing here?"

"Before I go, I'd like to leave something with you. It isn't a stick of dynamite, either. Here, take this damn pack of 'bargains' and keep them for yourself. But be sure and don't put them off on the people. I want to keep one of them." I pulled one out and stuck it in my pocket.

"What are you doing that for?"

"To show my authority." The truth was, I wanted to sell one more and go to the Paramount to a show. I sold that one and went to the show.

Then I went back to Mr. Hart at the Y.M.C.A. for more work. "Mr. Hart, that job's played out."

"What job, Jesse?"

"Oh, selling the garage bargains."

"Garage bargains!" He laughed. "Yes, I've got a job in mind for you. It is big enough for two good fellows. You know this man Horton that sweeps Science Hall?"

"No."

"Well, he is a preacher, and he's keeping a wife and baby on that job. It pays fifteen dollars a week."

"Good. Can I get it? Where is Science Hall, anyway?"

"You pass it every day. See that brick building over there?"

"Yes."

"Well, that's it. Now, there is a lot of work about it. It is supposed to keep one man busy all day long. Two boys are supposed to spend twenty-six hours a week there. I mean twenty-six hours apiece. Will that hurt you much, Jesse, in your graduate work?"

"Yes, that'll knock a big hole in my time, but I'll try to do it. You know I've got to have money."

"Well, you and Easton go down and see Mr. Abernethy right now. Six fellows are trying for the place."

Mr. Abernethy was a pleasant fellow to talk to. He told us he had worked his way at the university. We got the job. We started on Wednesday. I think my clothes helped me along as well as my tongue. He saw my worn shirt with split places around the shoulder.

Well, for nearly three months I worked seven hours a day and did graduate work. I went out at six o'clock and worked until seven. Then I went back at two and worked until five. I worked an average of two hours each day in the cafeteria. I went to the football games, and I took a notion to get a job selling programs. I was told I could not get that, as all the boys had been selected to sell the programs. I thought I would just go down and get myself an armload of programs and start selling. It worked beautifully. I made a little money and saw the games free.

But the work at Science Hall with a fellow as slow as Easton was getting to be monotonous. Of the thousands of men I have worked with, at fifty or more different kinds of work, Easton was the biggest donkey. He had gone to the hall, and Horton took him around and showed him how everything had to be done. When I began work the next day, Easton started showing me, and he tried to keep it up for weeks afterward. At first we started sweeping all the rooms together. I swept three and sometimes four rooms to his one. He was slow, and he was lazy. Finally I said: "Easton, I'll clean half the building and you clean the other half. Now, I'll divide the building and give you your choice, or you divide the building and give me my choice. Just the way that suits you."

When we did this, I had plenty of time to spare. Rister, our boss, lorded it over fifty-eight black janitors and two white ones. He told us to put in our time. He told us to stay there twenty-six and one-half hours each week.

I told him I could do my half of the building in one hour. "You can't do it and do it right."

"You stay with me and see." One night I did it in forty-six minutes. I cleaned the floors and the blackboards of six rooms, two halls, three offices, and two flights of stairs. I talked to Mr. Abernethy about leaving early. He said it was all right if I did my work well. Easton always watched for me to leave the building. He went then and told Rister that I'd slipped out. Rister went about trying to find more things for me to do. When I left early he went about looking for me. He thought I had a hiding place in the building. But I was going to the dormitory and studying.

One morning he sent me to the supply house to get eleven rolls of toilet paper and a gallon of antiseptic to drench the commodes in Science Hall. He came down a few minutes after I had reached the supply room. I ran a wire through the rolls of toilet paper and then wrapped them up with a wide piece of brown wrapping paper. I was ready to cross the campus now. "What are you wrapping that toilet paper up for?"

"I don't want those girls standing up there on the walk to see me carrying it across the campus."

"Oh, you don't? Well, all the other janitors do it."

"Well, here's one sure as hell not doing it, Rister. I am a janitor, but I'm not going up across that campus with an armload of toilet paper."

Rister looked at me. He said: "Well, ain't girls seen it before?"

"That may be true, but don't we have a certain amount of decency between us and self-respect? If we didn't, we'd all use the same toilets." Rister didn't like the attitude I took toward him. He wanted to say things to me, but by the way he approached me I knew he was afraid.

The job lasted only till January the first, then Horton was to take it back. Easton had quit now. I had one distinction. I was the only white janitor at the university. It was during the Christmas holidays that I made my last trip down to Science Hall. I went down to work. I was going over the woodwork and polishing it with wax. I got seven dollars per week instead of the seven and a half the colored janitors got.

I asked Rister about it. He promised me seven-fifty hereafter. But this morning was my last. I threw my broom across the room and kicked a light bulb out with the toe of my shoe. I had been trying every morning to break that bulb, but I could never kick that height before. I left the clothes I had worked in there.

And then I went again to hunt for work. I tried to get a job at newspaper reporting. I tried both city papers. I went all over Nashville trying. One night I stood at the corner of Church Street and wrote this on an envelope:

COURAGE BE WITH US ALL

Be with me, courage, for I walk alone,
Although I have no fear of night and gloom.
The earth is wide and there is spacious room
For human creatures on her streets of stone.
Be with me, courage, in this trying hour
When stars are hard to barter for thin bread,
(Be with us all in this dark hour of need)
The lonely poor with dreams, the rich with power.

The leafless tree in winter stands alone
Dreaming of leafy days and sunny Spring
When birds alighted in her boughs to sing.
Now somewhere out by changing winds I'm blown,
A yellow leaf to drift with time away
The silver moments of my swift brief day.

It was Christmastime, and people in Nashville were buying presents. The city was a busy place. The windows were decorated with Christmas-tree trimmings. I wanted to go home for Christmas. But I had used all the money I made sweeping at Science Hall as fast as I got it. I couldn't go home for Christmas. The cafeteria was not getting much trade, and for three days it was closed entirely. The workers there were cut to one-third of their regular time.

When I received my first-quarter grades at Vanderbilt University, they were so poor my legs weakened. I knew they were coming, but I wanted to make myself believe—I must believe—they were passing. The time taken up in the sweeping of Science Hall, the selling of "garage bargains" and football programs, and the work in the cafeteria had robbed me of too much time. And I had bought only a few books, too. But I had worked hard, and it hurt not to climb the hill. I'd have to try it all over again.

Would I register the second quarter with such grades? Why hell, yes. Why stand up and take a beating? Why not hand back a few blows? I was afraid of myself. Everybody was a stranger to me. I was afraid. Would I ever step out and be myself again? That didn't matter as much as fighting back now. I should fight back. Go away with both eyes blacked and be afraid to speak? I tried to make myself do better. But I could not. I was afraid.

Why didn't I take the time I spent on sonnets and poems and spend it on my regular classroom work? I had a little spare time I'd been using for writing stories. I could use it all to a better advantage. No one ever saw the sonnets I did. I wrote them and hid them away in a notebook. I had the notebook half full. I could have used this time learning facts. But facts didn't stay with me.

I registered for the second quarter on trial. If my grades were not better, I could borrow no more money from the university. I came back with a determination to be a better student. I intended to conform and study all required subjects.

It is somewhere between eleven and twelve. About twenty of us are listening to Robert Penn Warren talk about Elizabeth Madox Roberts. He goes on lecturing. I don't get it all. My stomach keeps on bothering me. It is empty. I forgot to drink water before I came to the class. Drink plenty of water, for water is good to drink. The head is dizzy, and the whole body feels sick. Drink good cool clear water and drink plenty of it, for it makes the sickness leave the body. Drink water when you are hungry so that your guts won't growl and the girls next to you won't hear and laugh. I don't mind a boy hearing, but I hate like hell for one of the girls to hear. But their guts would growl too if their stomachs were empty. I forgot to drink water. My stomach has ripped out a long growl. I bend over and press my hand on my stomach. It ceases slightly. My arm grows tired pressing down on my stomach. I remove it for a rest. My guts let out another long growl. Damn guts, I'd like to put my hands on them and squeeze them in the emptiness and confusion. I'd stop them from embarrassing me. I didn't quite get all that Warren said. It is only five minutes until the bell. I can see the clock in the tower from my window. I'll be glad when the five minutes are gone.

A man ought not to get hungry on eleven meals a week. One on Sunday, two on Monday, one on Tuesday, two on Wednesday and Thursday, one on Friday, and two on Saturday. The weekends were the hardest. I walked more then. The cold spells were a little hard. It took more food then to keep the body supplied with heat. My body was as strong on eleven meals as it would have been on twenty-one—still one hundred and ninety-two pounds and never stopped going. I know a little about food. I've worked a whole shift overtime in the steel mills without it, from eight to ten, or fourteen hours, without it. I drank water. Why not drink water at school? It is much easier to drink water and study books than it is to drink water and hook hot slabs of steel with a long rod of iron with a hooked end.

I have known hunger on a Kentucky hill plowing. I had to plow a piece of corn. I could not quite finish in one half-day. I would not go in to dinner until the field was finished. I always felt sorry for the mule. He pulled the plow, and I only guided it through the roots and drove the mule. He knew as much about plowing as I did. I didn't have to drive him. A mule knows right where to step. But he can't tell his driver whether he is hungry or not. And food, for the mule, is all he lives for. Give it to him. I don't live for food alone. I live on food and dreams. Give me mostly dreams. Cramp your guts when they growl. Push them against your backbone with your hand flat against your stomach. But don't cramp your dreams.

I have an appointment with Donald Davidson, a fine man and teacher, at seven this evening. He has passed me often in Wesley Hall. Sometimes he spoke, at other times he did not. He is a strange man. He is a man with dreams. There is something very fine about his face. I love to look at it. I think a lot of that silent man who slips quietly through the corridors of the hall and seldom speaks. But once I heard deep laughter outside the hall. I went to the window. It was Donald Davidson laughing. He was bending over and slapping his knees with his hands and laughing. There was a tall man with him on the street.

I found a kindred spirit in Donald Davidson. Just to speak to him or see him walking on the campus always made me feel better. Many a time from my Wesley Hall window, I saw a nice family scene on a Vanderbilt street when Mr. and Mrs. Davidson walked down the street with their very pretty small daughter, Mary. I often watched her skipping along the walk in front of her parents.

When I spoke to Donald Davidson, I didn't tell him half what I wanted to say. I wanted to tell him that I was a damned ass for not passing my schoolwork. But I hated to use that word to him. He would think it was unnecessary exaggeration on my part. But that is the way I felt about it. I should have passed all my schoolwork. He would say to me when I tried to explain, "Oh, yes, I understand." I wondered if he did understand. There was a lot to be understood that amounted to trivial dreams. What was I down there for, anyway, bothering Davidson? I had no business telling him my troubles. Davidson had a use for his time. He could write poetry. He could grade papers. He could sit in silence and forget teaching school. I could go on and be myself and get out of a spell of cowardice and fear I was going through. Hell, forget three C's. What were they? I was standing at one end of the class, Boswell was at the other. Somebody had to be last. But I felt better by talking to Donald Davidson. "You don't have to get an M.A. before the sun goes down. Take your time about it. You are capable of an M.A. from this university. Don't get tense about it. Don't worry. I understand." I got something off my chest when I talked to him. I had told somebody something and felt relieved.

I was enrolled in four classes. American literature, with John Donald Wade, a delightful man, a tremendous teacher, an individualist, and a personality. And I had Dr. Edwin Mims, never a man like him, anywhere at any time in any university. An individualist, a personality, a great teacher. I had a young teacher in "The Novel," a beginning writer, not too much older than his students, Robert Penn Warren. Then, I had Donald Davidson, also young, in Elizabethan lyric poetry, a delightful class. I didn't have any classes under John Crowe Ransom, much to my regret, but I saw him a few times on the campus. I talked to him a few times and got to know him. I didn't have Walter Clyde Curry, a well-known Chaucer scholar and writer teaching there then. But I got to know him very well. Allen Tate, living then at Clarksville, Tennessee, came often to the Vanderbilt campus, where I met him on a few occasions.

Vanderbilt's English Department was alive. I had found an English Heaven.

The excitement of my Vanderbilt English teachers (all the teachers I had were authors, from a few to many books) was constantly marred by my always wanting food. But the hunger of the mind, as strong and constant as the beating of my heart, overcame the hunger for food. And I had to have friends to whom I could confide my dreams and aspirations.

Once I told a student on the Vanderbilt campus I wanted to be a writer and he laughed and walked away. I remember his name quite well. But why record it here? On another occasion in John Donald Wade's American literature class, where I had made either the lowest or the second-lowest grade the first quarter, the young man who had made the highest, a little fellow who always wore a bow tie, I remember, told me that I shouldn't study English but should play football. The second quarter in his class, I made the highest grade in the class. And when I showed him my grade, I said: "How do you like this?" And he walked away, his Adam's apple moving up and down, moving his bow tie, although he wasn't talking. Mr. Wade was so delighted with my improvement he wanted to help me financially if I would continue school. This was charitable, but our parents taught us never to accept charity, and we never did. Thereafter I took a few trips with John Donald Wade and Ed Winfield Parks, just driving over Nashville in the car, stopping for snacks and sundries. These I appreciated as much as the conversation and listening to my companions quoting poems.

Unfortunately no one insulted me in Robert Penn Warren's class. I sat in class a little hungry, for it was near noontime and I'd not had any breakfast. Young men and women in this class spoke of writing "the great American novel." I actually took this course for credit, not dreaming that I would someday write a novel. Before going to Vanderbilt I had been told by a teacher that I could never write a novel. If one of my classmates in Robert Penn Warren's class has ever written a novel, I do not know of it.

If I had only had a retentive memory and time to memorize the long passages of poetry Dr. Mims required of us in his Victorian literature class; if I had only liked Tennyson then (and I did not), I might have done much better. I wanted to. In Dr. Mims's class one did or he didn't, and that was it. Once he said to me: "You shine like a star in *Sartor Resartus* [I

liked this book] and on Tennyson you fall to the depths."
And he was right.

I was always the first one to enter Donald Davidson's class
and the last to leave. I can't recall how I ever got a copy of
the textbook we used in his class. But I know it's marked
from cover to cover. There was a similarity between the
Elizabethan lyrics and the Elizabethan ballads I had heard
from earliest childhood in my east Kentucky hill country.
Donald Davidson loved the Elizabethan ballads and lyrics. So
did I. This strengthened my ties with Donald Davidson. I
was brave enough to show him poems I had tried to write,
poems imitative of popular poets of the time—Carl Sand-
burg, Rupert Brooke, and many other poets I had admired.
In a second sheaf, I showed him poems I had written of my
surroundings, poems which came naturally to me. Here his
decision was a quick one, a decison, I think, he never forgot.

"Your natural poems are the ones," he said. "This is your
trend to follow."

One of these poems, titled "Elegy for Mitch Stuart," he
went over and made a few corrections. "Send it to H. L.
Mencken, editor of the *American Mercury*," he said.

His telling me to send a poem to a big magazine, one of
the most popular in the United States at that time, scared me.

"But I can't even make the little magazines," I told him.
"I send to them, and all I send is returned."

"That is just it," he replied. "You're cut out for the big
magazines. Send it."

Then I told him about seeing an article in the newspaper
where someone had interviewed Mr. Mencken and he had
said there was no poetry being written in America at that
time fit to publish.

"His bark is bigger than his bite," Donald Davidson said
with a smile. I sent "Elegy for Mitch Stuart" to *The American
Mercury,* and it was accepted. For this poem I received
twenty-five dollars which came to me after I left Vanderbilt.

There, it would have been a small financial fortune. But the acceptance of this poem, and my teacher's saying I was cut out for the big magazines, an idea that had never occurred to me, meant more than any financial recompense. This gave me courage to send to the other Big Four magazines, *Atlantic Monthly, Harper's,* and *Scribner's* magazines. I did this within the next four years, and my poems were accepted. My teacher, Donald Davidson, had shown me the way to the big magazines when I was striving to make little magazines. That year at Vanderbilt meant a great deal for me. I had been properly shaken and stirred to the depths. Vanderbilt University had only sixteen hundred students then, but it was known nationwide. And of all of its faculties, the Department of English might have been the best known. Despite all my ups and downs, I had become a part of it.

I could not write a term paper in Vanderbilt University that would pass. I hated to write one. When I started to write a term paper, I would end up writing a poem. I wrote a term paper for Dr. Mims on Carlyle. I thought: "This will be an A paper. I have spent a week on it." Dr. Mims looked over the paper and couldn't find a single thing about Carlyle. He wouldn't take the paper. One day I got the paper out of my bureau drawer, and I couldn't find anything about Carlyle in the paper; only in three places I had imitated his prose.

I began to think about a thesis. I had to write one before I could get an M.A., so I must write a thesis. I went to both Vanderbilt University and Peabody College, and looked over the small steel corridors of thin black theses. They were all covered with dust. The only time they were ever used was when a student wanted to see what one was like before he wrote his own. He wanted to look at one for a pattern to cut his by, not for the dry contents, no, no, my heavens, no! Theses and hard work, reading and pounding a hard table with your fists for nothing, saying: "God help me! God help us all! God help this dry educational system! God give it a backbone to hold to and not dry theses, dust-covered, happy and contented in their steel corridors on a shelf at Peabody College and Vanderbilt University or anywhere. God! Can't you hear my prayer? My thesis is undone. My fists are sore. I am still beating on the table.

"No, the gods of education have not heard your prayer, but it will be heard fifty years from today. Go on and write your thesis. Measure your education in bushel split-bottom baskets like your mother used to make.

"The contents are cane seed. Put a paper inside so that the seeds won't sift through the cracks of the basket. Then stack on a few extra pints of bright red cane seed, a couple of extra quarts—maybe a gallon. Run it over and tell the people to look at your golden heap of education. Show them how it is running over, cane seeds and education. They walk hand in hand. Can't you see them! God, give me cane seeds and education. I have to have them. I have to eat. I have to carry my bushel split-bottom basket around to show my cane seed. Education, you know, is measured on dusty shelves. If you don't believe me, go wipe away the dust and read for yourself. Don't strike matches around theses or wear tacks in your shoes."

I intended to fill the basket by the fifteenth of April with golden cane seed. But one day in Wesley Hall when I was running the fingers of my brain through the seeds I'd gotten at the university, I heard a fire siren. I looked down, and the men were throwing on water. "Oh, it won't amount to much. It can't. Now I'll take out a little stuff and put it under that green tree in the yard." I took out three shirts and a picture. I put them in a suitcase. When I stood in front of Wesley, where I could see the fire, I thought that Wesley was gone; at least my room was right under the fire; I knew it was certain to burn. I ran back upstairs, and the smoke came in and blinded me. The building burned all night. The next morning only the brick walls stood, with smoke oozing from the pile of ruins. I lost the job where I had been able to eke out eleven meals per week, enough rations to keep strength in my body. I lost all the clothes but the suit I had on my back, and the crotch split in the pants when I was trying to save a few of my books from the burning building. I lost all I had, but the greatest loss was not the few old clothes I had—I lost my thesis, and the term paper I had rewritten for the fifth time, fifty sonnets, part of a novel, and several poems.

How could I stay in Vanderbilt University with everything gone? Hell, yes, I would stay even if the place where I worked out eleven meals each week did burn, even if the term papers, the novel fragment, and the sonnets burned, my textbooks and clothes and everything!

I marched away from those ashes on February 19 with Bill Chandler, a sixteen-year-old farm boy as poor as I was, and each of us promised the other that we would hang together. He carried his little bag of belongings thrown over his back in "turkey" fashion, as if he was going to a lumber camp. I carried mine in the same style. But it didn't look as if we would be able to stay in the university. I thought I would have to go home and lose the year at Vanderbilt University. I resolved again to stay. Clothes were gathered over Nashville for us, and there was one suit too big for anybody else, but it fit me, in a manner of speaking. I let it hang for a long time because I didn't intend to take anything given to me second-hand. Finally my pants went from bad to worse and they could be patched no more. I went over and got the big suit. It was a fit. It looked very good on me, but I always felt guilty wearing that suit of clothes.

I was able to obtain a free room in Kissam Hall. Bill Chandler was my roommate. I took a sonnet prize in *Muse & Mirror* and got five dollars. I got five dollars (donated) to buy textbooks with, but I saved this ten dollars for food.

I made four B's in my second quarter in Vanderbilt Uni-

versity after the turmoil of the fire. In the meantime I sent
to northeast Kentucky and borrowed a suit of clothes from
Lewis McCubbin, one of the teachers at the Greenup High
School, so that I would have a change. Then I went to the
registrar and begged him for another loan so that I could
register for the third quarter. He asked me about security. I
told him about a friend I had at Vanderbilt University who
had a job. He accepted him, and I took the note out as if I
was going to get him to sign it. I signed Ron East's name to
it and brought it back within an hour. I got the money and
registered.

The last quarter in Vanderbilt University, Dr. Mims asked
for an original paper written about our own selves—a short
autobiography, so to speak. I decided to make mine eighteen
pages at first. But that pleased me very much—the idea of
writing an original term paper—something that concerned
my own life. I heard many of the students laugh about their
very important lives and say it was an old-fogy idea Dr. Mims
had—and the students had to do this every year. I did not
think the idea was old-fogy. I had failed every term paper up
till now but one written for Donald Davidson. I had already
written two for Dr. Mims—on the first one I did not even get
a grade. The paper was too poor to grade, but he marked one
little paragraph in the paper I had written about my experience in the steel mills. He said it was interesting and fairly
well written.

After Dr. Mims had rejected my term papers, I wanted to
write one that would stick.

Ron East came to my room while I was working on my
term paper. "Stuart, I hear you're having it pretty hard, old
boy, since Wesley burned. Did you get registered all right?"

"Yes, I got registered all right. Getting a little grub's been
the worst trouble. Bill Chandler and I have been getting
moldy loaves of light bread, two big loaves for a nickel. We've
been cutting the mold off, and sometimes we have cheese to

go with it. Sometimes just water. But we are staying in the university."

"I just came over to tell you I've paid for you a meal a day at a boardinghouse on Highland Avenue. Sorry it couldn't be two meals, but I have to stay in the university, and I've got my wife to keep. I don't make much with that job I have down here in the slums."

"Ron, I'll pay it back. If I'm living, remember I'll pay it if I have to crawl to work to do it."

I started the term paper toward the last of March and finished it about the first of April. It took me eleven days to write it. I worked at night—sometimes all night long—and attended classes during the morning. I remember one day I did thirty-seven typewritten pages on that paper. Nearly every morning I would take my work to Robert Warren, and he would say it was good and for me to keep it up if I had to throw everything else aside.

Ron East came to my door again. He said: "Well, how are you faring now?"

"All right, Ron. I'm on the last chapter of my term paper that I'm writing for Dr. Mims. I'll have it finished tonight sometime. I've worked eleven days on the damn thing, but I've enjoyed writing it a lot more than I have enjoyed writing about dead authors. East, I haven't made one A in this university. If I ever do, I'm going to frame it in the school colors and send it home. I've had one term paper pass, and I got a B minus on it from Davidson."

"I hear the poems you slipped under Davidson's door are going well here. I heard he read them to the class."

"It's been a new Vanderbilt to me since Donald Davidson got those poems. Boswell, who made fun of me when I told him I wrote poetry, has been friendly like since Davison read those poems to his class."

The paper is done now. I shall not come back again and add to it. Blindly I beat the words out. They fell like drops of blood. I beat them with a hammer to make them paint the small pictures I have gathered in the album of my brain.

When I handed Mims my term paper—"Beyond Dark Hills," I called it—he sucked his pipe harder than I ever saw him suck it before. I let everybody get out of the room before I handed it to him. Then he said: "You write all of this for me to read. Stuart, you aggravate me—you are not passing my work, and then you go and write all of this." I humbly handed him the manuscript that I had bound down on a piece of cardboard with three heavy rubber bands so that he would not think it was as large as it was. I was really ashamed of imposing on him in the spring of the year, when all the term papers were due and a group of theses must be approved by him—and there were 311 closely written pages in my paper. I knew he would read it. When Mims required a student to write a paper, he read every word of it. He was one professor who read every word of a paper, whereas a lot of the college professors, I had been told, threw their papers in the wastepaper basket. He grumbled as he walked out of the room, tapping his cane every alternate step and smoking his pipe. He muttered words I could not understand and did not want to hear. But he had the huge term paper under his left arm, and the last time I saw him he was turning in at his office door with it under his arm and grumbling.

Approximately one week from that time, I passed by his office door. I had just finished a 479-line poem that I called "Whispering Grass." I was taking it to show to Robert Warren, and Dr. Mims came to the door and waved his cane at me and asked me to come in. He never spoke—he just looked at me. His eyes pierced me, and finally I let my gaze pierce him. I looked hard at him. He looked hard at me. If he was going to start a row with me, I thought I would not stand it any longer. And finally he said: "I have been teaching school for forty years, and I have never read anything so crudely written and beautiful, tremendous, and powerful as that term paper you have written." And then he smiled a hard smile. I couldn't believe that he was sincere. He absolutely floored me.

"Do you really like it?" I said.

"I took it home and let the family read it. It is a great piece of work—I can't go out with you to lunch today, but I am paying for your lunch—here, take this dollar and eat on me today." He handed me a dollar bill. I didn't want to take it, but I could not refuse. I had work pending with him, and I couldn't afford to raise a row.

When I got the dollar, I broke for the pie wagon to eat baked peach pie and drink coffee. I shall never forget the thoughts I had about Dr. Mims when I walked across the campus. "If he flunks me, I deserve it. I haven't done anything for him. I should not try to bring pressure to bear on him by doing other things and make him pass me in my schoolwork. If he passed me, he would not be the teacher I thought he was. If he flunked me or held my work up, he was a teacher. But he was an old fogy with regard to what he said about the work in the term paper." I really thought he knew the subject matter he taught but he was not up on creative work. I had been told so many times my prose was as rotten as dead leaves and my poetry would pass as fairly decent stuff. I could not believe now that I had ever done a fairly decent piece of prose.

The year at Vanderbilt University was over now. The classwork was finished. I would not wear the cap and gown even if my grades were good enough the last quarter to bring up my three C's and an F the first quarter. I hadn't written that thesis. We waited for our last quarter's grades in Calhoun Hall. It was in the literature class, where I had stood at the very bottom of the class the first quarter, that the grades were read. I had made the highest grade by two points out of a possible two hundred and twenty-four points. It was a victory, a victory!

My two next reports were A's. Only one class now to hear. I had to hear from Dr. Mims's class. I had not brought up all the assignments. He was the teacher I thought he was. The report was: "Work unfinished. No grade." There wasn't any grade on the term paper, either, only handwriting one had to interpret: "I've told you before what I think of this." I'd not made an A on any term paper throughout the year.

Vanderbilt University was a great school, but I didn't understand it until years later. I wasn't ready for it. It was strange to be in a school where teachers and students were writing books! If one wrote a book there, what of it? One was just in company with the rest. It wasn't anything to get excited about, as we got excited at Lincoln Memorial when Mr. Kroll wrote his first novel. Didn't they smoke in the class at Vanderbilt University—long cigars, pipes, and cigarettes? And if you got stewed at Vanderbilt University, wasn't that your own business too? If the university law found you meandering drunkenly on the campus, didn't he take you to the dormitory and put you to bed?

One of the ministerial students was the best poker player in the university and many of the professors kept jugs of corn liquor made in the Tennessee hills in their homes because they couldn't get legalized whiskey. It was strange that the students would go up before or after a class and fill their pipes from the professor's tobacco pouch, but they could not drink with him until after they had graduated from Vanderbilt University. That was a tradition there. And when I asked Dr. Mims if I could get an M.A. without writing a thesis, he referred me to the dry pages of the catalog and asked me to read it myself, and that was that. What a bunch of paradoxes. Vanderbilt University, upon a little hill, overlooking the city, unmolested throughout the years, going on quietly, watching the students come and go.

When I got ready to leave, my possessions all in a small borrowed suitcase, I said my good-byes to friends; then I went over to say a last good-bye to Donald Davidson. This was the the meeting, though I didn't know it then, that would change my whole life. "Go back to your country," he told me. "Go back there and write of your people. Don't change and follow the moods of these times. Be your honest self. Go back and write of your country, as William Butler Yeats is writing of his native Ireland. Your country has your material. And I wish you success. I hope you have a million readers someday."

I went back home to my father's farm and followed Donald Davidson's advice. In the following eleven months I wrote *Man with a Bull-Tongue Plow.* I have gone on to write, at this present moment, thirty-two books about my Appalachia.

Chapter 6

"WHEN A BOY IS SENT HOME FROM college, it's a disgrace," Mom said.

"But it wasn't my fault, Mom," James said, pushing his chair back from the breakfast table. James had gone to college when he was fourteen.

"It's never been your fault, when something goes wrong for you," Mom said. "Smoking a cigar and fighting!"

Mom sat looking across the table at James as she finished her cup of coffee. It was the spring of the year, in the early thirties.

"Every woman around here knows what's happened," she continued. "Every time I go to town, neighbors stop me and ask about you. They ask me if you're home and what you're doing. They ask me questions I don't want to answer."

"It's none of their business what happens to me," James said to Mom. "What about their boys! How many have ever seen a college? They can keep their noses out of my business."

"You're a failure, James," she told him. "You don't have to be a failure at anything. The metal in you can cut the toughest oak. You won't apply yourself. You've lost your ability to get down to work. You've got soft."

"I'd better get the horse harnessed," I said. "It's getting light enough now so I can see. The weeds are taking the corn."

I left Mom and James sitting at the table. As I walked toward the barn in the streaks of morning light, I wondered what would happen at our house. I wondered if James would went to leave home. Mom had always told us we should be kept busy doing something worthwhile. She told us that idleness was the devil's workshop. Never a day passed she didn't say to James and me: "I want you boys to amount to something. You have one life to give. You must make your life count."

I put harness on the horse and led him toward the field. It was getting light enough to plow now. I would be able to see the burned-off stumps in the new-ground balks before the plow hit them. When I passed the toolshed, I saw Mom and James. Each had a hoe.

"You're not goin' to the field, Mom?" I said. "You don't have to do this."

"That's just where I'm goin'," she replied. "I'm working with you boys."

"But we can do the farming," I said. "There's two weeks' work over there. Your place is in the house."

"A mother's place is with her children," she said. "I'll be with you until the corn is finished."

"She's even challenged me," James said. "Said she could beat me with a hoe."

"That's just what I'm goin' to do," Mom said. "When one of my boys is sent home from college, there's one thing left for him to do. He's got to get back to his early training. That training was hard work, sweat, honesty, and an ambition to do something worthwhile in life!"

"It takes a man and not my mother to challenge me in the

field," James said. "Mom, go back to the house. You can't last in the field."

I didn't listen any longer. I didn't want to see Mom in the cornfield again. She had worked in the fields when she was a young girl at her father's home. She had worked there after she was married and after we were born, to help feed us. I thought she had worked in the field long enough. She was fifty years old now. James was sixteen. How could she, mother of seven children, go to a tough new-ground cornfield and do as much as her son? Mom was like her own father. He had worked until he was eighty-eight. Then he sat in a chair in the yard watching others work. He cried because he couldn't work any longer.

The plowing was very slow, for there were stumps and roots. There were many rocks to plow around. Only last year, virgin trees had been cut from this slope. Giant white oaks, black oaks, and red oaks—beeches, elms, and maples had grown here. The broad mountainside was a graveyard of lost trees. Stumps were their monuments. Giant roots ran from these stumps under the ground. These roots were too big for my plow to break. My plow point often hitched on these roots; then I'd have to lift the plow over on the other side of the root.

Finally I got two rows plowed for Mom and James. I rested my horse to watch them start hoeing. I thought Mom would take the upper row, because it would be easier. She took the bottom row. She gave James the chance to rake weeds down on her row if he was a good enough worker to do it. She had really challenged him. She pitted her strength against her son's. I watched their hoes go up and down with the rhythm of their bodies. The hoes went up and down in unison. They worked the loamy new-ground dirt where the poplar, oak, and maple sprouts were taller than the corn. And it was barely light enough to tell the weeds and sprouts from the young, green corn that grew from the sweet-smelling new-ground earth. The few minutes I watched them while old Fred and I rested, Mom was barely keeping ahead of James.

Before noon, Mom was leaving James behind. But I saw his hoe going up and coming down faster. Soon James was close to Mom again. Once, while Fred and I were resting, I heard Mom say: "James, you hoe your corn and clean your balks like I do. Don't leave a sprout around any stump. Don't leave a weed in any row."

By noon Mom and James had cleaned the corn rows and hoed the corn high upon the slope. What they had done looked good. The sun had wilted the weeds they had cut. It was good to see the green corn blades waving in the slow-moving wind over the clean soft ground. When Mom and James laid down their hoes for lunch, Mom was far ahead in her row.

"You certainly have done some hoein' here this mornin'," I said.

"We got along fairly well," she replied. "James is a little soft. But he's doin' very well."

When we ate the lunch our sister Glennis had prepared for us, Mom, James, and I didn't talk much. James helped himself to the cornbread, soup beans, fried potatoes, and milk. Since he'd come home from college, he hadn't eaten with as much appetite. The food on our table hadn't suited him. Now he was not mincing over the grub we had grown on our hilly farm. This was grub Mom had often told us would stick to our ribs when we worked and would keep us from getting hungry.

After lunch James got up from the table and hurried out of the house. I went to the barn to get my horse. When I came back past the house, Mom was waiting to walk back to the field with me. James wasn't with her.

"Mom, where's James?"

"Look over there in the field," she said.

James had hurried back to get his row hoed up with Mom's.

"He can't stand for me to beat 'im," she said. "He's like my father. Pap could never let anybody do more than he could. In a short time, I'll have James back to his old self. Before this summer is over, he'll be wanting to go back to school, too."

The afternoon sun beamed down from the blue sky onto the loamy, pungent, new-ground soil. While my plow went slowly through the roots and around the rocks, Mom's and James's hoes beat rhythmically against the dark, rich, new-ground earth. Sweat ran in little streams down Fred's flanks and dripped onto the loose dirt. There was too much sweat on my arms and face for the sweat bees. They didn't want to try to sting me, for they got all the sweat they wanted. I was sweating enough to drown them. I watched James stop long enough to wipe his face with his red bandanna. Later I saw him pull his shirt from under his overalls and wipe sweat from his eyes. His bandanna was too soaked to absorb more. He wrung the sweat from his bandanna and left it on a stump to dry in the sun.

The afternoon was hot, but Mom and James never stopped to rest under a shade tree. They kept on hoeing steadily in their long rows around the mountain ridge. Mom was strong for a woman of fifty. She had worked in the hot sun before. That afternoon, Mom and James reached the first flat of the mountainside. I had gained only a few rows on them with the plow.

When we quit for the day, the sun had gone down. We heard cowbells tinkling on the high pastures around us, where children had gone to the pastures to bring the cows home to be milked. We heard the mournful songs of whippoorwills on the ridges. Evening shadows were spreading over the land. The cool of evening was bringing new life to the corn Mom and James had hoed. Blades stood upright toward the blue sunless sky, unmolested by weeds now, to accept the dew and coolness of the starry night.

"We've done a good day's work," Mom said as we three and the horse walked toward the house together. "I gained a row on James."

"Did you let Mom beat you?" I said, looking at his red sunburned face.

"I think she'd beat you, too," he replied quickly. "But she won't be beatin' me when I get used to work again. I didn't know I was so soft."

"My sons should never be soft," Mom said.

Tuesday morning, we were in the cornfield at daybreak, and we didn't stop work until noon. There was a new swath plowed and hoed around the mountain slope. James had kept his row up with Mom, too.

That afternoon we went back to the field in warmth from a sun that looked like a red-hot ember fanned by wind in the roof above our shut-in mountain world. James pulled off his shirt so the lazy winds could blow against his shoulders. James had met Mom's challenge. He was having it tough, too, and I wondered if James wasn't sorry he had laughed at her when she told him she could take the bottom rows and lead him through the field.

When we left the cornfield on the second day, Mom had hoed a half row more than James. She and James had left a wide swath around the mountain where the corn could breathe and feel the wind in clean rows.

James's appetite was growing. I had never seen him put away so much of the grub that stuck to the ribs before. Glennis had to fetch more and more grub to the table. James could have eaten about everything there was on the table by himself. She had to bake an extra pan of cornbread. We were all eating more, but James's appetite had increased the most.

Wednesday, Mom and James finished the second bluff on the mountainside up to the second flat. On Thursday they finished the second flat up to the rugged part of the field under the ridge's rim. It didn't seem possible when we had started at the bottom of this mountain that we would get to the ridge's rim in a week. But if we kept on going, we had a chance to finish it in two more days.

"It's goin' to be tough, James," Mom said as we went to the field before daylight on Friday morning, "but I believe we can finish this mountain this week."

"I can finish plowin' it," I said. "Fred can hold out all right. I think I can. The plow jars my shoulders and arms when the point hitches on a stump."

Every few feet my plow hitched on a rock or a root. The horse got some rest each time I had to lift the plow over to the other side of the stump. But we kept moving slowly toward the rim. Mom's and James's hoes sang a different song as they moved higher with the long rows. By sundown, when the evening shadows began to lengthen, they had hoed halfway up the last bluff.

Saturday morning, when the sun popped over the rim into our faces, Mom and James were working to finish the field. I had never seen James work like he was working now.

"We'll get done today," Mom said as we left the field for lunch. "It's a pretty sight to see corn blades wave above a clean field."

"Mom, you didn't gain on me this morning," James said. "Think I'll start takin' the bottom row."

"Anytime you want the bottom row, you're welcome to it," she said proudly. "But be sure you are ready for it."

When we came back to the field after lunch, James dropped down into Mom's bottom row. Mom looked proudly at him and smiled.

Saturday afternoon at four o'clock, we had finished the field. Mom's and James's hoes were worn so bright that when they lifted them up in the sun, the sunlight on them hurt my eyes. The bull-tongue plow on my sturdy plow beam was almost worn out. It was worn so thin I would have to put on another bull-tongue plow before I could do another field.

Mom looked over the big field. "You boys must not forget it takes work, sweat, and honesty to make you amount to something in life!"

"Cornfields don't have anything to do with college," James said. "But I do want to go back next September."

One day, three men came to me and said, "Is this where the Stuarts live?"

And I said, "Yes."

They said, "We're looking for Jesse Stuart."

And I said, "You're talking to him."

They said, "We want you, young man, back in the schools."

I said, "You're not getting me."

They said, "We want you for country school superintendent."

"Aw," I said, "why didn't you tell me that? Think of being over everybody—all the teachers of the county. I'll sure be that if I can get a certificate in time."

I got the certificate, and I became—because only one other person applied, and that person didn't qualify—superintendent of Greenup County schools at the age of twenty-four. I thought this was wonderful. Dad thought it was the greatest achievement that his son could have.

During that year we had thirty-two lawsuits. We won thirty-one and a half of them. The half ended in the state's Supreme Court. Three months after I was superintendent, the banks closed. We couldn't pay our teachers. I thought teachers would have to be given pep talks to keep that big school system going. When I went out to visit the little rural schools where the youth were walking barefooted, frost on the leaves, eating dry cornbread for their lunches—they weren't anemic pupils either, they were healthy-looking youth—I thought I would have to give pep talks. Instead, these teachers gave me pep talks. We stayed in that county and fought, literally fought, and kept that school system going.

But I have told in *The Thread That Runs So True* about those early years of mine in the school system. How I had to start going armed as a county school superintendent. That superintendency was worse for me than World War II. I talked to my board members about whether they would rehire me or not. They said, "Yes, we will rehire you, but we advise you to leave the superintendency."

I said, "Why?"

And they said, "You have done too much in too short a time. You have got the people riled against you."

What had riled them up? I hired married women as teachers. I paid teachers according to qualifications and experience. I wouldn't pay huge fees for menial labor—like cleaning out wells. I paid no attention to politics and politicians in running my school system. I fought a trustee system so top-heavy that one teacher had three trustees over her. I campaigned for consolidation.

Then they told me about places that were dangerous for me to frequent. Later, just a short time later, I caught it. I was in a drugstore with my back turned when a man hit me with a blackjack. I went to a hospital—but I don't know how— with three gashes on my skull and my shoes full of blood. That county school superintendent's position is something that I will never forget.

I told, too, in *The Thread That Runs So True,* how I was sent from there to McKell High School across from Portsmouth, Ohio. My board put me in there; they took me out of the superintendency. At McKell I wanted to build a model high school. I thought then, and I think now, that ignorance is dangerous. I wanted to go out and get all who were qualified to enter high school, and some of them if they weren't qualified, and bring them to my high school, old and young alike. First, my superintendent was against me. Then, my teachers were against me. But, finally, they let me do it. We brought them in; the oldest student I had was sixty-nine years old, the youngest eleven years old. That oldest one, at the age of eighty-four, wrote one of the best books I have ever seen of its kind.

Once I was a principal, I learned as never before the value of true teachers, inspirational teachers like Mrs. Hatton and Harry Kroll. Several great teachers worked at McKell. I think first of Alice Boswell, who taught mathematics. If Miss Boswell had been my teacher, I would not have failed algebra and plane geometry in high school. In later years I went back and mastered these subjects so that I could teach them. But I couldn't really teach them, even after I'd learned how to solve problems and reason propositions, until I sat in Miss Boswell's classes and listened to her.

Something in the personality of this teacher made her unforgettable, something that went beyond her teaching. I had often heard other women teachers whisper about Miss Boswell's clothes. She wore long dresses, longer ones than any of the other teachers wore, and they were always trimmed with frills and laces. Miss Boswell was large. She had thin lips, a tight little mouth, keen black eyes, and black hair. If a few hairs in her head changed color, she changed it back. Her eyebrows were carefully groomed, also her eyelashes. There was always a little curl on her forehead. Each day she wore a different dress and the curl on her forehead was slightly changed, so her appearance never became monotonous to her students.

Miss Boswell said that algebra was akin to poetry and music. An accomplished pianist herself, she coordinated the exactness of algebra and music and explained the rhythm of algebraic symbols and musical notes. In the beginning she never rushed her students but, lecturing daily, taught them by rote until they became interested in the subject. She told them algebra and plane geometry were as easy to learn as the alphabet. And the way she taught them, they were.

She went beyond mere subject matter. In her plane-geometry classes she taught the beauty of lines—just a straight line and an angle. She made her boys and girls aware of the lines in their clothes. Many times in the autumn she took her geometry class outside the schoolroom. With heavy white cording that wouldn't give and with stakes to set in the ground, they surveyed walks and made foundations for buildings. The immaculate white cords stretching over the brown, barren ground not only fascinated her own class but every student in the high school. Miss Boswell showed me the beauty in plane geometry and in algebra.

Of my three instructors in agriculture, two of them were practical men. They taught the boys what to raise on their farms to make money. They taught them methods of soil conservation, crop rotation, the better breeds of poultry, livestock, and swine. All their teaching ended with the value of dollars. This was all right, well and good. But the third teacher I had—a young, pink-cheeked man, Fred Hatcher—gave them this and something more. He mentioned dollars and cents only by implication.

Once I went on a field trip in the early spring with him and his agriculture class. We went to a field where the long-drilled rows of corn had just broken through the soil in an Ohio River bottom. Fred Hatcher took from his pocket a handful of shelled corn and called his class around him. He showed them how perfect these corn grains were that had produced the young corn in the rows. Then he had his students get down and observe the beauty of the slender stalks of young corn. He discussed the beauty of a stalk of corn until it became a flower. There on the spot I got the idea for a poem, which I wrote and sold to a national literary magazine. I had raised corn all my life, but this teacher gave me a new awareness of the beauty of the grain, the seed germination in the good earth, and the beautiful flower that helped to sustain man and animal.

When we discussed landscaping our large high-school playgrounds, this young agriculture teacher took his boys to the hills and gathered young trees and transplanted them on our school acres. What could be better teaching than this?

One of the most important high-school subjects had been the most neglected—home economics. Never in my teaching have I known it taught in its fullest possibilities. When I was a high-school principal, if my school had been big enough I would have departmentalized home economics. The majority of the girls we teach in high school will in a few years be homemakers. We know the importance of a beautiful, well-kept home in American life.

In my county school system I had a young teacher, Janice Starks, who taught in a remote rural school. She was teaching eighty pupils, from the first grade through the eighth. Her school was one of the prettiest of all the rural schools in our county. The majority of her pupils loved the schoolhouse Miss Starks made for them more than they did their own homes. They came to school early and often stayed late.

In the autumn months Miss Starks, with the help of her pupils, decorated her school with wildflowers and leaves. Here I saw sumac branches with red berries, sassafras twigs with bright leaves, and wild mullein plants. In winter her boys found holly, mistletoe, cedar and pine boughs, wild bittersweet, and greenbrier vines with their little clumps of dark-green berries. Briers were evil things until Miss Starks showed her pupils their beauty in decoration.

In her limited time for classes Miss Starks not only taught her pupils subject matter; she taught them the beauty they had overlooked, growing on their rocky, infertile soil. Every time I visited her school, I thought, "What if every rural school in America had a teacher like Miss Starks, who could teach boys and girls the beauty found in their drab surroundings and make a lovely home for pupils out of a schoolhouse that needs painting and repairs?" If every rural school in America had a teacher like Miss Starks, future generations would live in far more beautiful homes, regardless of their incomes. She is a builder for future America.

I visited her school often because I thought she was a great teacher. Miss Starks taught in a school so inaccessible in winter she had to ride a mule to get there. Once I asked her if she would teach a course in home economics in my high school. She refused because she wanted to teach youngsters on the elementary level. When she was transferred later to a graded school in a small town, she did the same thing there. She had the prettiest room in the school.

In my experience, the subject taught by the greatest number of good teachers is English. This is not to say they are all good. There are many English teachers who do not see beauty in language structure. Many fail to teach our great literary traditions in association with our country's growth. But in the schools where I have taught and in those I have headed, there has never been a time when I have not had an excellent English teacher.

Mrs. Lanning was one of these. She taught grammar in such a way that it became a concrete thing. Each part of speech was somehow related to building materials and carpenter tools. Verbs were hammers and handsaws, conjunctions were nails that held boards together, nouns were boards, and adjectives were various colors of paint. Mrs. Lanning's pupils, after acquainting themselves with tools and materials, built a house. First they worked on a sentence that was a part of the foundation. They diagrammed sentences on the blackboard until diagramming became almost an exact science and a thing of beauty. With these sentences they made a paragraph which was the end, side, or roof of a house. Then they tied a number of paragraphs together to make the whole. And when they had finished the process, they had an essay, a theme, a story.

At another time, Miss Winifred Madden taught our literature, English and American. Stories and novels and poems were things of beauty to Miss Madden's students. Her first object was to get their interest. So when she taught a story or a novel she briefed her students on the background of the story, its period in history, and the author's life. She took them back into another day and time, to when and where the story was created. If a poem was about a river, a railroad, or just a grove of trees, she took her class to such a place. Once when she was teaching that brief classic, "In Flanders Fields," she took her class to a field where poppies were in bloom and waving in the wind.

If we only had in America today more teachers who could teach beyond—and still include—the required subject matter, teachers who could inject beauty into their teaching, we could change the face of America. We wouldn't find the streets in our small towns and cities littered with piles of rubbish, and we wouldn't have our nondescript and ugly rows of houses in coal-mining towns.

Inspirational teachers can have a profound influence upon the youth who will later occupy state and national positions and influence a nation.

While I was principal of McKell in 1933, we were privileged to have some wonderful teachers on our staff. There was only one hitch. We did not have very many. Wages in the Kentucky school system were poor, and teachers were scarce everywhere. When McKell opened its doors in the fall, there were many classes for which there were no teachers at all. Senior students who did good work taught freshmen and sophomore students. Some of our students were rural schoolteachers returning to high school to earn diplomas after years of teaching experience, and some of these were among our finest student teachers. Everyone who could teach did teach, including the principal. I taught senior English classes the whole time I was principal. I shall never forget one youth I taught at McKell.

His name was Bruce Barnhill, but the pupils called him "Grassy" because he and his sister Daisy were the only ones who walked the eight miles from Grassy Valley to McKell High School in South Shore from 1932 to 1936.

Grassy was six-feet-two, with fair skin, large blue eyes, and a shock of hair as golden as ripe wheat stems. Daisy could have passed for his twin, except that she wasn't as tall. Although a year older than he, she was in the same class.

What made me remember Grassy was a theme he wrote for my English class when he was a senior. One day a week my students wrote on any topic they chose, then read their themes aloud. Grassy's theme was about jumping up and cracking his heels together. Because he was interested in math, time, space, and the universe, he wondered why the earth didn't move from under him when he jumped up and cracked his heels together.

He had practiced jumping so that he could stay in the air long enough to crack his heels together two and sometimes three times, and he had his sister Daisy time him with a stopwatch to see how long he was in the air on each jump.

The subject of Grassy's theme dealt with where he figured he should have been when he landed on the ground after his jumps. Using figures based on the rotation of the earth in space and time, he showed that when he cracked his heels together once in the McKell High School yard he should have come to earth in Fairlington, Kentucky, and after he had cracked them twice he should have landed on the west side of Portsmouth, Ohio.

When Grassy was reading his theme to the class he looked up from his paper partway through to see how the other students were reacting. They were smiling. Grassy had a hot temper, and he obviously didn't like those smiles.

"Read on," I said quickly. "This is a very interesting theme."

Grassy's face was flushed as he began to read the last part

of his theme, which discussed where he should have landed
after cracking his heels together three times in the air. According to his calculations, he should have come to earth on
the western border of Sinton County, Ohio. He closed his
theme by saying he hadn't been able to figure out why his
experiments hadn't worked.

Twenty-three students exploded in laughter. They
couldn't hold back any longer. Grassy's temper flared. He
was ready to start swinging when I hurried over and put my
hand on his shoulder. He was trembling like a dry sassafras
leaf in a September wind.

"That's the most interesting theme that's been read in this
English class," I said. "Now, of course, I don't know about
your figures. I'm not good enough in math to follow you."

"The figures are correct," he said, still trembling, "but I
can't understand why I dropped back every jump to the same
place where I was standing when I jumped."

"There is a thing called gravity that held you in place," I
said.

Now he smiled, and his classmates stopped laughing. They
looked at Grassy with puzzled expressions on their faces.

"How long have you been working on this theme?" I
asked.

"I've been thinking about it ever since last year," he replied. "This year it's taken weeks for me to practice my
jumps and for Daisy to get the timing. I had to figure my
distances too, before I could write the theme."

He handed me pages of figures to back up what he had
written.

"I've never had anybody work harder and longer on one
theme or put more thought into it than you did on this one,"
I told him. "It's the most original idea I've ever had a student
write about."

I gave him the only A plus I had given the class and showed
my gradebook to the students. Grassy smiled faintly; then his

face became serious. "Gravity" he sighed, "gravity."

Later I took Grassy's theme and his calculations to one of the math teachers and asked her to see if the figures were correct.

"Bruce is a genius with figures," she said. "If they're his calculations, I'm almost sure they're right, but I'll go over them for you."

Two days later she reported that Grassy's calculations were correct.

"Did his theme interest you?" I asked.

"The beauty in his calculations interested me more. There's lots of work behind every sentence of his theme. But his kind of thinking is a little crazy, isn't it?"

"I like his kind of thinking," I said. "He may never put it to any practical use, but he's certainly original."

"It doesn't make good sense. He ought to know, smart as he is, that people have jumped in the air before, and the earth didn't spin under them. I hope he can keep his feet on the ground!"

Now, I have remembered Grassy all my life just for that one theme. But as it happens, this story has a sequel that will show you how a teacher can sometimes be wrong in his estimate of a pupil.

In due course, Grassy and Daisy graduated and went to teacher's college. I heard that they were making A's and that Grassy was a track star.

In 1937 I left Greenwood to go to work on a fellowship, and when I returned I taught in Portsmouth, Ohio. I didn't hear any more about the Barnhills until one summer day in 1940, when I was back in Greenwood, and I met their father, Eif, on the street. He greeted me with a smile and a friendly handshake.

"I wanted to tell you that Daisy and Grassy finished college," he said. "There were over three hundred in the graduating class, and Grassy finished first and Daisy second."

"Where are they now?"

"Daisy is teaching at Plum Fork School," he replied. "And Grassy, well, he went to California."

"Is he teaching in California?"

"No, he's not teaching. He never tells us about what he's doing in his letters, but I think he's working in a factory."

In 1941, when the United States began fighting a war on two fronts, I enlisted in the navy. Years passed—1942, 1943, 1944. While I was home on leave at Christmas in 1944, I met Eif Barnhill again. I asked about Daisy and Grassy. He told me proudly that Daisy was teaching in a big high school in Nebraska.

"And Grassy?" I asked. "What branch of the service is he in?"

"Ah, Grassy . . ." he stammered. "He's still in California. When he writes, he never says anything about his work." Eif's face was flushed, and he looked away from me.

"I can't blame you for feeling embarrassed," I thought. "Your son was the best physical specimen in McKell High, yet as far as I know he's the only one of all the boys in his graduating class who's not in the service."

In the years that followed, I tried to keep from thinking about Grassy, but I never could forget him. Since he had never come home, I wondered if his hot temper got him into a fight that had landed him in prison.

In 1956 I returned to South Shore as principal of McKell High. One October morning a sunburned blond youth of about fourteen came into my office. When I looked at him, it was like looking at the Grassy Barnhill of twenty years before. Seeing him brought a strange, unpleasant feeling to me.

"Sir, did you used to teach Bruce Barnhill?" he asked. "Everybody called him Grassy."

"Yes, I did," I replied to the smiling boy.

"He's my cousin," he said. "My father is his father's youngest brother. Do you know where he is now?"

"In prison," I thought, but I didn't tell the boy what I was thinking.

"The last I knew he was in California," I said.

"He's been transferred."

I looked at this image of Grassy, who beamed with pride when he spoke of his cousin.

"He's at Cape Canaveral now," he said. "He's one of the high men working on missile projects down there."

Suddenly I understood many things. Now I was beaming with as much pride as his young cousin. "Well, Grassy," I said to myself, "you have certainly jumped higher and cracked your heels together more than three times."

And I remembered, then, telling his math teacher his kind of thinking might not have any practical use.

This teaching of youth is always exciting, since so many things influence the development of their plastic minds. Often they ask us questions that we think are a little crazy: sometimes we laugh at them! And in some instances we have given our questioners silly answers. And a few of us have been stupid enough to tell students they cannot succeed in this or that. This is dangerous. After many years of teaching and associating with young people, I have learned to respect the ideas of my students, particularly the ideas I didn't understand. And I have learned never to tell a student he cannot succeed in this or that.

One of the boys in an agriculture class asked me if it wouldn't be a smart thing to set black locust sprouts along the fencerows. "It's better to have living posts in a fencerow," he said, "than it is to have dead ones. I've been thinking about this as I've been replacing posts that have rotted off even with the ground."

"I cannot answer that question," I said. "Perhaps when the trees grow up, wind will weave the trees and slacken the wires."

Years later I saw a farm in Indiana where a farmer had successfully done this very thing.

Approximately twenty years ago one of my pupils conceived the idea of setting the barren slopes of his father's small farm in black walnuts. He had gotten interested in trees while taking a course in general science. His idea was that black walnuts grew quickly and that lumber saved from them was valuable for furniture and gun stocks. In twenty years, he reasoned to us, he would have a fortune. He said that he would get the walnuts, shell them, and make money from them as well as the wood from these trees.

I thought of this boy, who never had the money to execute his plan, when the government twenty years later sent me a letter suggesting that I set out a young forest of black walnuts. I don't know of a better move to replenish our dwindling forest on the well-worn Kentucky slopes that have been "corned to death." But a high-school boy had this idea twenty years ago!

But one of the funniest ideas I ever heard from a student was from one who longed to dress well though he wasn't able to. He admired boys who looked smart. Each morning before he reached the schoolhouse, he had to walk past a garage where he saw mechanics wearing unionalls working over automobiles. This youth said to me: "Mr. Stuart, why can't men change their clothing? Why do men wear the same kind of a suit year in and year out? Women change their kind of clothing. They always look better than we do! Looks like we'd make a change."

"I'm not interested in men's clothing," I said, looking down at my black old men's shoes, realizing at that time I'd never worn another color but black. Then I looked at him and asked: "What kind of suit do you suggest men wear?"

"Why not try a one-piece suit," he said happily, "something like unionalls! We think of unionalls as something to absorb grease in a garage—but I believe a one-piece suit could become the fashion. I don't see why we can't try it for a change!"

I had to laugh at his idea. It sounded so strange coming from a Kentucky student's lips. But when I was in Scotland, Hamish Brown told me about George Bernard Shaw's conceiving the idea of the one-piece suit. He said that Shaw not only conceived the idea but he had his tailor make his suit. He wore it down the streets of London, and everybody smiled. England was too conservative for this experiment. But what dashed through my brain was, a high-school boy once suggested this to me, and I laughed at his idea. The world's greatest dramatist had tried the same idea.

In our English class one day, one of the bright young girls asked me why we had to separate words with hyphens. "It seems to me," she said, "that we could improve our language if somebody would write a book and tie words together without hyphens. Look at the Old English language around Chaucer's day! We can hardly understand it now. The English language has undergone great changes, and it will undergo many more changes. So why not start improving the language by tying words together?"

James Joyce was writing at that time. But that was long before he had written *Finnegans Wake*. He, too, had this idea. But this girl didn't know about it. It was her idea; however, she was the type who probably would never have done anything about it.

When my students were dramatizing a short story for a one-act play, one of my boys conceived this idea. "Have two men," he said, "dressed in black dresses. Have them sit on the stage and let one be sewing with a long needle and white thread. Let the two talk about their age, the undertaker, and death."

Not one of us saw anything amusing about this boy's suggestion. We thought that he was ridiculous for having such an idea! For some time students called him "Undertaker." I thought about this incident when I was in the King's Theatre, Edinburgh, Scotland, and saw the most hilarious comedy I ever attended in my life. Everybody in the theater roared when two old men, dressed in robes of black, walked onto the stage with their sewing, long needles, and white thread (so we could see it) and talked of their ages, the undertaker, and death. I thought of the student we called "Undertaker" for suggesting this to us three years before.

Presently one of my students put this problem before me. He has twelve bushels of walnuts piled up to hull. He is trying to figure how many hulled walnuts he will have. He plans to figure this thing out. He told me how he was going to do it. Then he plans to measure the hulled walnuts to see how much he misses the problem with figures.

"It's a hard problem for you," I said, "but I believe you can do it."

"I know I can," this boy said. "What use is mathematics if you don't apply it?"

"It's your problem," I said.

"My math teacher will work with me," he said.

I didn't laugh at him. That was an idea. It was his idea. I would leave it to him and his math teacher. I know that it takes ideas to keep civilization moving; it takes ideas to write books, ideas to run a farm; and above all, it takes ideas to win a war. It takes ideas to do everything. Since we teachers are working with youth whose plastic minds are like young streams without channels we must be careful to direct each channel on its natural course.

And yet, over the years I have taught and worked with youth and teachers, I have seen that sometimes we must temper the encouragement we offer, particularly to the very bright pupil, with careful discipline.

Superior intelligence is a thing greatly to be desired in children, but how often we throttle its development in the young mind. Teachers all too often see how much can be crammed into the mind of an exceptionally bright child just because it can do the work. The child usually attends high school three years and one summer session and then enters college in his early teens with his name in all of the papers stating that he is a genius. If he is a genius, he stands a fair chance to be ruined, for the simple reason that he thinks he is superior and develops the wrong mental attitude. He decides too frequently that hard work is not necessary and develops a habit of dawdling. The result is that he is soon surpassed by all of his classmates.

I like to see a student put forth all the effort he has to lead a class, because I know that hard work is a factor in winning. Watch the students who are the steady, dependable ones, who can stand the test of school grind and monotony, and see if they don't more than average up. They usually are the geniuses in the long run when it comes to production.

I have in mind a boy who went to the same grammar school I did. He surely was the best pupil in the school. He set the pace through the school, carrying away the medal for being the best all-around pupil of his group. He was excellent. But nine years after we parted from this little school, I met a new gang of steel men working for the American Rolling Mills. I was working during summer vacation and was helping set a four-ton air hammer in a forge shop when I looked across the foundation and saw a familiar face. It was Chester tugging at some steel railings. I was anxious to know about him and his three brothers. So I began to question him and talk over old times, including our schooldays together. Chester told me that he had been working for four dollars per day and was glad to get that. He lamented that this would hardly keep him, his wife, and child and pay house rent and grocery bills. He said that he wished that he had gone on in school and that he had never started smoking cigarettes, because he had to keep paying for a desire that he had contracted himself. He said that he was sorry that he had ever led the class and felt like he had known it all. In other words, his opportunity was nipped in his childhood days. He said that he had often regretted that he was not the sticking type of student instead of genius type.

Average mental ability, plus ability to stick, will win where superior intelligence plus poor working habits will lose.

Character is a human trait one cannot buy. It is something acquired through home, school, and church training and through contacts with associates. One of the finest-looking youths I had in a high school, who was an A student and had set a record for the quarter mile in track, started giving us trouble in school. I talked to his parents. His father said: "Mr. Stuart, he's running with the wrong crowd." I knew he was right. I visited all the questionable places to see if any of my pupils were loafing there. I always found Ronald. Later in Ohio, a man was robbed. A cigarette package was picked up on the scene, traced back to a filling station near my school. Ronald Dorton had bought the cigarettes. He admitted his guilt. This boy served time in the Ohio state penitentiary. No more good days of high school for this teenage youth, nor cheers from hundreds when he broke the tape first on the quarter-mile run. When he was paroled, I went to see Ronald. He was restricted to an area of less than an acre around his home. He was embarrassed when I visited him again after the way I'd worked to save him. He wept bitterly.

I'd always liked to see pupils who could make A's in my school, but I came to the conclusion that I would rather have a pupil who made C grades and had A character than one who made A grades and had C character. If the morals and character of our people are good, our country rests on a firm foundation. But when the character and morals are degraded, our country totters on a weak foundation. The great majority of our people have good character and good morals, and this is what has preserved us as a nation. Let us fight to bring into the fold those whose morals have disintegrated and whose characters are not wholesome.

A legal whiskey store was located in the center of my

school district. Parents of many of my students often visited this store. My boys were getting whiskey, and I walked into this store and talked to the old man who was the proprietor. He assured me he wouldn't sell whiskey to a youth. But one morning early, I watched three of my boys go into this store. These three young fellows were unusually friendly with me until I called one into my office and told him what I had seen. He confessed everything. I got on the phone and called the prosecuting attorney. The proprietor threatened to send the high-school boy to the reformatory for lying about his age. The prosecuting attorney and I had different ideas. The liquor-store proprietor was fined one thousand dollars and forced to close the store. No other whiskey store moved in while I was principal of that school.

Another man, whose daughter I had in high school, I had jailed and fined many times. He was a bootlegger and sold my boys illegal whiskey. He detested me because I interfered with his livelihood. But he interfered with my dreams of America. My dream was to build men of character. Of his six sons, five served sentences in the penitentiary. Eighteen years later this man changed his way of life. He quit battling civil laws and accepted the Ten Commandments. He apologized to me then. He thanked me for the help I'd given his daughter, the only child of nine to finish high school.

It distresses me to bring up this problem, which is widespread over America. Our athletic equipment was carried off one night. One of my boys told me to go easy. He knew the right ones and would get it back. I didn't like the idea. And I figured he was involved. This boy did get it back, and he didn't have any part in stealing it. We got back the much-needed equipment but didn't have a single clue about those implicated.

Stealing, as I'd never before experienced, broke out in the high school. We had faculty meetings to try to break it up. Each member of the faculty, behind closed doors, suspected a different person. But one day a little girl came and said to me, "Mr. Stuart, I caught a boy in my locker, and I have the only key to it." I asked her who he was, and she didn't know. Our school was rather large, and not all the pupils knew each other. I had her wait as my pupils marched in. She identified the boy. I couldn't believe it. He was one of two youths in my school on a spending allowance. He was my best half-miler in track. I let him get to his homeroom and then phoned his teacher to send him to the office. He came in smiling and didn't suspect anything. "Give me that ring of pick keys," I said so quickly he got them from his pocket without thinking. I locked the office door, pulled the window shades, and turned on the lights. In that office was some drama.

When I told him what he was doing, for I had the evidence with the bundle of thirty keys, he didn't deny it. He admitted he did it, just as one might tell his principal about understanding a lesson. He thought it was clever. He said, "I suppose you'll suspend me for this."

"No," I told him, "I couldn't do that."

"Then you'll spank me," he said.

"Not a man," I said. "What good would that do? You're no longer a child."

After we talked, and I explained to him that among hill people nothing was more unforgivable than stealing, he stopped smiling. He got serious and he trembled. I was upset and walked the floor.

"Do something with me," he said.

"What am I to do?" I said. "This is serious. I can't suspend you. This will be found out if I do. You'll be ruined for generations to come if you still live here, as your people have for five generations." Then I shed tears, and he wept. "Can you," I asked him, "if I never tell a teacher, never tell anybody, so this won't ruin you as a man in later life here, go home and sin no more? Will you promise me? Will you be as good as your word?" I thought he was going to hug my neck. No one knew he was the culprit. This ended our stealing. This boy helped me by giving advice to other youths. He fought through the North African campaign with distinction, through southern France, and was in Austria when the war ended. He came home and taught school. He is today one of our finest citizens.

In this community it was our school against a community. Once in a talk I told my boys and girls only they and not their parents could make this the best community in the county. Ten or fifteen years later, it was. Today, a boy I accepted in the school at an older age, against the advice of my faculty, is superintendent of a church. He had been a professional boxer and later an alcoholic. He and I took long walks together and talked of the future. Any human being, in any possible way, should be saved. Another athlete, six-feet-four, 242 pounds, redheaded, with a mouth like Mussolini's, used to gouge me in the ribs as he stood and looked down on my head and said: "Mr. Stuart, today we play Rosten High School, and I'm tackling John Phelps and carrying him six yards. I'll make them white ivories rattle until you can hear 'em on the sidelines. No foul play, but he won't stay in a game." And he would do just that. His brother, the same type and size of boy, was later farmed out by the Dodgers. Then this boy went to a funeral. It was the death of a child of one of his classmates. There was no minister there, and the child would have been buried without rites. This big redheaded boy, the farthest from religion of any youth I knew, rose up and said there would be rites for the child. He preached the funeral and said a prayer. Today he's a lay member in a church.

Our pupils at McKell had little in material goods in those Depression days. But there were many, many young people in our school who had character and generosity. Many were truly poor, but their hearts were in the right place.

"Mr. Stuart, can you help us work out this Christmas program?" Helen Riggs asked.

"Yes, we've got a problem," Jim Tackett said.

Helen Riggs and Jim Tackett were seniors, and I had appointed them to work out the Christmas program. McKell High School had twelve teachers, a full-time librarian, and three hundred students. The time was 1936. Some families had a father working at the steel mill and a mother at the shoe factory. Many families had only a father or a mother working as breadwinner. About half the families represented lived on small farms where they could barely eke out a living. Only two teachers at McKell High School owned automobiles. Students either walked or rode a school bus. A few students lived in such remote roadless areas they could not ride a bus. And less than a dozen of these students walked from six to ten miles to McKell High School. Not a student owned or drove a car in this Depression year.

"What is your problem?" I asked Helen and Jim.

"We think we ought to get a present for Dr. McKell," Helen said.

"Yes, he even buys our football uniforms and headgear," Jim Tackett said.

"He has furnished most of the books in our library," Helen said. "We have one of the finest libraries of any small high school along the Ohio River just because Dr. McKell is our friend."

"Yes, he certainly is," I replied. "He's done everything for this school but pay the teachers and build the schoolhouse. And I think he had something to do with putting a better roof on McKell High School to stop the leaks."

In an area that was to grow and develop, Dr. McKell had given forty acres of valuable land for the new McKell High School, to be built in the western part of the county and to be named for Dr. McKell. He was proud that Greenup

County in Kentucky would name a school for him.

"A living monument," he said proudly.

McKell High School students, faculty members, and principal didn't know how much Dr. McKell was worth financially. We didn't inquire and try to find out. But we knew Dr. McKell was worth a lot of money. He was a very rich man who had come down from Chillicothe, Ohio, and bought land in the western part of Greenup County. He was the first man to practice soil conservation on his land, to set trees to protect, and to feed wildlife. Dr. McKell was a medical doctor who didn't practice medicine except for people in western Greenup County too poor to pay a doctor. He owned refractories in Ohio.

As I have said, people didn't care how much Dr. McKell had. No one in western Greenup County envied him. They loved this small, balding man who wore tennis shoes winter and summer, and in spring and summer walked over his land hunting snakes (copperheads were his favorites), grasshoppers, and bugs, and discovering all living things that walked, crawled, or flew. He often took his own four small children with him. Often he had McKell High School students. And very often I went with him on the snake hunts. When he bought headgear for our football team, he insisted we strike a bargain.

"I will buy your helmets, the very best made, but only if you will never remove your helmets even for a second in a game," he said. "You must be very careful about head injuries."

Dr. McKell was ahead of his time. Today I believe this is an athletic rule in most states for high-school, college, and professional teams. Once, while our team practiced football, Dr. McKell appeared from nowhere, climbed up the goalpost, walked with his hands out on the crossbar, and chinned himself fifty-two times.

Coach Wilson, the football players, and I stopped to watch

him. When he had finished, he walked back over the crossbar with his hands and scooted down the goalpost.

"Boys, I just want you to see what it means to stay in shape," he said. "I chinned the bar fifty-two times, for I am fifty-two years old today."

Dr. McKell was loved by the people as well as the students and faculty of the school that bore his name. When he walked, as he liked to do, many people followed him but had to run to keep near him. He walked fast. He loved people, and everybody wanted to live on his property to get his free medical service. Whatever they grew on his fine fertile land was theirs; he didn't take any share of it, if they'd agree to feed the birds and wildlife. Dr. McKell paid the taxes, kept the property in good repair, and gave them free rent. How could students at McKell High School buy this rich and fabulous man a Christmas present? They'd worried for the three years I had been their principal. Now they'd come to me for advice.

I suggested they buy a desk set. "A fountain pen and pencil set. I think you can get it for about ten dollars."

In 1936 ten dollars was a lot of money at McKell High School and the surrounding area. Teachers made from eighty to ninety dollars a month. Half of our faculty had M.A. degrees. Coach Wilson made a hundred dollars a month. I made twelve hundred, and I worked twelve months. Laborers at the steel mills were paid higher than teachers. Workers at shoe factories made wages in proportion. Anyone then was content just to have a job. Work and money were scarce. Farmers were helped by the government, and many people worked on WPA, and still some few others, not many, were on "relief."

On Monday before Friday, the last schoolday before our holiday season, Helen and Jim came into my office to give me the present the students' pennies had purchased for Dr. McKell.

They had brought a desk-set fountain pen and pencil for me to post to Dr. McKell.

"Oh, that's a nice present, and he'll love it," I bragged to Helen and Jim.

They had worried so much about this present. They had worked hard to get it by collecting a thousand pennies.

After the day was over and I went back to my hotel room, I placed a long-distance phone call to Dr. McKell's residence in Chillicothe. Luckily, I caught this very busy man at home.

"Dr. McKell, are you too busy on Friday afternoon to come to McKell High School and give the presents out from under the Christmas tree to our students?" I asked him.

"I'm a busy man, but I'd be delighted to do this," he said. "Do they want me?"

"They certainly do," I replied. "Students want you, teachers want you, and I want you!"

"I'll be there," he said.

On Friday morning students brought their gifts for each other. Teachers brought gifts for one another. There must have been four hundred little gift-wrapped packages lying under that tree before our program began. I walked down to the pile of little gifts and shoved one back under the pile. This was the gift a thousand pennies from three hundred students had purchased for Dr. McKell.

As Dr. McKell had promised, he was in my office at one o'clock Friday afternoon. And now our students were marching down to the gymnasium-auditorium to take their places and to receive their gifts.

"I'm touched the students love me and want me," Dr. McKell told me.

"We feel wonderful to have you," I told him.

After they had gone down and were seated, Dr. McKell and I walked in. He was dressed in his dark business suit, white tennis shoes, a white shirt with a stiff white collar, and a black tie. When the students saw him, they rose. With his hands he motioned for them to be seated.

"Dr. McKell, whom you know so well and love so much, has come to read your names and give you the presents," I said. "Now, this will have to be done quickly. Remember, there'll be nearly four hundred names called after we sing some Christmas carols."

"We will have time for two carols, 'O Little Town of Bethlehem' and 'Silent Night,' " Mrs. Juergensmeyer said. Mrs. Juergensmeyer led the singing without music. Dr. McKell joined in the singing. To be with our youth and to join with them singing hymns made his face radiant. After we had sung the two hymns, Dr. McKell walked over to the tree and said, "This is a pleasure for me to do this. I've never done anything like this before!" Then he reached down and began reading the names on the packages.

Girls had cut and embroidered handkerchiefs for presents. Boys had made wild-bird feeders and had given them. This present made Dr. McKell smile. Out in the country areas, far away from the stores, so many of the youths had had to make their presents. Embroidered hand towels and pillowcases were made by girls and were given as presents.

In the industrial areas, where youths lived in South Shore and Fullerton and were close to Portsmouth, Ohio, across the river, there were all kinds of stores, small and large, loaded with holiday merchandise. And students from this area, where they could purchase from the stores, gave different gifts. Girls gave boys pocket combs, handkerchiefs, little nail clips, pencils, small pocketbooks, socks, and neckties. They gave inexpensive tidbits of merchandise in this Depression year. Boys gave girls hair clasps, ribbons, perfume, lace-edged handkerchiefs, and small boxes of candy. This was a gay affair. Dr. McKell was a happy man.

"What a wonderful teacher he would have been if he had not inherited a business world," I thought.

Dr. McKell had given most of the presents to students and

teachers and was now getting down to the bottom of the pile. I was sitting in the front row of the senior section, near Helen Riggs and Jim Tackett, when Dr. McKell picked up the gift Jim and Helen had wrapped for him.

"Well, here is a present for me," he said. "To Dr. McKell from the students of McKell High School. I thank you. I shall open my present here!"

Then he took the wrappers from around his present. He held it up.

"Beautiful," he said. His voice faltered. "Beautiful . . . I thank you!"

"Dr. McKell, three hundred students contributed pennies for your present," I said. "Every youth in this school had a part in your present."

Dr. McKell tried to speak, but the words wouldn't come. He turned his face away from the students. He didn't want them to see him overcome by his emotions.

"I thank . . . you." And he motioned for me to come up and read the names on the last presents. He walked away across the gym with his back toward us. He went to the back door of the gym. And he eased out carrying his present. After I had read the names of those yet to receive presents and Coach Wilson had led us in reciting the Twenty-third Psalm, we were dismissed. The program was over, and the students marched to their homerooms to be dismissed for the holiday season. School buses were waiting to take those home who rode buses as far away as twenty miles. And in a minute scores would be walking to their homes in inaccessible areas where buses couldn't run. There were no good roads then. They walked and ran, or ran and walked. They were happy with their presents and looking forward to their holiday season. When I reached my office, Dr. McKell was waiting.

"I'm not given to too much emotionalism," he said, "but I was deeply touched. I'll keep this present all the days of my life. It will occupy a conspicuous place in my home. Just to think they brought their pennies for a gift for me. You know, a rich man gets few presents. Everybody seems to think he and his family have all they want. Well, say they do, but a present bought with pennies, given from three hundred hearts and minds . . . ah, what a gift! I just wanted to tell you that I've never been made happier in my life. All those pennies' worth of love!"

Chapter 7

AFTER TEACHING IN RURAL
schools, after being a high-school teacher and superintendent
of Greenup County schools, I knew I needed more know-
how to meet the educational problems of my day and time.
I decided to study at George Peabody College for teachers,
Nashville, Tennessee. Here I spent four summers, equivalent
to one year of graduate work. Had I written a thesis, which
I never did, I would have received an M.A. degree there. But
at Peabody, where graduate students outnumbered undergraduates, I got more than a sheepskin.

Although I didn't realize it at the time, my teachers at
Peabody College were educational giants. One of the most
outstanding was Dr. Alfred Leland Crabb. I had philosophy
of education under this remarkable teacher-writer-lecturer.
He asked our class of graduate students to write a paper on
our philosophy of life—I thought this over while sitting in
class. I came to the conclusion my philosophy (being one of
the younger ones in the class) was not solidified enough—that
I couldn't write my philosophy yet. I thought I should write
on the philosophy of an older person. And who would I

choose? I decided before the class was over.

After the bell ending the class, I went up to Dr. Crabb's desk.

"I don't have a philosophy of education," I told Dr. Crabb. "I feel that I can't do your assignment. But I have a substitute if you'll let me do it."

"What is your substitute?" he asked sternly.

"I'd like to write on the philosophy of my Uncle Martin Hilton," I said. "He's my mother's brother, a very positive man. He certainly has a philosophy of life!"

"Is he a teacher?" Dr. Crabb asked.

"No, he's only an eighth-grade graduate," I said. "And he is a Kentucky mountain hillside farmer. And he sat in the shade reading *The Rise and Fall of the Roman Empire* while weeds took his corn!"

"Sounds like a very interesting man," Dr. Crabb said. "I'll let you take your uncle for your philosophy-of-education paper."

On the date Dr. Crabb had wanted our papers, everyone had his paper ready. At our next class meeting, Dr. Crabb announced: "Today I am going to read the philosophy-of-education paper which I think is best. It is titled 'Uncle Mel,' and was written by Jesse Stuart." I had been an unknown in this philosophy-of-education class up until now. I had asked a lot of questions. Dr. Crabb read my paper while the old graduate students, many of them Ph.D. candidates, listened. This paper created quite a stir. I remember one woman who was working on her Ph.D. said it was more like a short story than a paper on the philosophy of education. One person wiped away a few tears. He said my uncle reminded him of one he had, but he had never thought of him as a subject for a term paper.

This time Dr. Crabb asked me to stay after class. He said he wanted to talk to me about my paper. And I waited until all members of the class had left the room.

"Stuart, I've been at Peabody a long time," he said. "Each summer and each year I have my students taking philosophy of education do this paper. This is the best one I have ever received and. . . ."

"Well, thank you, Dr. Crabb," I interrupted him. I was really pleased to have this compliment from him.

"And I think you might sell this paper to a magazine," he said.

"Which magazine would you suggest, Dr. Crabb?" I asked.

"Any of the quality magazines," he replied.

After talking to him, I hurried to my room, put the manuscript in an envelope with a self-addressed and stamped envelope for its return if it were rejected. I sent it to *Esquire*.

That summer I had brought my brother, James, with me to Peabody. We had to live on half enough money to support one of us. I had been teaching for a small wage, and James had been working on my father's farm. We came thinking we could get part-time employment. Some days we didn't know where our food would come from. There was a small restaurant where I could put a nickel in a machine and pull the lever. If the right combination of numbers came up, I was paid off in meal tickets. And I had always been lucky. Once for a nickel I got thirty meal tickets.

"Uncle Mel" had been gone just over a week when my self-addressed envelope, almost flat as a pancake, was returned to me. I tore it open. And here was a fat check—just as if they knew my predicament. But they certainly didn't know I had a brother with me whom I was trying to support!

"Hurrah, hurrah," went through my head as I waved the check. I wanted to celebrate. I ran to Shorty's Restaurant, where I had won so many free meals for us. I bought a cigar! Then I went up the street of the Quadrangle to the administration building. I knew Dr. Crabb would be in his office at this hour. And he would rejoice when I showed him my check.

Inside the administration building I hurried to his office. Up I went, waving the check and puffing my cigar. "Dr. Crabb," I said in a half-breath. "It sold! Look at this!"

"You get out of here!" he yelled. He grabbed a large book. "Get out of here with that cigar!"

When he came after me with a book, I started running. I could have pushed my excellent professor aside easily. He was three-fourths my size and twenty-six years my senior. But I ran like a chicken out of the administration building, down the steps, and down the street. Dr. Crabb followed me to the steps. But I was off and gone.

I had forgotten Dr. Crabb's hatred of tobacco. No one could smoke in his house. A classmate of mine who got his Ph.D. degree at Peabody lighted up a cigar while he waited to form a line in the graduation processional. Dr. Crabb came up and pointed a finger. "If I had known you would have done this, you wouldn't be wearing that cap and gown this evening," he told him. He meant it too.

After selling this paper to *Esquire*, where it was published as a story, I sent more poems, articles, and stories to magazines. Things changed for James and me at Peabody College. We ended up eating in the Peabody College cafeteria. I no longer gambled for food. I paid James's and my way in full, and when James and I went home, we didn't go back the way we had come. We went first class on the Pan American—a great southern train. We ate steaks in the diner too. And the money I had sent home to help my father on our farm was enough to purchase some new mule-and-horse-drawn equipment, a new hay rake, a new mowing machine, a new disk, new plows, and a lime spreader. This was one of the most profitable summers I ever spent in college—thanks to Dr. Crabb.

The following summer, when I returned to Peabody to further my teacher education, new plants came up in Dr. Crabb's garden. He didn't know exactly what they were. He hoed the plants and coddled them. They grew up, beautiful plants with large leaves that flapped in the wind. Beautiful small blue blossoms appeared in the cone at the top of the stem. Dr. Crabb didn't know he was hoeing and loving tobacco plants—something I had worked with many years of my life. It was the money crop on our Kentucky farm. Dr. Crabb, so I learned later, was furious over his mistake. And he never learned who planted those seeds in his garden. Dr. Crabb, giant educator that he was, thought tobacco plants were flowers.

Dr. Crabb suggested that I apply for a Guggenheim Fellowship. I applied and got it. I applied for and got a leave of absence from McKell High School. I went to Europe, where I visited twenty-seven countries; I visited schools in those countries; I visited farms.

"Why don't you go to America, James?" I asked a Scotch friend of mine while I was in Scotland. He was a talented architect and painter and was making seventy-two dollars a month. "You'd make money in America with your talent."

Since I had told him my salary as a teacher in Kentucky, he smiled at me. "You'd better stay in Scotland and teach school," he said. "We pay our teachers more than you make in Kentucky."

And I found that he was right. Though the wages in industry were frightfully low in Scotland (the land of my father's people) as compared to those in America, teachers were better paid. The reason teachers were well paid, so I was informed by knowledgeable sources, was that it took years to prepare a teacher—and it was expensive—whereas a skilled tradesman could learn his trade in a short time and was usually paid something while he was learning.

The teachers I talked with in Edinburgh were earning well over the two-thousand-dollar mark. I did not tell the Scots that I remembered the time when good teachers, well prepared to teach, left the rural schools in Greenup County, Kentucky, because they couldn't live on their low salaries, and sought employment in the five-and-ten-cent stores in Ohio.

However, I didn't fail to tell school administrators and teachers everywhere I visited in Europe that our forefathers had planned a more democratic school system than I had found in any country in Europe. Free high schools did not exist in any country I visited. In England, Scotland, Wales, and Ireland, they had free elementary schools which corresponded to our grade schools and probably reached our junior high schools, since algebra, Latin, mechanical drawing, and plane geometry were taught. But the students left school at about fourteen and went to serve an apprenticeship for some trade.

Our American school system has less snobbishness than the English, and I say this with all due respect for the fine literature and sense of freedom and respect for laws that these great people have given to the world. In America every boy and girl, regardless of family and money, has a chance. In England a coal miner's son is expected to be a coal miner, though if unusually talented he may not be. It made me glad I was born in America.

But I found out that schoolteachers in England are not only well paid in comparison with other professions, but they are respected as they are few places in the world. The English are smart enough to know that the fate of their people is decided in the schoolrooms of England. Adolf Hitler, too, was smart enough to organize his schools the way he wanted them organized; he put teachers who were really teachers (and not Nazi puppets) in concentration camps, so he could proceed to sell his ideas to the German people. We know the results.

I visited schools in Denmark, Norway, Sweden, Finland, Estonia, Latvia, Lithuania, Poland, Holland, Belgium,

France, Switzerland, Czechoslovakia. In every country I visited—whether or not the people were poor, and most of them were exceedingly poor by our standards—they paid their teachers well in comparison with the wages paid others. Next to England, Sweden paid its teachers best.

America is my country—and I'm as much a product of America as a stalk of Indian maize corn. Therefore I have a right to criticize and praise. And I say that we certainly departed from what our forefathers established in this country. They would have been shocked to see how, although the schools have had the lion's share in bringing about our country's accomplishments, we have let some of our best teachers depart for vocations where they can make a better living. And who can blame them?

Our federal and state governments have not acted to avert disaster in the schools. What we did in Kentucky was to lower the standards so that any Tom, Dick, or Harry with a high-school education could get an emergency certificate, though he never had a day's teaching experience.

During the war I met a former student who was working in industry. "I just want to show you something," he said. He took a slip of paper from his pocketbook and handed it to me. It was a statement showing that he had earned $138.52.

"I made that in one week."

"Just $1.48 short of what I make in a month as a teacher," I said.

I had taught him four years in high school. He had finished with barely a C average—just enough to "get by." Yet he was not doing manual labor but had taken a six-week course in blueprinting.

At this time, I had approximately seven years of college and university training and ten years of experience. I had spent thousands of dollars for my training. And as superintendent, I was receiving the best pay in our system—$140 a month!

I cannot understand how this nation can underestimate the worth of its schools, when it was founded on the basis of free schools and free religious worship. I am not proud of the way my native country has treated its teachers.

In Edinburgh, Scotland, I kept getting letters signed "Nancy Astor." I didn't know Nancy Astor. She was asking me to come and visit with her in London. I didn't answer her letters. Finally she wrote me in disgust, "Are you or are you not coming to see me?" I had rented a room from Mrs. Hastings, a kind Scottish woman of about sixty. Since I thought someone I didn't know might be trying to blackmail me, I took Nancy Astor's letters to Mrs. Hastings. She said, "Who are you? Who do I have staying here with me? You are receiving letters from Lady Astor! I am in her party, I work for her. I never got a letter from her in my life!"

When Mrs. Hastings said, "Lady Astor," I knew who was writing to me. Lady Astor was a Langley from Virginia who was related to the Stuarts of Virginia. It was distant, but still kinship. I sat down and wrote her I would be there. After leaving Scotland, I visited Northern and Southern Ireland, revisited Wales before getting to London. Then I went straight to Lord and Lady Astor's. It was the largest house I had ever stayed in. I had Godfried Van Cramm's (the great German tennis player) old room at Lady Astor's. Several mornings I ate breakfast with Lord and Lady Astor.

"What is it you miss most in England that you are used to in America?" they asked me.

"A good cigar," I said.

"Just a minute," she said. She got up from the table and handed me two large cigars.

"Cigars Mr. Winston Churchill left here," she said. "Try these."

"It's a great cigar, Lady Astor," I said. "But I couldn't afford these."

Once the telephone rang in my room and I answered.

"Sir, this is the ambassador of Belgium calling," said a voice.

"You've got the wrong number," I said and hung up.

Lady Astor took me to the House of Commons. Once I sat six seats away from the Queen Mother, King George VI's mother. I never had a better time than at the Astors'. Lady Astor gave me a key to the house, a tiny key that unlocked a big door.

Evenings I joined struggling British, Irish, and Welsh poets who had come to London to make literary careers. They certainly were poor and struggling. I liked them and they liked me. The poet-writers would follow me home after our parties broke up, and they'd watch me unlock the door and go into the Astors' big home. But this wasn't the biggest home. It was at Clivedon on the Thames River. And I went there with Lord and Lady Astor for more parties and a two-day stay. I had never worn a tux, but I dressed in my dark $22.50 suit. I looked all right and I felt at home with some of the guests, especially beautiful Lady Astor, whose sons were older than I—I especially felt at home with her in her home. I spent two wonderful weeks with the Astors and was invited to return if and when I ever revisited England. When I left the Astor home, I went to the Continent for more travel and later for home to America.

When I returned to Kentucky I found that things had changed in our educational system. A rigged election had changed the school-board members. The new members did not want me back at McKell. I had challenged the liquor dealers and the bootleggers. I had rocked the boat. These new board members did not want me in their system at all. I crossed the river to Ohio, and there I got a fine job teaching remedial English in an excellent high school in Portsmouth.

During my schooldays I came to the conclusion that if I ever taught school I'd teach English differently from any teacher I'd ever had except Mrs. Hatton and Mr. Kroll. They were the best, and it seemed to me they got results. Each taught creative writing one day a week in their English courses. Mrs. Hatton couldn't write a good line of poetry or prose herself, yet she could tell her students how to do it. Mr. Kroll was a novelist. These teachers were opposites but obtained very similar results. I have no way to measure the results of their teaching except by remembering the work that was read in each class.

My early training left me with the idea that writers were not exactly human beings, that they walked, talked, loved, breathed, and ate like the rest of us living mortals here, but yet they were different. They wore long beards and chin whiskers. I wanted to be a writer, but could I ever qualify according to my preconceived image? I wonder if any students today feel like that. Well, if they do, it is nonsense. Writers are real human beings.

When I first meet a new class of English students, I tell them that I don't want them to feel that they aren't a real part of things. I want everybody to feel as welcome as the flowers of May on the big earth. I tell them that I seldom flunk an English student, and this usually pleases the class. It is true an English student has to be downright hopeless before I flunk him. I want my students to have absolute freedom and see what they do with it. That is something I seldom got when I was a student. Teachers sooner or later will find that the students themselves create their own interest. The classwork will become fun, and once there's interest in the classroom, discipline naturally follows.

In order to get things going, I tell the students to write about anything they like and put it in any form they please. The race begins. They envy each other. They try to do better work than their friends, and they jump so far ahead that I find some students start copying. They don't intend to be outdone. I have seen teachers who would throw a student out of the class for a trick like this. But why should the student be thrown out? You understand he has pride, and he hates to let another surpass him when he stands up and reads before the class once a week. It is usually the girls that will not be outdone. The boys can take it better than the girls.

My first aim is to get them to write. I don't grade off for periods and commas and colons and semicolons when I'm getting them interested in putting their thoughts on paper. Remember, there are a few in the class who can't write a line. They are afraid to let themselves slip on paper, as they would be afraid to skate the first time on ice. I take these students one by one, find out an impressive experience they have had, and ask them to write about it. It is not long before they find out they can write themes, poetry, articles, and short stories, in a fashion. I want them to feel free and flexible. I want them to put their hearts on paper, and they do it.

I let the students have memory work once a week, and this is optional too. If it is an American-literature class, I ask them to memorize American poetry; if the class is English literature, I ask them to memorize poetry from the English poets.

Many students ask to memorize more than one selection of poetry. I can hardly think of a good minor poem, English or American, that has not been recited in one of my English classes. The minute a student gives a poor poem for memory work one can see the students looking at each other. They set their own standards of memory work and give as much or as little of it as they like.

Written work grows like memory work. First the themes are brief. Then they get longer and still longer, until they become quite lengthy. We have taken up a whole period on one theme, discussed it pro and con, and each student raises his voice and gives his opinion. We let everybody's point of view count. If a student doesn't fit into our English class, we try to find the reason and to remove all obstacles. We discuss the form of the poetry when it is recited. We try to forget that the author was a literary figure. We find lines in his poetry that show he was a real human being like the rest of us. Then, when we study his life, we hunt for poems that relate to incidents of his time. It makes the English class fun.

I read poems from my own book to my English classes, and I often find one or two of the students start to imitate my work. I read stories to them and articles. I find that my classes are critical, and when the majority say a poem is good, or a story, it sooner or later finds a place in print. This has happened too many times to be an accident. I've been thoroughly disgusted at times, when they'd turn their thumbs down on my work. But they stuck to their judgment, and they were usually right.

All members of the class agree at the first of the year to write about the things in our own backyards. We would write about anything and everything except picnics (that was a subject worn out long ago) and trips to New York, unless the student had actually been there. We decided to write about our own people, our trees, stars, grass, flowers—old apple orchards in the sun and tumbling fences, people getting drunk, elections, public officials, love affairs that the students actually know of (one of their own if they want to write it), snakes, turtles, terrapins, birds—all living things that walk or crawl on the earth. There is no barrier to keep them from writing about anything. Length and style are left to them. Outside students want to leave their classes and come in and listen to the students read on theme days. Often a student reads a theme and another says, "Why in the world didn't I think about that and write it?" Here it is—just as simple as falling off a log, and someone happened to stumble onto the idea and put it into words. That is the way great art is born —it is often done when the author doesn't realize what he is doing.

One year I couldn't get any poetry from the class. This was back at McKell. The students wanted to write prose. I asked for poetry time and again. It never came. One day a student from our little Writers' Club (which at that time was composed of five boy members) handed me five poems. I handed them back and asked Clyde to read them aloud. I asked him if he had ever written poetry before, and he said he had, but he had never brought it to class. I thought it was the best poetry I'd ever received from a high-school student. He had scribbled these five poems down in a chemistry class on the backs of his test-question sheets.

I had to suspend another one of my best creative English students twice and threaten to keep him out indefinitely for drinking. He was tall, high-strung, and extremely nervous. The boy could actually write, and he had a mountain of an urge in him to write. He would sit in another class, answer the questions thrust at him by the teacher, and in the meantime be writing a short story. He told me many times that he would rather write than eat. I would not change his style of writing for anything on earth. He was a little rough, but sooner or later as he grew older he would make the necessary changes and shape himself up into a regular style.

One of the girls wouldn't read a theme in class. One of the teachers told me, "Virginia is afraid of you."

I said in astonishment, "That certainly is strange. She has no right to be afraid of me. No human being needs to be afraid of me. Why, animals are never afraid of me."

"Yes, but Virginia is," she said.

One day I asked Virginia to remain after class. She told me she couldn't talk as she'd like to talk, and when I called on her to read, it scared her. And she thought she couldn't write. I asked her if she could not talk a little. She acknowledged that she could. "Write just as you talk," I told her. The next day she came to English class with a short story. From that time on, she led that English class, with plenty of points to spare. I never found a better all-around English student than Virginia. One day before Virginia graduated, I said to her,

"Virginia, see how much a teacher misses when he doesn't understand one of his students. Look at the difference in your work the first semester and the last semester of this year."

Virginia replied, "And how much the student misses when she doesn't understand the teacher! I don't even know what my grades have been this last semester, I've enjoyed my class so much. I've really learned how to express myself on paper, though I do not intend ever to be a writer."

Before the year is over we cut the production down to a certain extent and do a little work on sentence structure. We practice a little technique. At the first of the year, ideas for writing are the things we fight for. Now it is our work to arrange them properly. I have always felt that if the young plastic mind of the student is taught to create—or rather, is directed in its own creation—that the technique would take care of itself. Almost anyone can get to the place where he can punctuate, but can he put his ideas on paper? My feeling is that they cannot when they are hampered by restrictions such as assigned topics to write about, and arguing all day about where a period or comma should be placed. They cannot get anywhere.

I have received letters from English teachers asking me how I teach the short story to high-school English students. These teachers seem to think I should be a better teacher of the short story than those who have never written a story. If anything, this theory should be reversed. The teacher who has never written a short story will not lean to any particular type but will teach each type, written by many different authors, with the same interest.

One thing I do is not to teach the short story as it was taught to me. I used to dread coming to a short story in my literature book. I didn't know anything about the short story; yet I had to dissect it. I had to find the climax, the anticlimax, and about a half-dozen other things in the teacher's formula —a formula creaking with age. I received low marks on dissecting the short story. I graduated from high school hating the short story.

My students, no matter how poor they are, will not leave my English class hating the short story as a medium of literary expression. I shudder at the thought of the English teachers who have ruined their students' love of the short story by age-old tomfoolery. I want my students to enjoy the short story, and they do.

In my assignment of a short story in the text, I ask my students to read the story before we get to class. There will be a few students who have not done this. I make allowances for them. Paragraph by paragraph, we read the story in class. There isn't any hurry with this first short story. Many of the students will not like this story, and they are free to tell me their opinions—maybe they are right. I tell them there are many stories that I do not like, but we go on. We read the story; then we discuss the author, the type of man he was, and why he would write a short story of this type. We also connect the setting and characters with the author. We talk about the words he has used. We discuss this story in general. We do not have a skeleton to analyze the story by; we do not take it apart and piece it together again.

After we have read a few stories in our textbook, we make comparisons of the short stories of certain authors, for instance, Edgar Allan Poe and Washington Irving. We find that each was a great short-story writer, that Poe depicted the very essence of gloom in his stories, while Irving had a great sense of humor. We do not say one is greater than the other; each student takes his choice. My students often tell me the reason Poe was so morbid in his writing was that he did too much drinking. I tell them that he couldn't have done all the drinking credited to him, since when he died at forty he had written forty-two books. Then we discuss Poe the entire period. Our class is not on schedule; we never finish a lesson in our allotted time.

You would be surprised what these discussions do. They motivate my students to find out all they can about Poe and bring their information to the next English class. They will tell me that I am wrong about this or that. I listen to the student, often agreeing with him, for I know that I have him where I want him when I get him interested. Interest will bring about love for any subject. Lazy boys get interested in my classes. All of my students get interested. They do not take the textbook for everything. They go to the library of their own accord and look up material.

I tell my students that America is the home of the short story. We go back to the beginning of our literature in America and go over the early giants. We link the writers together, one after another, up to the present time. We discuss the short story from Irving and Poe to Bill Saroyan. I know Bill personally and I tell them about him and many other American authors whose work they study. I try to get the idea out of their heads that all writers wear long beards, that there is something different about them. I tell them authors are human as students are and that someday one in my class may become a fine writer and that he may be a student to whom I have given low marks.

We do not read a short story with sober faces. We relax and take it easy. I want students to laugh in my class when they find something funny in a short story. And if one finds something that would cause him to weep in my class, I would want him to weep. I like most to hear rich laughter in my classes. We read the short stories for enjoyment and with this enjoyment comes knowledge.

We sum up our adventures at the end of the school year in our reading of the various short stories. We note the different periods of American literature, the airtight plot of an O. Henry short story. Many of the modern stories have, as we term it, a subconscious plot. We read the modern story and think it's pointless, but there is some part of it that lodges in one's brain. This type of story, I tell them, is not the planned money-making commercial short story. It is one the author had on his brain and in his heart and had to write. We go in for all these little details in the short story and discuss them with laughter and heated arguments.

My teaching, I'm proud to say, has been felt by college and university English teachers. One lady remarked to me that she was always glad to get my students in her English classes. "They have a broad view and scope of American literature," she said. That was one of the finest compliments that has ever been paid me. I would have felt insulted if she had told me they knew the exact place to put a comma. They have a pretty good knowledge of grammar too, for I lay it on, but the English language, and the great literature that it embraces, is something bigger than mere technicalities. And of all the forms of its literature, the short story is most definitely American.

In my later years of secondary-school work I became weary of tests and testings. And also distrustful. And for very good reasons. My remedial students in that Ohio school have amounted to more in later life than their fellow students classed as excellent. Other pupils in the school used to come to our remedial classes and listen to my pupils read their themes and poetry.

But I am a Kentuckian, not an Ohioan, and after my time in Europe and in Ohio, I wanted to go home. Still our local school system was dominated by politicians who cared more for their power and their jobs than they cared for Kentucky schools. They had no use for me. I bought a farm in W-Hollow next to my father's farm. I married my girl, Naomi Deane, whom I had courted for years and could never marry on the salaries Kentucky paid her teachers. I settled down to farm the land, as my father had before me, and to write. I said that I was through with teaching and schools forever. I have said so time and again, but education is in my blood and bones. I am a schoolman, whether I like it or not. I always come back.

I did write during those first years after my marriage. I wrote poems and short stories and novels. *Beyond Dark Hills,* which I wrote as a term paper for Dr. Mims at Vanderbilt, was published then. It was the first book I had written, but the fourth I had published. *Harvest of Youth, Man with a Bull-Tongue Plow,* and *Head o' W-Hollow* all came into print before it. *Taps for Private Tussie* I wrote in six weeks of hard work at W-Hollow. *Foretaste of Glory* I wrote while serving in the navy during World War II. *The Thread That Runs So True* I wrote and published after the war. Teachers liked this book. The National Education Association voted it the most important book of 1949, and I received many, many invitations from that time onward to address high-school youths and college youths and teachers and principals.

My father, Mitch Stuart, who couldn't read, was a great teacher.

Greenup was the center of my father's universe. He never traveled a fifty-mile radius from this town. He went to town on Saturday, dressed in his overalls, clean blue work shirt, overall jacket, his soiled weathered cap with a shrinking bill, and his turned-at-the-toes, stump-scarred brogan shoes. He walked a path four miles over the bony hills to the town, as he had done since I could remember.

One day I went with him. He talked to a group of men on the courthouse square, where the men from all over the county meet on Saturdays with the men from the town, where they walk, tell their stories, chew their tobacco, try to whittle the longest shavings with their pocketknives while they listen to the courthouse bell calling men inside the courthouse for justice. While they talked and chewed tobacco from long home-grown twists of burley and spit mouthfuls of ambeer spittle on the courthouse square, I heard a man say, who was standing in another group of men not far from my father's group, "There's old overalled Mitch Stuart. . . . See 'im in town every Saturday." This fairly well-dressed man, teacher of a rural school, pointed to my father, and the men in his group looked and listened while he talked. "Never amounted to anything in his life. Never will amount to anything. But he's got smart children. His boy is a book writer, you may've heard about."

Pert Maldin didn't see me as he went on telling the men in his group how my father loved to come to town on Saturdays and loaf, just loaf and try to whittle the longest shavings, how he loved the sound of the courthouse bell and how he'd listened to it for a half-century. And he told them he'd known my father that long and how my father had gone to the same little tavern, run by the same people for a half-century, and got his beer on Saturdays, and after he had a few beers, how he talked to his old friends and told them big windy tales. He told about his seeing my father have a few fights in his younger days and how time had slowed him down. Since Pert Maldin talked confidentially to the men that surrounded him, I couldn't hear all he said. I did hear him say my father wouldn't know his name if he would meet it in the road, that he couldn't read a beer sign, and he couldn't write his name.

I thought about walking over and popping Pert Maldin on the nose when he talked about my father. But I stood silently and listened as long as I could, and many thoughts flashed through my brain as the ambeer spittle flashed brown in the November sunlight from the mouths of the men in the group where my father was talking, where they were laughing at some story one of his group had told. I thought a pop on the nose would serve Pert Maldin right, and then I thought, "What's the use? What does he know about my father? And what does he know about education, though he is a schoolteacher?"

My father never read anything about soil conservation in

his life. He could not read. I never heard him use the word "conservation." I doubt that he would have known what it meant. It would have been a big word to him. He called it "pertectin' the land." And if anyone had read to him about how to conserve the soil or protect the land, and if he had sat still long enough to listen, I know he would have said: "I did that fifty years ago."

For fifty-five years, ever since I was big enough to tag at his heels, I could vouch for that. He had done everything I've read about soil conservation, and more.

He couldn't understand why everybody didn't "petect the land." He wondered why more people didn't use a little "horse sense" to keep all their topsoil from washing away.

Despite his not being able to read, in magazines or books, he read the surface of the earth, in every slope, hollow, creek bottom, on every piece of terrain he walked in his day and time. He loved the feel of the soil against his shoe leather and of the fresh dirt in his hand. He almost petted the earth beneath him as if it were something to be fondled and loved.

When he bought the first and only land he ever owned, fifty acres of hill land in the head of W-Hollow, half of this small boundary was considered worthless. He bought the fifty acres for three hundred dollars. The only part of this farm that was not streaked with deep gullies was the timbered hill slopes. The slopes that had been cleared and farmed were streaked with gullies deeper than a man's height. My friends and I used to play on this farm. We cut long poles, and our favorite sport was pole-vaulting from one side of the gully to the other with a sixteen-foot pole. This gives some idea of the ugly scars that marked the earth's surface and gleamed yellow in the sun. Now, no one would know that the skin of this earth had ever been scarred by ugly wounds that cut down deep into the earth's flesh. For this land grows four crops of alfalfa each season, and a mowing machine rolls smoothly over it.

Even when we were cutting logs to build us a home on this farm, he saved the branches and the tops of these trees. The branches from the pine tops especially appealed to him for the kind of soil protection he planned. He laid this brush down in these scars, putting the tips uphill. "When the water comes down the gully," he said, "all the grass, dirt, and little twigs it carries will catch in this brush. The gully will soon fill up." These were deep gullies, and it took wagonloads of brush. We seldom put rocks in one of these gullies. If we did, we put them on the bottom, down deep, so they would never work to the top of the ground and be a menace to the plow or the mowing machine. And we stacked the brush high above the earth's surface in these deep gullies, because the weight of snow, the falling of rain, the wash of sediment weighted it until the brush was finally below the surface. Then we added more brush, finer brush, always placing the tips uphill to meet the avalanche or trickle of water.

My father always said if a cut on the surface of the earth was properly handled, it was like a cut on a man's body, and nature would do wonders to heal it. Nature did wonders where we piled this brush. Nature edged in with her sediment wash. Nature pushed the skin of her surface over, trying to heal the ugly scar. For a year or two or three, we plowed up to these deep gullies. We plowed all around them. The dirt went over and into the brush. Soon we hauled wagons of oak leaves from the woods and spread them over the place where the brush had sunk. We pushed in more dirt from the sides, healing the great scar, and then we started plowing over. We reunited the earth's skin, leaving it without a blemish. It did not take long to do this. My father was always against building rock walls across the gulleys. He said it took too long to build the wall, and nature would not work as gently and as fast with rock walls as it would with the brush and the leaves and the pine-needled branches. This was the way we handled the gullies that were from five to fifteen feet deep.

The little gullies, those from six inches to five feet, were much easier to handle. We used what we had cleared from the land to fill them. We pushed the dirt with mattocks and shovels until it united over the brush-brier and leaf-filled gullies. We closed the little scars on the earth's surface before they grew to be big scars. We crossed over the scars with a plow the first year, reuniting what had once been joined. But man's folly had lacerated this earth's surface. Then man had abandoned this land as worthless, never good again for crops, to the wind, rain, and freeze.

"An ounce of prevention is worth a pound of cure," was an old saying my father used when he and I worked on his farm together. Never did I see him one time ever drag a plow up or down a hill and leave a mark that would start a ditch. Maybe that was one of the many reasons why everybody we ever rented from, before he bought land of his own, wanted him to remain on his farm. Instead of dragging a plow with a mule or a mule team hitched to it as I've seen so many other one-horse farmers do in my day, my father would drive his team ahead and carry his plow. He was that careful with other people's land, more careful than the owners themselves, because he loved the land.

Another thing he did from the time I could remember was to follow the contour of the hill with his plow. We never farmed anything but hills in those days and many of them were very steep. These hills didn't erode for my father. He could judge the nature of flowing water, what it would do to the land he plowed. He didn't let it do anything; he never gave it a chance. Even on these hill slopes were deep ravines. My father plowed into them and straight around on the other side, making a perfect contour, never up or down. And he never had a ditch to start down his slope.

Today it is recommended by the Department of Agriculture, and this information is carried to us by our county agent, that we farm corn on our level acres and sow our hill slopes in grass and use the uplands for pasture. My father learned this long ago. Again it was a matter of "horse sense" and he learned, perhaps, the hard way. On our "worthless" (never worthless to us) hillside acres that wouldn't grow timber but only shaggy brush, we cleared this land and farmed it three years straight in corn. We did this to prepare it for grass. We used fertilizer even when we planted the corn with a hand corn-planter. Dad planted the corn, and I followed and dipped fertilizer from a bucket with a spoon. This was before fertilizer became popular in this section. It was before any great farm program was developed. Our first year gave us a fair yield of corn. Our second year the land was easier to plow, since we'd torn out more roots and stumps, and we got a better yield of corn. Then the third year, we got about the same yield as we did the first year.

Then it occurred to my father that this land was already infertile to begin with and that he would not "corn it to death." So my father stopped growing corn on the hillsides altogether. We cut the brush, put it in the ditches if we had them; if we didn't have them, we burned this brush and sowed the land in grass.

We learned the stumps were better left in the ground to rot and fertilize the ground instead of farming the land and tearing out stumps with the plow, digging them up or blowing them out with dynamite. Though we had to cut the sprouts and briers with mattocks and scythes in July and August of each summer, we soon had a better pasture on the steep hills by doing this than we did by raising corn three seasons to prepare the ground for grass. We lifted the fertility of our little creek bottoms, the flats on our hill slopes, and the level hilltops by using oak leaves, barnyard manure, and commercial fertilizer.

We had two places on my father's fifty-acre farm that gave us trouble. One was a steep bluff, not far from the house, that was cleared and farmed. In the first place, this land should have never been cleared. But my father learned this after it was too late. This bluff started slipping off down into the valley in big slides. Again we hauled brush and laid it down in the valley to catch the slides. Then my father did something else. He suggested that we set this slope back in trees. It was a difficult type of erosion, the kind that he thought only the roots of trees would cure. And this would have to be done quickly by trees that had good roots and grew quickly. He decided on the yellow locust sprouts to set on this bluff. Because this tree grew all over the farm, we could find small sprouts to dig and reset. He chose this tree because it had roots like iron ropes, grew rapidly, and made good fence posts when it grew up. He chose it too because the grass would grow under its shade. These locusts stopped the slides on this steep slope. The scars were soon healed, and the land reset itself in grass.

The other problem we had was where a stream sank in our pasture field and left a deep hole. Here is what we did about it. For some time we used this hole for a trash dump. We hauled the old tin cans, trash, cornstalks, and whatnots and dumped them into this hole. But we couldn't fill it up with all of this flimsy material. Then we hauled wagon loads of rocks. They sank down too. Again my father hauled brush and put it into this hole to form some sort of bottom. Then he went about the farm and gathered all the old rolls of barbed wire that we had taken down and rolled up. He hauled these bales of worthless rusty wire, for he was always afraid to leave them about on account of the cattle, mules, or horses, which might get tangled up in them. These he put on top of the brush, and this held the wash that poured into it. The place healed over, and grass covered the spot. No one, except we who remember, because we worked there, would know where it is today. My father worked carefully with nature, and she healed her own wounds. Not a scar was left on his eroded fifty acres seven years after he bought the farm.

All his life, he waged his war against erosion. He used a

sled to haul tobacco, hay, and fodder down a hill slope. He would not use a wagon because the wagon wheels cut deep and help to start ditches. Sled runners slide over the dirt and hardly leave a trace. He would not drag logs straight down a hill unless the ground was frozen. Old log roads are another good way to start erosion. And if nature, with a bountiful rain, a freeze, or a thaw, broke the skin anywhere, he immediately did something about it before it got a head start. This is why he had no erosion on his farm. He did not learn the second-hand way, through words on a printed page, but he read the language that nature scrawled upon her rugged terrain, and he understood that language better than any other man I have ever known.

Let Pert Maldin talk on the courthouse square. Let him talk about my father's not having an education, that he wouldn't know his name if he'd meet it in the big road. I could tell Pert that he didn't know about education. He was speaking about these secondhand things called books when my father's people had lived an education while they were helping to build a nation and a civilization. Yes, they had taken the law in their own hands, for they had to do it, since the law didn't protect them while they fought their enemies; helped to build the railroads through the mountains and bridges to span the rivers, and blasted the turnpikes around the rocky slopes. They cleared the fields and broke the first furrows through the roots. They built the log cabins from the giant trees they didn't split into fence rails; they hauled giant saw-logs with yokes of oxen to the edge of the Big Sandy and waited for the spring rains, when with spiked boots and with long poles with spikes in the end they took their log rafts down the Big Sandy and the Ohio River to the little town of Cincinnati, the Queen City of the West.

I could tell Pert Maldin that my father, son of these figures of the earth, with the blood of these men flowing through his veins, was an educated man. He was educated the same as they were educated—but maybe his education didn't fit the time he was living. He couldn't sit behind a desk wearing a white shirt, a necktie, a neatly pressed tailored suit, and shined shoes, with a pencil behind his ear. He couldn't live in a world of figures and words. They would be playthings on the wind to him. All he'd say, even if his mind were trained to do these things, is, "To hell with this." I knew him well enough to know that he would say these words. For what did he say about my books? "A lot of damned foolishness."

I could tell anybody that my father was an educated man. Though he was a small man with a wind-parched face the color of the autumn earth, my father had the toughness in his muscles of the hickory sprout. He had a backbone like a saw-log. In his makeup fear was left out. That word was not in his vocabulary. I never heard him say, in my lifetime, that he was afraid of anything.

My father could take a handful of new-ground dirt in his hand, smell of it, then sift it between his fingers, and tell whether to plant the land in corn, tobacco, cane, or potatoes. He had an intuition that I could not explain. Maybe Pert Maldin, with all his education, could explain it. And my father knew when to plant, how to plant and cultivate, and the right time to reap. He knew the right trees to cut from his timber for wood to burn, and the trees to leave for timber. He knew the names of all the trees, flowers, and plants that grew on his rugged acres. My father was able to live from sterile, rugged mountain soil. He raised enough food for his family to eat, and his family ate about all he raised. Money did not mean food to him, as it does to many in America today. Money was some sort of a luxury to him. It was something he paid his taxes with. Money was something to him to buy land with. And the land and everything thereon was more than a bank account to him; land is something durable, something his eyes could see and his hands could feel. It was not the second-hand substance he would have found in a book.

I could tell anybody in America that if my father wasn't an educated man, we don't have educated men in America. And if his education wasn't one of the best educations a man can have, then I am not writing these words and the rain is not falling today in Kentucky. If his education wasn't as important as mine—this son of his he used to tell every day to go to school, since he had found the kind of education he had didn't work as well this day and time in America as the kind of education where a man had a pencil behind his ear and worked in a world of figures, words, dollars and cents, when to buy, when, where, and how to sell—then I am not writing these words.

"Come with me, Jane," I said. "It's time for your after-school lesson."

Our daughter Jane had come from school and had laid away her books. She was about twelve years old then.

"I'm ready, Daddy," she said.

Jane was always anxious for these little walks we took unless she was reading a book. She was especially ready if her mother had some little task for her to perform. "We're going over on Breadloaf Hill this afternoon," I said.

Jane and I walked in the clean young wind of an afternoon in April. It was about four, and the sky was blue and the sun rather warm. We walked down the W-Branch and Jane left me, ran full speed forward, and leaped into the air, over the stream, and landed on the other side. She was not much given to any athletic performance, and I was very happy to see her do this.

She remained on the other side and watched me walk down to the stream's edge and step gently over and climb the other bank.

Then Jane and I followed a faint path that cattle had made

years ago and the elements—rain, freeze, and thaw—had not completely obliterated. There was a dim outline, an indentation in the earth for us to follow. We gradually climbed, following this path that angled up and around the hill, until we came in sight of the first trailing arbutus.

"Oh, Daddy," Jane said. "Here it is! Look! What pretty blossoms! I believe it's prettier than percoon!"

Jane walked up to this beautiful wildflower that grew in a soil almost too poor to grow pines. It was almost too steep to stand on without holding to a bush or tree for support. Below us were the cliffs, and not very deep beneath the surface of this sterile soil was the solid rock. And down below the cliffs was the stream, W-Branch, that carried the bright clean April water from the entire watershed of this valley.

We stood in a beautiful setting with barren trees all around us except for the evergreen pines. At our feet were a few clumps of trailing arbutus, one of our earliest-blooming wildflowers. The small blossoms were shell pink, almost the color of shale stones I'd seen slivered from this hill after a winter freeze. The trailing-arbutus leaves were green and beautiful, just an inch or so above the cold April sod.

"Jane, what kind of leaves remind you of the trailing-arbutus leaves?" I asked her.

"Sand-brier leaves."

"But there's another leaf more like it."

She became studious and thoughtful as we leaned over, touched, and fondled the trailing arbutus.

"Daddy, it must be a sweet-potato leaf," she said. "Trailing arbutus got its name because it grows close to the ground, and sweet potatoes vine over the ground but don't have blossoms."

"Right," I said. "You got that one."

We spent several minutes in this nook of trailing arbutus. And this brought back memories to me. The first time I had ever been on this hill was in the spring of 1915, when my father and mother moved to the house where we live now.

My oldest sister, Sophia, and I were playing on this hill, and we found this flower. We didn't know what it was, and Sophia took a small spray of these exquisite blossoms to the house to show our mother. Mom told us what they were as soon as she saw them. Since 1915 we have often returned to see trailing arbutus in blossom, to show it to our children and our friends.

It doesn't matter how cold the winter gets, how deep the ground freezes, how poor the soil is, how near the greenbriers and bushes crowd in, the trailing arbutus, so fragile in its beauty, is a rugged little flower, and it holds on to life despite hard winters and rough terrain.

As we sat there, I explained all of this to Jane. And I explained that flowers often remain in the same ground for over a century.

And since our house has stood, with the exception of new additions that we have built, since 1840, I wouldn't doubt that children and adults for 115 years have come each spring to this very same spot to fondle, touch, love, and enjoy the fresh spring beauty this little flower gives. Jane was fascinated with all this.

"The trailing arbutus grows on this bank like our people live in this valley," she said.

"Only the trailing arbutus has been on this bluff longer than we have been in this valley," I said.

Jane looked thoughtfully back at this wistful flower as a cool, brisk April wind whined close against the earth and made its blossoms tremble. We continued our walk up and around the old cattle path.

"What is this?" I asked her, pointing to a tree.

"An oak."

"What kind?"

"I don't know the kind."

"It's a chestnut oak," I told her. "You can tell by the bark. See how big, thick, and tough the bark is."

"How do you know?" she asked me.

"My father and I used to peel chestnut oaks for tanbark," I explained. "The bark was used in tanning hides. That means to take the hair off skins, and the skins were made into leather, and the leather into shoes, pocketbooks, saddles, briefcases, suitcases, and a hundred other useful items. This chestnut oak has helped to do all that. Now, will you remember a chestnut oak next time you see one?"

"I believe so!"

"What's this tree?"

"Oh, it's an oak too," she said, smiling. "It's a white oak. I'd know it anyplace by its gray bark."

"You're right. Now, what's that tree?"

"Is it a beech?"

"No, you missed," I replied. "What tree do we get sugar and syrup from? Syrup that's good to eat in the morning with pancakes!"

"It's a sugar maple," she shouted.

"Do you suppose you'll remember this tree when you see it again?" I said. "It does resemble a beech a little, but when both trees leaf, you can tell the difference by their leaves. I want you to be able to tell them apart in the wintertime after they've shed their leaves and they are somber, barren, and sleeping."

"I know what this is before you ask me," Jane said, stopping beside our path to touch a tree. "It's what you make fenceposts of. This is a locust."

"Right this time," I said. "There are two kinds of locust that grow here. This is the black locust."

"How can you tell?"

"By the bark," I told her. "But don't you try to do this yet. Black locust bark is finer than yellow locust bark. I'm going to wait until I've promoted you to a higher grade in this subject I am teaching you, which we call naturelore, before I start giving you the hard problems."

Jane ran and leaped like a spring butterfly flitting from the brisk April wind. She jumped up and down, and the wind lifted her pony tail of brown hair, which was the color of many of the leafless trees that grew in abundance on either side of the dim prints of the path we followed.

We stopped a minute to listen to the singing April wind among these briers and barren trees and to listen to the mumbling April stream, full of clear water, winding down its rockbound channel and singing on its long journey to the sea.

I knew this was a beautiful classroom for my child. It was so large, well ventilated, and decorated with beautiful and wonderful things to inspire a child's thinking.

And I knew similar classrooms existed nearby or not far distant for other children. Many of these classrooms have different decorations from ours, since they're in all parts of America. But parents, teachers, and leaders of youth can take pupils to this kind of classroom everywhere. And I know it gives them a sixth, seventh, and maybe an eighth sense of fundamental knowledge that helps with health and all other subjects, including regular classroom textbooks.

This is an interesting classroom, where, if and when a child finds an interest, there is never any delinquency. And this is the kind of classroom that hurts the trade of the psychologist and the psychiatrist.

Jane started asking her own questions and giving me her answers. This was very good. I knew that in a matter of minutes in nature's big book where there are so many unwritten things to learn, she would trip herself on one of her own questions. Even in this primary course of simple identification, she could not go far.

"Greenwood moss here, and this is mountain tea," she said.

She stopped to pick some leaves to chew, and so did I. And among the mountain-tea stems were ripened red berries that we ate.

"What's this?" I asked.

"I don't know."

"Wild-huckleberry stems."

"And this?"

"It's a maple."

"No, you really missed on that one," I said. "Did you ever see a maple with white blossoms on it? That's a hard one. That's the same tree my father took me to see when I was a small boy. That's a service tree, a serviceberry tree, and many of the older people, including my father, called it a white-beam tree. I didn't expect you to get that one.

"But remember, it blooms before the dogwood, wild crab apple, and redbud. I've seen it white with blossoms in a March snowstorm, and I couldn't tell its petals and the falling flakes apart.

"It's blooming late this year," I told her. "This has been a late spring. And we've got to get back down home. Look at the sun going over the hill, won't you! Our big classroom will soon be filled with shadows, and the night animals and birds will awake in holes underground, in hollow logs and trees and big nests of leaves up in the vines, and all start stirring in the night world they know. Even the foxes will come from under the cliffs."

"There's a lot to this course," Jane said.

"Sure, there is," I agreed with her. "More than you or *I* either will ever know."

"But it's fun to learn it, and I feel so good getting out where I can run," she said. "I even like to talk in my classroom."

"Yes, the big hills catch your voice and hold it," I said. "Your voice is lost on the air and mocked by the wind. We are very small in nature's classroom. And so are the ants which we must study at some later date."

We turned on the path and started back down toward the cliffs, stream, the valley, and home. Jane was as happy as I had ever seen any child who had come from a classroom. For the wind among the barren trees was mocking our voices, and the water in the stream below was singing, and the sunball was a red zero of flame.

They were good years and fruitful years, living with Naomi Deane and Jane in W-Hollow, writing and farming and leaving the valley only to go on speaking tours. I wrote *Hie to the Hunters* and *Kentucky Is My Land* and *The Good Spirit of Laurel Ridge,* and in one year I gave eighty-nine talks in thirty-nine states. In 1954 Kentucky made me her poet laureate, and I made more speeches than ever.

In the fall of 1954 I gave a talk at Murray State College. It lasted an hour, and when it was over I was supposed to go and catch an airplane to Flora, Illinois, to give another talk. But I did not take the airplane, and I did not give another talk that day. I fell to the ground with a massive heart attack, and it was a year before I stood on my feet again.

When I was released from the hospital, still a weak man, I went back home to W-Hollow to recover.

Whatever I am or ever shall be—schoolteacher, tiller of the earth, poet, short-story writer, upstart, or not anything—I owe it to my own Kentucky hill-land and to my people who have inhabited these hills for generations. My hills have given me bread. They have put song in my heart to sing. They have made my brain thirst for knowledge so much that I went beyond my own dark hills to get book knowledge. But I got an earthly degree at home from my own dark soil. I got a degree about birds, cornfields, trees, wildflowers, log shacks, my own people, valleys, and rivers and mists in the valleys —scenes of a fairyland childhood that no college under the sun could teach me.

I have learned from walking through the woods in W-Hollow at night where the wind soughs through the pine tops. I have learned where the big oak trees and the persimmon trees are; I have learned where the blackberry thickets are, where the wild strawberries grow, where the wild crab-apple trees blossom in the spring. I have learned where the large rocks are in the fields, where to find the red fox and the gray fox, where the squirrels keep their young in the hollow treetops, and where the quail hides her nest. I know the little secrets of nature, of the wildlife that leads me to these things. I have tried to write about them in my humble, crude fashion. I have enjoyed doing it more than I have eating food, visiting people or cities. My love is with my own soil and my own people.

Slowly, in my own house on my own soil in my own country, I regained my strength and my health. And then I surprised everyone and I surprised myself. Once again, I became a schoolman. I was invited to take over my old school, McKell, again. McKell had gone downhill in the years since I had been principal there. We had had a fine school there in the early thirties, in spite of our problems, but things had changed by 1956. There was a new generation; there were new problems; there was a weak, watered-down curriculum; there were Kentucky teachers leaving the state by the thousands for better-paying jobs in the North; there was an overcrowded building; there was no school spirit among the youth at McKell. McKell had gone down sadly.

The superintendent asked me if I would take over my old school once again and help out. I consulted my doctor. I consulted my wife. My doctor approved. My wife did not. I approved. And I went back to McKell that fall of 1956 as principal.

Chapter 8

McKELL HIGH SCHOOL WAS BUILT
for three hundred pupils. When I took it over in 1956, it had
six hundred and twenty-five. Many lads wore their hair in the
long duck tails then fashionable among young rebels. Many
wore their jeans as low on their hips as they could ride without falling off. Many drove hot rods. There was gambling at
McKell and in the neighborhood at illegal pinball joints.

Unfortunately, on my very first day I had to break my
doctor's only instruction—not to climb stairs. In a second-
floor classroom, a roughneck boy told one of my finest young
lady teachers to "kiss my —." I was up those stairs and had
that boy by the nape of the neck before I knew where I was.

When I accepted the job of principal, I was given a list of
the teachers on my faculty. There were six. For weeks I
scoured the countryside in search of teachers. The first I
recruited was a strong young man who had gone to school
to me twenty years before. He had been a tough young
hoodlum then, until I disciplined him—with my fist. Now I
asked him to come back and teach for me.

"I consider it an honor and a privilege," he told me. "Do
you know what made me a teacher?"

"No," I said.

"Your fist," he replied.

I brought a few older retired teachers back into the school-room. I brought a few younger ones. When school opened I had thirteen teachers to teach six hundred and twenty-five youths. I recalled teaching without teachers at McKell once before. If we could do it then, I thought, we could do it now. I appointed senior pupils who were good in their studies to teach freshmen and sophomores. And I beefed up the curriculum, adding Latin again and increasing requirements in the other subjects.

We housed many of our students in prefabricated dwellings near the high school. We held classes in the gymnasium. We made the work of helping to maintain the school property an honor rather than a chore. Our coach assembled a winning football team, and our handful of dedicated teachers began to pull our demoralized pupils together into a group of young people proud of their school and willing to work.

One day one of the senior boys came up to me and said, "You know, I'm that rebel without a cause." For days his teachers and I had been watching the peculiarities this boy had developed, how he was going around twisting his body and shaking his head. He had been a good solid youth, with good grades, and a fullback on our winning football team. At that time I didn't figure it out, for I had never seen the movie *Rebel Without a Cause*. Very soon we had so many boys going around mad about nothing, trying to be James Deans, that I went to see the movie that had influenced them. The idea was: Be mad at the world for nothing. I have seen many silly pictures, but this was the superior silly. Nevertheless, it influenced elementary and high-school students, for they are great imitators in those years. Well, James Dean was their image for a time. But he forgot, in his role of make-believe, that a high-speed engine could make four wheels leave the road. So he's no longer a rebel without a cause. But his movie influenced more youth in my school than I wanted to admit.

When school opened we had young hoodlums who had dropped out riding up at the noon hour on their motorcycles to disrupt our pupils. We sent them away. We had vandalism, but as the best of our pupils showed their pride in their school, the worst became ashamed and stopped their destruction. We had smoking, but when the pupils learned that the staff as well as the students were forbidden to smoke on the schoolgrounds, there was less smoking. And we had gambling and profanity on the schoolgrounds, but when a few of these offenders visited the office with the coach and me for a conference with the Board of Education, as we called our flat wooden paddle, we had less gambling and profanity on the grounds.

We had a truancy problem. The boys would take off in the afternoon to loaf around the poolhalls and pinball parlors. But the boys were not the only ones who played truant. One morning in my office there were seven girls among the truants. I asked for an explanation.

"Grace, Ethel, Faye, and I, who got on Mr. Gardner's bus, had to go shopping for clothes," said one of the girls. "We rode the bus to Kensington, and when Mr. Gardner stopped to pick up some pupils, we got off!"

"Where did you shop? Kensington?"

"No, sir, we caught the Kensington-Portsmouth bus and went to Portsmouth."

"But I cannot excuse you for a day's absence to shop," I said. "Missing school is serious business. Do your shopping on Saturdays, or let your mothers do it!"

Each girl made a plausible excuse why her mother couldn't go shopping for her. Her mother had to stay home because her little sister was sick, or she had peaches to can which would have spoiled if she hadn't canned them yesterday. Each girl vowed she had to have clothes before she could come to school. Each girl was deadly serious.

"Your excuses sound all right," I told them.

Mrs. Markham wrote their names down on admittance slips and I initialed them.

"How are you classed this year?" I asked.

"We're sophomores," one said.

"That's all now," I told them. "Go to your first-period classes."

They didn't thank me for the admittance slips. Each girl acted as if she had been insulted by the new principal's prying into her personal life.

The other three girls, who were on another bus, had a similar story. I initialed their admittance slips and sent them to their first-period classes.

"I'm not satisfied with their excuses, Jean," I said to one of my student secretaries. "My idea might not be any good. So don't breathe a word of what I ask you to do. I want you to check back into the teachers' classroom books of last year to see how many times these seven girls were absent," I said. "See if they were absent on the same days!"

Only a few days later, I had the finished report. I studied it and then said, "This is really something. Quite a coincidence when seven girls from Shannon Creek are absent on the same day twenty-one times in a school year! Tell these girls I want them back in the office!"

When the seven girls walked in, one—who was as pretty as springtime and who wore an expensive sweater and blouse and costume jewelry that clanked when she moved—spoke for the group. "Did you send for us?" she asked.

"Sure did. You seven girls have certainly done a lot of shopping together, haven't you?"

"No, sir. We haven't," she said.

"You've missed school on the same day a lot of times, haven't you?"

"No, sir."

"Then the records have lied."

Now the rose-petal color in her cheek spread over her face.

"Something is wrong here! Last year each of you missed twenty-one days of school. You missed on the same day too!"

Not one of them said a word. They looked silently at each other and at me.

"I have no jurisdiction over last year," I told them. "Last year is over. Now, this year you have begun that same practice. It's not going to work with me. I am warning you not to let it happen again!"

"It won't happen again, Mr. Stuart," said the pretty one, who was evidently the leader of the group.

"You know and I know you didn't stay out of school twenty-one days to shop."

"No, we didn't, Mr. Stuart."

"You didn't shop yesterday either, did you? I want the truth."

"No, sir, we didn't. Well, we did a little shopping too," she said. "We saw a movie!"

"I'm putting you on probation," I said. "Your record from this time on will be carefully watched. You know you can't do wrong and get by with it. Whatever you do will come out."

Some weeks later Mrs. Nottingham, who taught English, came to me.

"Mr. Stuart," she said in a soft voice, "I have a little problem among the girls. Two of our girls got into a fight over a pocketbook on the school bus. Each one claimed the pocketbook and said she bought it at a certain store in Portsmouth."

"Have you got the pocketbook?" I asked her.

"Yes, I have. This happened last week. Last Saturday when I was in Portsmouth, I went to both stores to see if the kind of pocketbook they fought over was sold at either, and it wasn't. I showed a clerk at each store the pocketbook and asked if they had any more in stock and was informed that the brand of pocketbook had never been handled there."

"What kind of girls are they?" I asked.

"Nice-looking girls," she said. "You'd be surprised. You'd never think they'd fight on a school bus over a pocketbook. You know," she whispered, "I believe the pocketbook was stolen."

"What? Girls stealing?"

"I'm not sure, but I'll find out," she said. "It might take me two weeks to get all the details, but I'll work it out."

It was not until more than two weeks later that Mrs. Nottingham came to me again about her problem.

"Mr. Stuart," she said, "you remember the pocketbook two of my girls claimed to have bought?"

"Yes," I said.

"Well," she said, "after I visited the stores they claimed to have bought it in, I knew both were lying. When John came home, he and I tramped the streets in Portsmouth all day Saturday examining merchandise in stores to find where this pocketbook was sold. We couldn't find it."

Mrs. Nottingham had the pocketbook with her. She let me examine this nondescript item of merchandise which had caused the trouble.

"Then last Saturday John and I started hunting again," she continued. I listened and looked at the cheap item, wondering how it could ever cause a hair-pulling squabble between young women on a school bus. "Finally we found these displayed in a second-rate shop window. Yesterday while you were dealing with your problems with absenteeism, gambling, and parents, I had these girls back in my little office upstairs, and one broke down and confessed to stealing it. When she confessed, the other girl was so badly scared I thought she too was implicated in stealing. While the girl who had confessed was weeping, I sat there waiting, and soon the other girl confessed. She broke down and started crying too."

"Both were involved?"

"More than two were involved," she continued. "These

two girls involved five more. I have confessions from seven girls who have played hooky from school to steal from the Portsmouth stores."

"It's bad enough for a boy to steal, let alone a girl," I interrupted, shaking my hand in disgust. I gave the pocket-book back to her. "How long has this been going on?"

"Last school year, last summer, and this school year," she replied. "I have all of the story, too. Now, Mr. Stuart, you temporarily halted their stealing this year. You remember the seven girls whose names you checked on the last year's absentee lists because you found when one missed a day this year that six others missed on the same day! That's the gang!"

"Looks like a gang that large would have been suspected and caught."

"No, they're smart," she said. "When they got to Portsmouth, they divided in pairs, and each pair went a separate way. After a day of looting stores they had a common meeting place! But we've run into another problem. Just what will we do with them? They can't take this material back, confess stealing it, pay for it, and apologize. They've worn out many of the things they have stolen."

"I agree with you on that," I said. "If all seven were to take back a few things and admit they stole them, there'd be headlines in the papers that would ruin them for life and this school eternally. What do you propose to do?"

"In my vacant period I expect to call them into my office room, two at a time, and lay them across the desk and set them on fire with one of your paddles," she said. "I intend to lock the door. The women's lounge room is small and soundproof, so no one will hear or know what goes on inside. They must not get by without punishment. If they do, I don't know what might happen to them. We shouldn't tell anyone —not even another teacher or their parents."

"I agree with you."

When Mrs. Nottingham had gone, I sat behind my desk

and thought about these seven fine-looking girls, and about
how we had decided to punish them ourselves and not disgrace them. And I thought back to when I was just a little
fellow, and took apples from Mrs. Collins, and how my Mom
switched me all the way to the Collins' house and made me
tell her I had stolen her apples. But I wasn't yet ten then, and
"Grandma" Collins was kindly. So Mom had her way, and
we had ours. Two different ways, but both, I knew, could
work.

That afternoon, when I went down the corridor to the
teachers' meeting, I met the two members of the gang who
had fought over the pocketbook. Their eyes looked as if they
had been crying as they passed me hurriedly to get on the
school bus. Mrs. Nottingham was coming down the steps
behind them very slowly.

"I didn't punish all yet," she said softly. "I got the leaders
today. Tomorrow I'll take care of the followers."

That was the end of the group and of stealing for all of
those seven girls. Today all seven are fine citizens. Three are
teachers themselves today.

Morning was a busy time for me in McKell High School.
Among the six hundred twenty-five pupils enrolled, there
were always those returning who had been absent the day
before. They formed a single line in my office when they
explained their absences. I gave, or didn't give, them a
chance to make up this work. And this November morning
wasn't any different from other mornings except a young
girl, June Quarrels, came into my office with her blue eyes
sparkling and a broad smile on her face. She had walked
around the line of waiting students.

"Do you have a problem, June?" I asked. "You'll have to
get in line."

"I have a very pleasant problem, but it can wait until you
have finished with the others," she replied.

"Wish mine was that pleasant," Willie Smith grumbled.

He bore more weight on one leg and rested the other as he stood in line.

"It must be nice to have pleasant problems," Carol Keeney sighed.

There were other mumbled remarks among the standing and waiting pupils while June sat down and waited. She smiled and listened as the line grew shorter. She waited until I had finished with the last pupil.

"All right, June," I said. "What is your happy problem this morning?"

"Mr. Stuart, I want to ask you what you think about my getting married?"

"Who is the lucky man?" I asked.

"Ronald Ratcliffe."

"Wonderful," I said. "I don't see a thing wrong with it. You're seniors in McKell High School. You've grown up together and you're classmates. You're about eighteen, and he's. . . ."

"Ronnie's nineteen," she interrupted. "I'm eighteen."

"Do your parents know about this?"

"No, we thought we'd discuss this with you first."

"I appreciate your confidence."

"We'll tell our parents when we go home this evening," she said. "I'm so happy about this."

"When did you get engaged?" I asked.

"We've been going steady for about a year now, but we didn't get engaged until this morning."

"You're certainly a nice couple," I said. "I'm all for this marriage, but I'd like to make a suggestion to you. Since you're eighteen and nineteen years of age, I suggest you have dates the rest of this year and that you get married in the spring."

"We'd planned to marry about Christmas," she said. "Ronald wanted us to marry then."

"Really, I'd suggest you marry in June," I said. "It's the month of brides. June brides! And June is your name!"

"Oh, yes, Mr. Stuart," she said, "I think June is the right month, and I'll tell Ronald. I'm sure it will be all right with him. You see, Mr. Stuart, what one suggests, the other agrees to, and what one likes, the other likes. We're in love."

"I hope you and Ronald enjoy your days from now until June," I said. "These will be romantic days for you. You'll remember these days in later years, and maybe you might even thank me for my suggestion that you make June your wedding month instead of December. June, you will make such a beautiful June bride."

"Oh, thank you, Mr. Stuart," she said. "I'll tell Ronald about your suggestion. Thank you again and again, Mr. Stuart! You have been so nice. I'm inviting you to our wedding."

I wrote an excuse for June. This happy young woman, so full of youth and springtime and romance, stood before me with tears in her eyes. She was about five-feet-four, with dimples in her cheeks, had large blue eyes and black hair that was done up in a bun. She had a half-dozen books in her arms when she left my office.

"Too young to marry now," I thought. "She should take time to enjoy the too few springtime years of her life while youth is here. The years of youth are too few, and marriage is a long-time contract."

After she had gone I looked into the files and got Ronald Ratcliffe's registration card. He had a study hall the second period. I expected him to come to my office too to tell me about his and June's engagement.

I was right. Big Ronald, fullback on the football team, brown eyes, black hair that was cut short and stood up like bristles, appeared wearing a suit and necktie and shined shoes. He stood before me smiling.

"You already know our good news, Mr. Stuart," Ronald

said. "June has already told me. You know she told me between class periods. Our lockers up in the senior section are
very close. See, Quarrels and Ratcliffe—the Q's and R's are
close to each other. And, Mr. Stuart," he said with a broader
smile, "one Q and one R are going to be a lot closer next
June."

"Have a chair, Ronald, and let's talk a few minutes," I said.
"My office work isn't pushing me now. I'll write you an
excuse so you can get back to study hall."

We talked for a while, and Ronald seemed as full of love
and happiness as June had.

June and Ronald's coming to my office to tell me of their
engagement was on Monday morning. On Tuesday morning
Mr. and Mrs. Joe Ratcliffe came to my office and introduced
themselves. Mr. Ratcliffe was an average-sized man with
brown eyes and slightly graying hair. Mrs. Ratcliffe was a
plump, middle-aged woman dressed in a matronly fashion.
They lived in the country not far from Fullerton. They were
in their middle forties. There was sadness on her face, and
Mr. Ratcliffe's eyes danced with resentment.

"Mr. Stuart, we have come to see you about Ronnie," he
said. "He came home last night and told his mother and me
that he was engaged to June Quarrels. And when his mother
and I objected, from all he told us, you practically told our
son marriage was the right thing for him."

Mrs. Ratcliffe, who had been wiping tears from her eyes,
burst out crying. I walked over and closed my office door.

"In other words, you are taking over the custody of our
son," he shouted.

"Calm your voice, Mr. Ratcliffe," I said. "I can hear you
better when you don't shout."

"But you know Ronnie has a football scholarship at State,"
he said. "And you know he's a good student!"

"Yes, I know these things," I said. "But I also know at
nineteen he thinks he is a man. And he is a man. He is ca-

pable of making some decisions for himself."

"But he isn't," Mrs. Ratcliffe wept. "He's still my little boy. I know June is nice. But we don't want him to marry yet!"

"Do you think, Mr. Stuart, it is wise for our son at nineteen to marry a girl who is eighteen?" Joe Ratcliffe asked me.

"No, I don't," I said. "They had planned to marry in December. So I asked them to postpone the marriage until June."

"Yes, we know all about that," Mrs. Ratcliffe sobbed. She had the handkerchief over her face. "Ronnie told us last night all you said. And when we objected, he said, 'Well, Mr. Stuart didn't object. Mr. Stuart is the young people's friend.'"

"And we do object, Mr. Stuart." Joe Ratcliffe spoke loudly again. "We want you either to discourage this or to stay out of it. To be frank with you, this is none of your business."

"Mr. Ratcliffe, I've worked with thousands of youth," I said. "I've seen them come and go. Although I have only one child of my own, your children are my children here, and all the parents and guardians who send their children here are my children too. I want the greatest good for the greatest number. I want each one to attain the highest level in life. I'm not trying to take your son away from you and. . . ."

"But what do you call this?" he interrupted me. "You're encouraging them to marry! You've even set June for their wedding month!"

"You don't know youth, Mr. Ratcliffe," I said.

"I don't know youth," he repeated heatedly. "I've got seven children, and you've got one. And you tell me I don't know youth!"

"You don't know them like teachers and principals who work with thousands of teen-agers," I said. "You think of Ronald as a little boy. He isn't. He's grown up."

"He's still a child," Mrs. Ratcliffe cried softly.

"But don't you see I've got them to postpone their wedding until June," I said. "They were determined to marry in December, just one month from now. And they would have done it if I hadn't talked to June."

"Mr. Stuart, what would you do with a boy who would steal a car?" Joe Ratcliffe asked me.

"This hasn't anything to do with your and my problem," I said. "But I will answer your question. I would see to it the boy had a car to drive if it had to be my own."

"That's just why I asked you," he said. "Then you know the boy, Booten Halbert, who drives places in your car, once stole one."

"Yes, I know that," I said. "That's why I trust him with my car. And he goes places, does errands, and always brings the car back."

"I don't understand your way of thinking," Joe Ratcliffe said. "I think he should have gone to the reformatory for stealing that car. And I don't think you should have encouraged our son Ronnie to marry, either. I want you to break this up and break it up in a hurry."

"Mr. and Mrs. Ratcliffe, I'm doing what I believe is best," I said. "Your son has made up his mind to marry. Miss Quarrels has made up her mind to marry. Now, I can tell you how you can make them marry before June!"

"Ah, don't tell us," she sobbed.

"But I will tell you," I said. "You keep on fighting this the way you are, and they'll marry now. And then," I added, "when they marry, and if their marriage is successful, they'll always resent what you said and did to them."

"Come on, Nannie, let's go," Joe Ratcliffe said. "We can't get anyplace talking to Mr. Stuart. He's for this marriage."

"But, Joe, don't talk like that," she said, rising from her chair. "He did do one thing. He got it put off until June. We can have Ronnie home with us a few more months!"

"Yes, Mr. Stuart, we do thank you for that." He spoke grudgingly. "Good day, sir."

He took his wife by the arm and they left my office. Had their son been dead, Nannie Ratcliffe couldn't have grieved more than she had in my office. Had a wayward driver struck Ronald and injured him permanently, Mr. Ratcliffe couldn't have been more resentful toward that careless driver than he had been toward me.

On Wednesday morning Mr. and Mrs. John Quarrels came to my office. I had never seen June's parents before. They introduced themselves.

"Mr. Stuart, June came home Monday and told us that she was engaged to Ronnie Ratcliffe," John Quarrels said, "and. . . ."

"Now, we weren't shocked about this, John," Mrs. Quarrels interrupted.

"But just a minute, Clarinda," he said. "Let me tell Mr. Stuart."

"But tell him, John, you married me when I was eighteen and you were nineteen, and that Joe Ratcliffe was eighteen when he married Nannie, who was seventeen, and we heard they're about to die over Ronnie's getting engaged to our June. And, believe me, they have no kick coming, for I think Ronnie Ratcliffe is getting a bargain. We should be the parents who do the kicking!"

John Quarrels was a tall, thin man with brown hair and blue eyes, and he couldn't keep from smiling when he tried to talk. Mrs. Quarrels was a willowy, handsome woman, prettier than her daughter. She couldn't speak to anyone without smiling. They were this side of forty and full of fun and vitality.

"Now, Mr. Stuart, what I have been trying to tell you is, we really don't want June to marry at eighteen, for we have plans to send her to State Teachers' College," John Quarrels said. "We have saved for this, since we have only one child. We just have the one egg in our basket. And it looks like we might have two—and one will be a goose egg. I think I'd rather have some other kind of egg in the basket and. . . ."

"I agree with John about the eggs," Clarinda Quarrels interrupted him again.

"I'll say schoolteaching is interesting when we have problems and I get to meet the parents," I said.

"Well, what we've come to say is, we don't want this marriage, Mr. Stuart, even if we have. . . ."

"But I told John I thought it was wonderful you got this wedding put off from Christmas until June," Clarinda interrupted again. "We will have Ronnie around for Christmas, at least. I think we'd better be going, John, and let Mr. Stuart get back to his work."

"We thank you for getting it put off, but we don't want you to encourage their getting married," John Quarrels said.

"And since they've made up their minds, I told John we might as well encourage it," Clarinda Quarrels said. "Come on, John, let's go and let Mr. Stuart get back to his work."

I did not see the Ratcliffes nor the Quarrelses again for months. November passed, and December came. Often I caught Ronald and June walking in the corridor holding hands, and when they saw me their hands came apart and I smiled and they walked on. He was wearing her small class ring on a little chain around his neck, and she was wearing his big class ring on a chain around her neck. All the pupils in McKell High School knew they were engaged, because June was wearing an engagement ring.

The Christmas holidays came, and I was glad of them. It had been a hard autumn, fighting to bring a once fine high school back to a decent level when it had fallen so low. My doctor was not as pleased with my health as he had been. He wanted me to spend the holidays relaxing, and I did, with Naomi Deane and Jane. The most energetic thing I did was to take long walks with Jane.

When my daughter wanted nothing more than to take a walk on a winter night with me, then I was going. What could be better than taking a walk together? The very idea meant a better understanding of each other. Now, at the age of fifteen, Jane needed her mother and me as much as she had ever needed us before.

Before we were married and had a daughter of our own, I had had vast experience dealing with teen-age youth. Many a group of young fellows who I thought were slipping from our school's discipline, I took for autumn or winter walks. We'd take food, build a fire on a lonely hilltop, and sit around the fire and cook and eat. Often the women and men teachers of our school would take girls and boys out on these little get-togethers, which proved very effective. I learned by teaching school one way that parents can be close to their children.

I learned it in my own home. I had wise parents, though I didn't realize it when I was a youth. We took long walks through the woods on Sundays, identifying trees, wildflowers, and plants. We made a game of counting up our scores to see who could identify the most. This was a lot of fun, and, simple as it may seem, tied our family into a strong, indivisible unit.

So when my daughter asked me to go walking, even if the night was cold, I knew I should not refuse.

And what could be better, I thought, than seeing stars in the high dark sky? What could be better than a cold wind stirring enough to rattle the leaves still hanging to the white oaks? These belonged to the creator of the universe. The winter sights and sounds were enough to inspire us, even if we had to brave the nippy weather to see and hear them. I was sorry when vacation was over and our walks had to be less frequent.

When school reopened, we still had our share of problems. The hardest was getting the illegal gambling joints where our pupils gathered closed. This was difficult and dangerous, but we got it done. Then we were short of funds, and our school building was robbed, and we had trouble with the State Athletic Association that had to be ironed out.

But our two lovebirds had no problems at all. When school resumed in January, June Quarrels and Ronald Ratcliffe walked up the corridor holding hands. January and February came and passed. March came, and I didn't see June and Ronald walking up the corridor holding hands.

On an April afternoon, June came to my office.

"Mr. Stuart, I'd like to speak to you, if you don't mind."

"Sure, June," I said. "How is everything with you?"

"Not good, Mr. Stuart," she said as she burst into tears. "I've come to thank you."

"Here, June, have a chair and sit down and tell me your troubles," I said. "Tell me why you have come to thank me."

"You've saved my life by getting us to put off our wedding," she said. "I'm not crying because I'm sad. I'm crying with joy. Every time I think, 'What if I had married Ronnie Ratcliffe in December," I shudder. Mr. Stuart, I've had time to find him out. He's not what I want for a husband. He's almost a brute."

"Now, June, he's not that," I said. "He's a nice boy."

"Don't try to encourage me, Mr. Stuart," she said. "If you do, I'll lose my respect for you."

"Oh, I'm not trying to encourage you now," I said. "You know what you want in a husband."

"And I know I don't want that Ronnie either," she said. "See"—she held up her hand—"no ring. I gave it back to him with thanks. Never that Ronnie, Mr. Stuart. You saved me. Did you know this would happen?"

"No, June, I didn't," I said.

"Oh, Mr. Stuart, he's not for me," she said. "I've found him out. He's even a double-crosser, Mr. Stuart. I wish you knew him better. If we were the only two people left on an island, he'd have to keep his part of the island, and I'd certainly keep mine."

June Quarrels, a pretty, unsmiling girl, walked out of my office.

In the last period before school closed, Ronald Ratcliffe came in.

"I won't sit down, Mr. Stuart," he said. "It won't take that long. I've come in here to thank you for putting off our wedding last December. If I'd married that June Quarrels, Mr. Stuart, it wouldn't have worked. I hate to tell you, but she's a wildcat. She even scratched my face here last Sunday week. I could never get along with her. Really, by putting off our wedding I had time to find her out."

"I have always thought she's a pretty girl. . . ."

"But pretty is as pretty does," he interrupted. "You don't know her, Mr. Stuart."

"No, I don't know her disposition except as a student," I said. "She seems nice and pleasant, and so do you. I thought it might be one of those real marriages that I've been told are made in heaven."

"Made in heaven, my foot," he said, his voice rising. "That one would have been made in hell. Sir, last night after I went to bed I couldn't sleep. And I went back over the whole thing. You saved me from a marriage that would never have worked."

"Do your parents know about this?"

"Yes, I told them you saved me," he replied. "They're coming in here to thank you. I'll be going to State this year, and I'll be carrying the pigskin there too."

He gripped my hand in enthusiastic gratitude before he left the office.

When his parents dropped in to see me a week later, both were smiling.

"Now, about your letting Booten Halbert drive that car," Mr. Ratcliffe said. "I've thought a lot about that. He hasn't stolen a car since. And he told me the other day he was tired of driving the car for you. Said he'd lost interest in driving."

"And I'm thankful our Ronnie has lost interest in marriage," Nannie Ratcliffe said. There was no sadness on her face now. Her brown eyes were filled with sparkle. They danced like stars. "That was a wise move, Mr. Stuart, getting that marriage put off until June. I want to thank you from the bottom of my heart. It wouldn't have worked, so Ronnie said, and Ronnie knows."

"We've just dropped in to thank you," Joe said. "Nannie and I have thought that maybe you had thought it wouldn't work from the beginning and that's the reason you suggested they marry in June."

"No, I didn't think that," I explained. "I thought it might work fine. But I didn't think they had taken time enough to know one another."

"Well, Mr. Stuart, thank you for your patience with us," Nannie Ratcliffe said.

"Not patience with you, but with youth, Mrs. Ratcliffe."

"Well, thank you anyway."

"Yes, and our apologies over the way we acted in your office when we were here before," he said.

When they left the office this time they were happy and smiling parents. I had not expected John and Clarinda Quarrels, but on a Monday morning in May, June told me that her parents were coming to see me. And shortly after school had begun and I was alone in the office, I looked over at the door and there stood two happy parents.

"Come in," I invited.

"We won't take much of your time," he said. "But we would like. . . ."

"To thank you," Clarinda interrupted. "Oh, I've just told John that what is to be will be. And he said that wasn't true. He said we ought to thank you for postponing that marriage. You understand now, Mr. Stuart, about the two eggs in one basket and one's being a goose egg?"

"But, Clarinda, don't talk this way now," John warned her. "Be thankful our June isn't married to him."

"Mr. Stuart, our June plans to go to State Teachers' College," Clarinda explained. "And we are so happy. Oh, how smart you were, Mr. Stuart. You knew, didn't you?" I stood in silence. "You knew it wouldn't work all the time, didn't you?"

"No, I didn't," I told her. "No one knows that, not even people who get married. Look at the divorces. But I wanted them to have more youth and springtime and to know each other better. Parents make the mistake of thinking their children are small, that they haven't grown up. I know youth are intelligent but often act too quickly. I think they're capable of making up their own minds."

"Well, you handled it right," John Quarrels said. "We owe you a debt of gratitude. June told us if it hadn't been for you, her life would have been ruined."

"Well, maybe it would have been," I said. "We can't tell what act or what spoken word, maybe spoken by a stranger, will change the course of our lives and maybe our destinies."

"We know you're busy, and we won't take any more of your time," John Quarrels said. "We must be going. But I would like to know what caused you to suggest to June and Ronnie that they delay their wedding until June."

"Have you got time to listen to a little story?" I asked. "You know, we learn by doing. I was a teacher for twelve years and have been a principal for ten. Once when I was a younger and more inexperienced principal, I had a similar experience at Greenup High School. John Mapes loved Mary Boggs. Mary Boggs loved John Mapes. So Mr. and Mrs. Boggs came and told me not to let their Mary see that John. They warned me to break it up. Mr. and Mrs. Mapes came, and they told me not to let their John look at that Mary. They told me to break it up. This was in November too. And by Christmas this couple ran off and got married. And it didn't last a year. I learned then that trying to keep a young couple apart wouldn't work. The young couple, John and Mary, were fine people. They hadn't had time to know each other. We didn't give them time, for their parents and their high-school principal were after them. They thought if their getting married was important enough to cause all the trouble, they would marry anyway. I learned my lesson. I was determined never to do this again, regardless of all the pressure put on me by the parents."

"Oh, I'm so happy," Mrs. Quarrels said. "June said no one knew that Ronnie. She said she pitied the woman who ever married him."

"June wasn't the right one," I said. "They found this by waiting. He will find the right one, and she will find the right one."

When Mr. and Mrs. Quarrels left my office, I walked over to my desk and knocked on wood. It was the first problem in a long time in this school I had managed where everybody was happy with the solution. And to solve a problem and make everybody happy happens too few times to a high-school principal.

Commencement time came. We had taught school for a full year in an overcrowded building with too few teachers, too little money, and problems with local racketeers. But a few dedicated teachers had changed a lot of young rebels without causes. Discipline had brought both boys and girls to appreciate their heritage and their opportunities. We had made McKell High School a real school in one short year.

My doctor ordered me to resign my post. It had been a hard year, full of hard battles, and they had taken their toll. But it was worth it. That summer I rested happy, knowing I had made a contribution.

With football in the clean, cool, crisp autumn air, I returned to McKell High School to see how everything was going. No teacher, principal, or superintendent is ever an indispensable person, because the vacancy is filled and the school goes on.

When I walked in unbeknownst to anyone, I never saw a pupil in the corridor. Then, I followed my old beat up and over the second corridor. I never found better discipline and a better-organized school. There were many reasons for this, but the principal reason was the school's principal, "Lucky" Clifford Lowdenback. He got that name in athletics because he was always considered "lucky." In this particular case, McKell High School was lucky.

The year before, Mr. Roscoe Stephens, Greenup County school superintendent, had said to me, "Should you leave us at McKell, will you have somebody in mind to take your place?" It is very rare when a high-school principal gets to recommend his successor.

Knowing McKell High School as I did, having taught two generations there, I went over the names of those I had taught. I looked for one of my pupils who loved to teach and who would rather accept a challenge than to eat when hungry.

I narrowed the list down, one by one, and it came to "Lucky" Clifford Lowdenback, six-feet-four, weighing 165 pounds. He never got hungry, for he never liked to eat. He had always been in the best of health, too. He was skinny and tall in body and still taller in the mind.

Clifford Lowdenback came to me at Greenup High School when I was a young principal. He was not valedictorian of his class, but he was very close. He was an A Student, an A athlete, and he was A in character. In football, he played end, and if my memory is correct, he didn't have a front tooth left after the season, and our local dentist fixed him up free of cost or for a minimum fee. He was determined his goal line would not be crossed. Many a time, in an addled state of mind, he'd be swinging and wouldn't leave the field, and the coach and I would carry him off the field. He never gave up easily.

Clifford Lowdenback is example enough to dispute a lot of nonsense about the pupils from broken homes. He was from a broken home, and practically made his own way in high school by mowing lawns, working in stores, and doing odd jobs where and when he could find them in the Depression years. His not having a home made him more ambitious than ever to do something in life. He left a fine set of grades at Greenup High School, and a good athletic record.

A classmate of his and I took him to Lincoln Memorial University one late summer day, where we left him with one change of clothes and five dollars. We left him, happy as a lark, sitting in the kitchen among strangers stringing beans. He had already learned to adjust himself among strangers.

He wasn't a stranger long at Lincoln Memorial. He didn't know he could pitch ball, but he tried out and was one of the leading pitchers in the Smokey Mountain Conference. This small college won Tennessee state championship a number of times and furnished several league players. Clifford for a time thought of big-league baseball for a career.

He liked teaching and returned to Greenup County and taught a rural school. Quickly he was transferred to high school. Once, when the pupils tried to riot against a helpless principal, he stood at the door. When violent youth came up the steps to "get" the principal, Clifford piled them up so deep the last ones couldn't get over the fence of sprawled youth. Excellent with his fists, he was an English major who loved poetry and wrote many poems in his youth.

The rest of his career was all schoolwork except four years in the army in World War II. He coached at McKell High School prior to World War II, and Elby Nickels, University of Cincinnati star and later captain of the Pittsburgh Steelers, was one of his McKell team.

"Lucky" Clifford Lowdenback coached at Ludlow High School, and his smaller team beat Ashland's Tomcats in its heyday of power. Coaches of large high schools over the state know Holmes High School in Covington and its football teams. Clifford was line coach there for a number of years.

Then he followed me as principal of McKell High School, where he instituted a coach's discipline. His school year was preplanned and preorganized long in advance. Similar to men on his former football squads, each pupil in McKell High School knew in advance where he belonged, his course of study, and what was expected of him in discipline. So after I could no longer be there, McKell High School could stand up and be counted as one of the well-planned, well-disciplined schools in the state.

Chapter 9

TO TEACH CREATIVE WRITING IS never a cinch. Teaching it at the American University in Cairo, Egypt, presented a combination of problems that seemed insoluble to me when I arrived on the scene as visiting professor of English for 1960–61. I had been invited by the president of A.U.C., Dr. Raymond McLain, who had read my books.

First among the factors that made me doubt my sanity in accepting the invitation was my own background. I had grown up free as the wind in the hills of Kentucky. I had taught with the same freedom. I had lived in a country where my views on any subject (if not obscene or treasonable) could be freely expressed. Given my American political heritage, my Western culture, how could I teach in a country where newspapers, magazines, publishing houses, radio, and TV were "nationalized"?

In the second place, my students would be of many nationalities and from countries with many forms of government—monarchies, dictatorships, democracies, limited democracies, and communist-infiltrated. I would be teaching

Muslim and Christian. I would have all colors of skins, from the blondly Nordic Finnish to the deep ebony of the Sudanese. All of this diversity, racial and geographic, meant that I would be abysmally ignorant about the personal backgrounds of my students and could not possibly brief myself by carrying out my usual practice—visiting in their homes and with their parents.

Finally, I would have so little time. The semesters at the university are only four months long and are fragmented by a succession of holidays, religious and political. For example, because the Muslim counterpart of the Christian Sunday is Friday, we did not teach on either of those days. I won't enumerate the special observances—there are so many.

Against this negative array stood one big positive factor: I believe there are few, if any, more "quality" schools than the American University at Cairo. There was a faculty of eighty-five for fewer than five hundred undergraduates and hardly half a dozen graduate students. The average student-teacher ratio was five to one, which meant that the eleven students enrolled in my first-semester class in creative writing represented a really full house.

When I first looked into my students' faces, a new fear struck me. Some of the countries from which they came were hostile to the United States. Had national attitudes rubbed off on these young men and women? Would personal hostilities nullify my efforts to teach them?

In a very short time I began to learn more about the American University at Cairo. Even before school began I saw a number of teachers and students talking and laughing together. I found students sitting on the stone steps or on little stone benches under the palms. They sat anyplace they could, drank Coca-Colas, Turkish and French coffee, and had the best time on earth just talking and looking at each other. This was before school began too. Anytime students could make a plausible excuse to come through the gate, they came.

These students loved, honored, and respected the three-and-a-half-acre campus and this small, compact university, under its sheltering palms. Why did they love this school?

In America students don't love a school this much, not any more. Many American students dread the start of a school year. They remain at home until the day of registration. Here they wanted to live on the campus. I didn't know that Muslim girls didn't date boys as girls do in America. I didn't know marriages for young couples were arranged by their parents and many a groom and bride didn't see each other until the day of their wedding. There were many things I needed to learn about this world. Jane learned more quickly than I. At eighteen she could talk easily to boys and girls here, and she took a fancy to the carefree life on these three and one-half acres.

She wanted to live with the students on the A.U.C. campus before school began in September. At the start of school, less than a half-dozen students came every day. Then the number increased, until there were a dozen, a score, and then more, three dozen. This was one effect of the fence and gate. Was it to lock freedom in or freedom out? Was it to lock America in? Had it not been for the fence and gate, there wouldn't have been standing room on this campus.

"Daddy, you know the kids are smart here," Jane said. "They don't know many TV programs but they've read good plays. They've seen the best movies that come here. They know the best music. They've read the best books. But when it comes to boy meets girl and date, they don't. They go in groups. They're like children!"

"They're probably smarter than you think!"

"No, Daddy, honest," she explained. "I feel desperately sorry for them. The Christians here are Copts, Armenian Orthodox, Greek Orthodox, Roman Catholics, and Protestants. There are many Muslims and a few Jews. And while we Christians here can date, though not as freely as the Christians in other lands, the Muslim girls can't. And, you know, Daddy, they're so lovely—so beautiful, so wonderful—I feel sorry for them, Daddy—I can't help it. I know Hoda, a pretty Muslim girl, likes Latif, who is a Christian, for when Latif walked away with Lila, who is a Christian girl, Hoda cried like a child. There wasn't anything she could do about it!"

"Oh, don't tell me that," I said. "She could do something about it! She could have walked away with him too!"

"Oh, no, Daddy, this world of young people here is different," she said. "It is something—yes, really it's radical for girls of Muslim faith from some countries in the Near East to go to school with boys. It's radical for them to sit as we sit and talk to each other. You'll soon learn all of this. We have such good times together. I love the Muslim girls and boys. You know beautiful Nadga I introduced you to?"

"Yes."

"When she goes back to her little country, she'll have to wear a veil. Always."

"That's a shame," I said. "She is really beautiful. She has a nice smile. She speaks perfect English-English!"

"Daddy she writes excellent poetry too."

"Tell her to get in my English class," I said. "I'm going to speak of freedom in that class!"

"Be careful, Daddy," Jane warned me. "You have to watch what you say in your classes here. We're in an American school, but we're not in America! I've been told in every class somebody is there to report what you say to the government."

"I don't give a hoot," I said. "Let them report."

"But I want to stay here, Daddy," Jane pleaded.

"Don't tell me anything more," I said. "Let me find out everything for myself. Let me learn my way."

"But don't blunder, Daddy," she said. "You know the police have a record of us, and they watch what we do and find out what we say. The students here know this, and it hurts the young people that the government is like this. They're embarrassed, Daddy!"

We had come eight thousand miles to this little three and one-half acres of American University college-campus freedom which was locked in with a big padlock. But freedom cannot be held behind a gate. It jumps over a fence and becomes a fresh-blowing wind. Freedom can start from my tongue that can generate hot words for a hot wind. It can start from many tongues. And to hell with the stooges and spies! I'll teach school when the teaching starts!

When we left America to come to A.U.C., some people thought the U.S. government or an American agency like Ford or Rockefeller foundation paid me a large salary; I'd come for five thousand dollars, which is less than I'd made in 1956–57 when I was principal of the McKell High School in Greenup County, Kentucky. We had come not to make money but to do a job in the Near East to help the people, and by doing so to buy goodwill for our country.

For A.U.C. stands as a monument to the philanthropy of the American people who give money each year to keep it going. No one comes here for a big teaching salary. Nowadays, if it were money the teacher was after, he'd stay in America. And students come here from the countries of the Middle East, North Africa, and a few from Asia and Europe.

Only a third of A.U.C. teachers are Americans, and about two-thirds are from the Middle East, but many of these are American- and European-trained. A.U.C. is located right on the battle line of Western and Eastern ideologies. Why had it not grown to be as large as the American University at Beirut? Because Lebanon is approximately one-half Christian. Lebanon is not in the United Arab Republic. It has more freedom, no censorship. It is more progressive and has a richer economy. In Egypt no one wonders why A.U.C. has not grown larger. People wonder here how it has been allowed to remain.

A.U.C. is not recognized by the United Arab Republic because it isn't nationalized and state-controlled, but it is recognized in America and Europe. There are approximately five hundred undergraduate students in A.U.C., and an extension school gives courses to another six or seven hundred. Then there is a small graduate school. In all, one thousand to fourteen hundred students are enrolled annually at A.U.C. The year I was there, the extension courses were not advertised. Five thousand applied. Due to the lack of classroom space and teachers, only five hundred could be accommodated.

To this place we had come to do our part. Jane would take her freshman year here. I would teach in A.U.C., while Naomi taught at Maadi, a private elementary and secondary school. Here, too, was an American-style school, with pupils from all over the world.

Before the semester began, we learned about the preparation our Egyptian students had had.

All children between the ages of six and twelve, if able-bodied, were compelled to go to the elementary school. After twelve, schooling was not compulsory. If the pupils wanted to continue their education, they could go through grades seven, eight, and nine, which was called secondary education. They had to make certain grades before they were recommended to go on to receive an education at the government's expense. This consisted of another three years, tenth through twelfth grades, followed by another division of training and then college.

Not all rural areas or all the villages have elementary schools, of course. In certain areas fewer than fifty percent of Egypt's children get even an elementary-school education.

If a youth had dreams of a medical career, and if an aptitude test showed he was inclined toward bookkeeping, then he became a bookkeeper. The government decided for the ambitious students what they should have been permitted to decide for themselves. Regardless of what the tests showed, a boy who wanted to study medicine would have done better in the subject he liked than one the government said he should take. This one policy killed mental incentive. This wasn't a free education at all.

Only if a student was bright enough to meet the high standards set for him was he entitled to a free education beyond ninth grade. And then, only if he were willing to accept the vocation the government selected for him, could he continue beyond that. It was different from America. I was to find out how different.

It was my privilege in Cairo to have as a colleague one of the greatest, most inspirational teachers I have ever known. He was only thirty-eight, with the body, arms, and hands of a wrestler and the round face and blue eyes of a cherub. He was a political-science teacher at A.U.C. If anyone thinks his subject is easy to teach in Cairo, let him take over and try. Old Carl would do exactly this. He turned over his classes to the students and sat back and listened with an impish grin. He enjoyed this sort of thing, for he has a sense of humor.

If Old Carl didn't know the Near East when he went there, nearly two years before I did, he learned it quickly. His political-science courses didn't fill up to capacity at Marshall University and at the University of California. But in the Near East political science is a most important subject, for the students think their very existence depends upon this one subject. And when it comes to political science, students in the American University at Cairo are no babes in the woods. They know something about what goes on in every country in the world. And if a teacher doesn't know his subject, these students will keep him jumping. But not Old Carl.

Now, students at A.U.C. didn't call him Old Carl. He was Dr. Carl Leiden to them. He taught what can be the most controversial subject for any teacher to try to teach in the

Near East, where the ideologies of the Western and Oriental worlds meet and battle along a long invisible line of thought. He was never ruffled when a storm suddenly turned relations bad between two or more countries in the United Arab Republic. Old Carl taught students from over thirty different countries and from six continents. When there was trouble in the world, and there always was plenty, this was bound to have repercussions in his classes, for students are highly sensitive in the Middle East, where nationalistic fervor runs high. But there was no trouble in his classes. This Swede (and he is all Swede, on both sides of the house) will always be in control of his classes and any situation.

How did he do it? The weather was quite warm in Cairo, and instructors just about had to keep their windows raised and the doors propped open. So, I've stood back behind the corridor wall and listened to him teaching a class. He's like some of the old teachers I used to know in the one-room schools in the Kentucky hills. There is a little rostrum built above the floor with the teacher's desk up there where he can look down like a feudal lord at his pupils and teach down to them. Not Old Carl.

He brought his chair down on the same level, and he talked right out to them. He never talked down, and he never talked up. At first I thought he was a little hard of hearing, and maybe he is, but even this works well for him. He would sit with his students in a circle around him. And if and when a student had a good opinion, no one was prouder than the teacher, and he told that student so. Students left his classes laughing and talking. A classroom period was never long enough for them.

Now, the big friendly Swede with the wrestler's body and the cherub face isn't one to be pushed. One had as well try to push the sphinx. If he were being deliberately pushed, he wouldn't give ground. One day I asked him how he got the scars over his face. "Street fights and playing football in

Boone, Iowa," he said. "I never liked to give an inch of ground when I was on the defensive." He's such a friendly big fellow, one might assume his thinking is shallow. But he can read a dry book of seven hundred pages in a night and tell you all about it the next morning. He'll tell you the book is dry and no good and not to waste your time reading it.

"How many books do you read in a year?" I asked.

"Last year I read two hundred and sixty-seven," he said. "I've got a record of them and what I thought of each one!" This made me wonder when he found time for other things. Yet, Old Carl had more time than any other teacher in the American University at Cairo.

Another thing he could do was kid his students and make them like it.

"I know your Prophet Muhammad was a tolerant man, but he wouldn't approve of your smoking that cigarette," I heard him say to a young fellow in his class. He slapped him on the shoulder good-naturedly. "But Muhammad understands. I don't think he'll report you to Allah."

Then the young man and his teacher laughed together. No doubt this young man thought over later what his Dr. Leiden told him, because the good Muslim doesn't smoke.

He prodded his students and fellow teachers jokingly about religion, and if they believed in shooting and if so whose side was God on in some ancient battle. And he was constantly asking Christian Copts, Orthodox, and Protestants why their groups and denominations engaged in battles against each other and why they're all going to school together. "American University is the future world in a teacup. Be nice," he told them.

And he would call a boy over and say: "What is it you don't like about Tito?" Or he would ask a youth: "Do you like Mr. K.? Don't you believe Bulgaria, Hungary, and Czechoslovakia are parts of a colonial empire?" He kidded the students with a smile. But every joke would have an implication.

"Sir," a senior said to me, "I hope to go to your America as soon as I finish here." His face was beaming when he thought of going to America.

"To what school do you plan to go?" I asked him.

"Any that Dr. Leiden can persuade to give me a scholarship," he said.

"Are you having any luck?" I asked.

"Not yet, but I will, for Dr. Leiden has written to about fifty schools for me."

"Why do you want to go to America to school? Why not England or Germany?"

He didn't answer my questions, but instead he looked puzzled because I had asked him this question.

Then he said: "Are all Americans like Dr. Leiden?"

He had answered my question, but I wouldn't answer his. I stood looking at him. Here was a part of Old Carl's teaching. He just didn't stop. He worked as if they were his sons and daughters. They had such confidence in him they'd ask him to recommend a dentist to clean their teeth, or a store for clothing or books. And their Dr. Leiden would not only be glad to tell them, but would say: "Come on, I'll take you to the dentist. I'll show you the way. Let's go now and make a date, and you can go back later. I have some free time right now." Old Carl always had free time for students. He would take the student in his little British car, which made a lot of miles on a little low-octane gas. And if that student didn't have enough money to have dental work done, his teacher would help financially.

"Where do you get all your money?" I asked him once. I saw him give Muhammad, the watcher over cars at the university gate, a pound.

"Since we've been together a lot, I'll let you in on it," he said. "See, I just love money. I actually hoard the stuff." He laughed, and his eyes twinkled. "First I worked my way at college. And I married Mary before I'd finished my graduate work. I started teaching in college at twenty-two. I'm thirty-eight and I've not missed a year. There's not much beyond making a living to be made in teaching, but I found other ways. I have been a part-time professional photographer, a plumber for a summer, a pollster, and a variety of other things. But while I was in Huntington, West Virginia, I made my pile. I got a raise in Marshall University, and we bought a home. So being handy at woodwork, bricklaying and pouring concrete, I improved that home. And I built a very fine garage. So when we left Huntington, I sold my home and the garage I had made with these hands for a handsome profit of fifteen hundred dollars. That's my pile, Stuart. Sure, I got money!"

He laughed good-humoredly at his wealth, and I laughed with him.

One of Old Carl's favorite pastimes was telling stories about college and university teachers and presidents he had known and worked with in his sixteen years of college and university teaching. I never knew there were so many funny ones until I heard him lecture once to his fellow A.U.C. faculty members. After that I heard him entertaining teachers at several parties. He saved these stories for the teachers when the parties started getting dull. We thought his stories were about the funniest things we'd heard. I always asked for more than he could tell at one sitting. And I liked to watch him act the part of the one he told the story about. After the dramatic ending to a good evening, when we got ready to leave, there was always a strange silence. This was the time when each teacher at the party had time to reflect on the stories. There was always a story to fit each one of his listeners. Each teacher had seen himself or herself in one of these stories. The teachers Old Carl told us about have done some funny things, and they have been a little lower than the angels too.

Now, when he told stories to his students, he never told

about teachers. He told them stories about students he had taught in far-away America—Iowa, West Virginia, and California. He had two volumes of these stories that he carried around in his head, one about teachers and the other about students. After he had kept me laughing until midnight once and our host was ready for us to go, I said: "Why don't you write these stories?"

"Who'd read 'em?" he said, looking inquisitively at me. "There are too many dry books published anyway." He got up and stretched his big frame; then he suddenly broke into loud laughter. "If I were to write these stories on paper, what would I do for stories to tell?" he said.

In Cairo it is often said by teachers that students in the Middle East are without a good sense of humor. When Old Carl told them stories, their faces first lighted up and then beamed like a bright morning sun over a yellow sea of desert sand. They would hold back and try to keep from laughing, but suddenly they would break loose like the first avalanche of flood waters coming down the dry Nile in September.

But after Old Carl told them his stories about students in America, which were so funny they couldn't hold back their laughter, they would drift back to that rigid Oriental silence. When storm winds blow away the sands of laughter, the pyramids are still there. For each student in the class had time to reflect, and he saw himself in one of those unbelievable, fantastic, funny stories of which Dr. Leiden acted the parts as he told the story. Those funny students in America were just like so many students in Dr. Leiden's classes in the American University at Cairo, Egypt.

No wonder teachers from ten and students from thirty nationalities and all the cleaners and repair men at the university and car watchers on the streets and the bowabs at the gates and men of 101 shops and men at the museums and pyramids and even in the streets knew this big, lumbering Swede with the Mediterranean-blue eyes, white teeth, burr haircut, and smiling angel face on the wrestler's body.

One night Old Carl and I were walking toward the gate after our eleven o'clock classes.

"When do you leave the Near East?" I asked him.

"I've got another year here," he said happily. "Then I need to go to America and buy another house to improve and build a garage. I need another windfall. It doesn't take long to dissipate a windfall at a piaster a pitch. You know, I like money. I want to be rich again."

"Do you have a teaching position when you go back?"

"No, but I've got two thousand dollars' worth of wood-working tools stored over there," he said. "I can build a house, and I can lay blocks and bricks, and I'm a fair plumber. And I've got a stamp collection my students have helped me collect. But I'd have to get awful hungry to sell it."

I was walking beside the greatest teacher, natural diplomat, and super salesman of goodwill to mankind I had ever known outside of America. Youth from many lands idolized him as a symbol of an honest, down-to-earth, friendly American who would rub shoulders with the masses. They knew he couldn't be held behind an American university or an American embassy gate.

On seven o'clock one Sunday morning Carl Leiden and I were in his little Morris-Minor and on our way to pick up Muhammad, who was to take us to his village. This was the village where Muhammad grew up and where the mother of his present wife lived and cared for Muhammad's son by a former marriage. This trip provided Muhammad a way to visit his son, his cousins, and his uncle. And he promised to take Dr. Leiden and me to the village school.

Dr. Carl Leiden furnished the car, and I furnished the gas and candy for the youth. I also had three pounds changed into three hundred piasters.

We drove down the street beside the Nile until we reached

the old building where Muhammad lived. He lived in two rooms with dirt floors. One room was roofed with straw, and the other had no roof. Muhammad was waiting for us. Then, the three of us were on our way down the Nile. We followed the Nile until we came to a bridge. Here we crossed the bridge and followed the canal.

Giant trees grew on either side of the hard-surfaced canal road. There were so many things to photograph. We passed people on their way to Cairo with loads of vegetables and buffalo cows' milk. Men were riding camels, asses, horses, and bicycles.

Although it was the middle of November, the leaves on these giant trees were as green as the leaves on the trees are in midsummer at home. And on either side of the canal men and women were working in the fields. They were digging with short-handled hoes, planting new crops while they gathered cabbages, onions, corn, cane, and potatoes.

"Stop here," I said. "I want to take a picture of the man turning the Archimedean screw!"

"But we're going to a school," Carl warned me. "And the village is over thirty miles away."

He brought the car to a stop, then backed to a place where sunlight filtered through the trees onto the man on the other side of the canal. He turned the Archimedean screw like we used to turn the wheel on an old cider press. He hummed a song while he turned this device used for 2,200 years to lift water from the canal up to the ditches, where it flowed into the most fertile earth in the world.

"How much does that man make a day?" I asked Muhammad, who got out of the car and was following me.

"He'll make six piasters a day," he replied. "If he's lucky, he might get seven."

His wage was from fifteen to twenty cents a day. The man was barefoot. He wore short, loose pants that came to his knees. I took a couple of pictures. He never stopped turning this ancient device, but he stopped singing and shouted something across the canal to us.

"What's he saying?" I asked Muhammad.

"He wants money," Muhammad said. "He wants two piasters, but he's across the canal and we can't get money over to him. So let him go. He can't get over here to get it. You don't owe him anything."

Before we got ten steps back to the car, a fellow rode up and stopped on his bicycle.

"Come on," Carl said. "We'll never get to the village school."

"Get out of the car and look at these cabbages," I said. "I've raised cabbages all my life, but never like these."

The fellow was on his way to market in Cairo on his bicycle. He had two cabbage heads, and each would have weighed twenty-five pounds. He had a basket of eggs much smaller than our pullets' eggs. On either side of the bicycle was a milk can filled with water-buffalo cows' milk. Then, on the front of his bicycle was a smaller can filled with creams. A nice young fellah was on the bicycle. He was barefoot and wearing a soiled galabia.

Muhammad and I got in the car, and we were off again. We came to three loaded camels with riders sitting high upon them. We passed the little gray asses pulling big cartloads. I'd never seen a world like this! The pages of time had been turned back—and except for the hard road and an automobile now and then, I was in a world where they lived like people when Menes was king of Egypt, five thousand years ago.

A woman walked down the road with a tall, slender jug balanced on her head. No wonder people in Egypt were straight as ramrods, with their heads erect and their eyes looking forward. This carrying everything on their heads made them this way. Three women passed with baskets of fruit on their heads. Their hands fell limp at their sides. They walked with dignity. They looked straight ahead.

"Look ahead," Carl said. "A dead horse in the road."

He pulled up to a stop. Two teen-age fellahin were out trying to get the horse up.

"He's still alive," Muhammad said.

Muhammad and I got to the horse first. Carl pulled over to the side of the road and parked the car. He got his camera out.

"Now, this is a picture," he said. "But the light is bad."

One boy started to whip the horse.

"No, no," I said. "Don't hit that horse."

Muhammad said something to them, and they talked to him.

"He said, horse was down ready to die."

"Let's check the harness," I said.

Muhammad didn't understand the word "harness." So I went around to the other side, and one shaft was still fastened to the collar. I unfastened the shaft. Then I motioned for them to push back the wagon—the wagon was heavy enough for two horses. Now I examined the shoes on the horse's hooves, which were worn slick as glass. The horse had slipped and fallen on this road. He got the breath knocked out of him. He was not done for. He wasn't about to die. They had been driving the horse too fast.

By this time Carl was out taking pictures.

Now I took hold of the bridle, and the horse came to his feet.

Then I said to Muhammad, "Tell them to rest the horse. Tell them to wait thirty minutes before they put him in the wagon. Tell them not to run him. Tell them I am an American horse doctor."

He told them what I said. One took the horse over under the shade of a tree, while the other backed the wagon off the road. "Tell them not to run the horse and to feed him well," I told Muhammad. And he told them. I was never treated with more respect than I was by these young Egyptians.

They saluted me before I left. I returned the salute and got in the car.

"We're never going to get to the village," Muhammad said.

"Nor the school, either," Carl sighed.

We passed the finest date-palm grove I'd seen in all Egypt. I begged Carl to stop the car so I could photograph this grove. Carl pretended not to hear me. He kept on driving.

"We get to my village soon," Muhammad said. He pointed. The village was nestled among date-palm trees on the bank of another canal.

When we entered the village, someone who knew Muhammad threw up his hand; he greeted Muhammad in Arabic: *Allah is Good.*

"My cousin," Muhammad said. "He's glad to see me. I kin to many people here. I have many cousins and uncles and aunts."

Muhammad lived thirty miles away in the big city of Cairo, which was a distance to the villagers. It was too far for the horse or the ass to pull the cart to take them. It was too far to ride a camel or a bicycle or to walk.

We entered the village, where the ancient walls of cracked stones and mud bricks were joined in irregular squares, and between these were winding, narrow little unpaved roads filled with sheep, goats, chickens, turkeys, asses, camels, and pushcarts. Among animals and fowls, children from babies to teen-agers ran and played. Sitting on the ground, leaning against the wall in the sun that filtered through the date-palm leaves, sat mothers nursing their babies and occasionally brushing the flies from around their eyes and mouths. I saw one small boy with large black clumps around his eyes. I wondered what was wrong until Carl had to stop for a flock of geese that came up the bank from the canal. Then I discovered the black spots around the child's eyes were clusters of houseflies. If any country in the world has more houseflies and takes fewer preventive measures against them than

Egypt, I don't know that country. These pests whip the children. Children finally give up and let them hang on in little black knots over their faces.

"Shoo, shooo," Muhammad said to the geese. But the geese didn't shoo. We waited until about a half-hundred crossed the dirt street and went up an alley. Only the geese knew where they were going.

Muhammad said: "Over there the mother of my wife lives. She has my son! Let's go!"

"Come on, get in," Carl said. "We'll never get to the school!"

I got in the car, and we went another couple of blocks—very slowly, for villagers ran in front, on either side, and the older ones followed. Old Carl drove over and parked in front of an open door in the corner of an irregular square, where a large date palm, maybe sixty feet high, came up through the thatched roof. Here we parked. Down in the canal women were washing clothes. Between Carl's little car and the canal, a small girl, about ten, was busy loading dung into baskets, which fit over a little ass's back like saddlebags. She worked while the teen-age boys followed us. I took a picture of this child while Muhammad got out and went in at the open door. He came out smiling with his mother-in-law and his son. His mother-in-law was thirty-one years of age. She had five children before she lost her husband. She was very pretty, dressed in her Arab black. Muhammad's boy was a very handsome child. She was keeping this boy while her daughter, Muhammad's second wife, about sixteen years old, was expecting a child. Muhammad sent her about two pounds (five dollars) a month, which was a lot of money in the village.

Now the crowd gathered until there was hardly standing room. But Old Carl got his camera out. He took pictures. I took more pictures. Through Muhammad's limited English, we talked to these happy and very friendly villagers. I pushed my way to the door and looked in. There were no chairs.

There was practically nothing but mats used to sit on, sleep on, and pray on five times a day. A few pots and pans were in the middle of the floor. The time of our Lord Jesus Christ, two thousand years ago, must have been modern compared to this. Animals stayed under the same thatched roofs with the people. I never saw anything like this. I couldn't jot a note down. I was too busy seeing.

Then, generous Old Carl went for the candy. He began giving the children one piece each—but the older people wanted candy too. He could go only so far.

"We need a truckload, Carl," I said.

"We sure do. No, no," he said to the older man who held out his ancient shriveled hand that looked like an old paw. Carl looked at the old man. "Well, you can have a piece," he said kindly. Carl knew he, too, was a child and wanted candy. Everybody wanted candy. Their wants were so simple. They didn't know about homes filled with furniture, two automobiles for every house, a fine job with paid vacations, time and a half for overtime and double pay for Sunday, Social Security and eternal security. All they wanted was a penny piece of candy.

Muhammad held his son up affectionately. And the Egyptians are really an affectionate people. I will never see them as soldiers. Not when a policeman will not offend a person! Their past history has been one of subjugation—thousands of years of the other man's rule—imposed on them! And no wonder! This village is an example of what has been. The fellahin are peasants, slaves of the soil, and followers. They are not aggressive.

"No, no, no, no! No more candy," Carl said. He got in the car while Muhammad got the people back.

Carl backed over and up the narrow alley. I got in beside Carl. And Muhammad pointed the way toward the village school. We crossed a bridge over this canal and drove beside it about half a mile.

"Stop here," Muhammad said.

Actually we were supposed to have permission from the government to visit this school. But permits to see this and that are long in coming from the Egyptian government. I'd applied last September, and this was the middle of November, and I hadn't got one yet. Why? No one could tell me if I'd asked a thousand people. Muhammad got out.

"Come," he said.

I looked for a building higher than the others. I couldn't locate the school. We were parked on a high road which had been made from the dirt of the canal. Somewhere below us was the school. There were many buildings down there.

We followed Muhammad and a fine-looking, very large fifteen-year-old cousin down the path, through a gate under grape arbors, past two dozen beehives. Then we came onto a square.

"This is the school," he said.

"Carl, this is the school plan that is becoming popular in America," I said. "Look how this is laid out!"

"Well, this is an old school," Carl said. "Look at the buildings. Egypt didn't model on our buildings. We modeled on theirs!"

The April before, in Columbia, South Carolina, I'd visited a new high school located among the pines which was built on the same pattern. Paul Blazer High School, then under construction in Ashland, Kentucky, and considered the most modern and up-to-date school in our area, was on the same plan as this one—several small buildings, one story high, which made a neat little village with playground in one area, and plenty of space between the buildings. It was 11:30 when we reached the school. We'd been almost five hours coming thirty miles.

We were taken to the office of the headmaster, who couldn't speak English. Only one teacher could. These teachers had been educated in Egyptian schools—everything here was strictly Egyptian. And after seeing the village, I was in for some surprises. This school, which was only an elementary school, was far more advanced beyond the community level of that little village than our schools are advanced beyond our community levels in America.

The headmaster was a small man and not well dressed. How could he be, on a teacher's salary in Egypt, where teachers start teaching for fifteen pounds ($37.50) per month —and a few at the very top never make over seventy dollars a month. The headmaster here probably made twenty-five pounds—certainly not over thirty pounds.

Again we were accepted with friendliness. The young man who spoke English took us to all rooms—from the first through the sixth grade. There were four hundred pupils and fourteen teachers in this school. Not a classroom had over thirty-five pupils. There were ten men teachers and four women. The discipline was excellent. The rooms were clean. We saw the teachers in action. They appeared to be doing a good job of it too.

The little cafeteria, one which wouldn't begin to measure up in comparison to our more modest ones, was the apple of their eye. And I agreed how wonderful it was but at the same time suggested they expand it. Then I saw one room covered with matting where first-graders sat on the floor. This was the only room like this. I didn't inquire, but I thought that for village youngsters not used to chairs, the mat was probably a preparation.

Through the interpreter the children greeted us. We greeted them. Once I wrote on the board from one to ten in Arabic, and I didn't do a good job—my three was too much like the two—and all the children laughed. From the schoolrooms we went out to watch the youth go through physical exercises. Here, they excelled. They were really good. A lady teacher gave the calisthenics, and she knew her work. She was excellent.

"Now, come," said our guide-teacher.

"Isn't this all?" I asked.

"No, no," he said.

On the edge of the schoolgrounds was a building. Here was a school to teach the blind—a few were children, and others were grown-ups. They were using scissors and cutting rope. They were making matting and carpets. The instructor was blind. He went to his library and found a book in Braille and read instructions and then told a blind woman what to do.

The next building was unforgettable. Here were elementary youth making mosaics, painting pictures, doing artwork that pupils in the best of our secondary schools should see. The Egyptians have artistic imaginations: They can do beautiful things, but they neglect the practical details of life that count for so much.

"Come, come," said our guide.

We followed him to a poultry unit, where I saw the large breeds of American chickens.

"We are changing things," he said.

"This is the right place and the right way to do it," I said. "This is the village where people farm."

Then we went to the rabbit hutch. Here I saw where young boys were taught to breed and raise rabbits for meat supply. Then, the last building on the schoolgrounds had a young bull, of the Egyptian breed, chained to the wall. He was almost as tall as a young camel. He was marked all over where he had been in a fight.

"He's been to the hospital," said our teacher-guide. "He is a valuable animal," After looking him over, I wouldn't dispute what the guide had told us. "Now, come inside," our guide said. "I'll show you!"

Inside were three stalls. In one stall was an enormous brown Swiss bull. "Is he gentle?" I asked.

"Very gentle," the teacher said.

In the second stall was a Holstein bull.

"We got him in Europe," the teacher said. "He's very gentle!"

In the third stall was the largest bull I'd ever seen. His square horns lay back against his head, then turned down like oxbows. The ring on his nose was fastened with a very large chain which was fastened to a steel link embedded in the concrete floor. When we went in he bellowed, like the growl of low thunder. He pawed until I thought he was shaking the concrete floor.

"What about him?" I asked.

"He's dangerous," the teacher-guide said. "He hurt the bull outside."

This bull was not fat but he would weigh over a ton!

"I would take no chances on him," I said. "I would watch youth around him!"

"We do," he said. "But our youth must learn about cattle!"

In college I'd helped make brooms, while many of our students made chairs and other pieces of furniture. In our high school our students learned to use tractors to plow, plant, and harvest; we didn't have animals, fowls, and rabbits on the schoolground; I explained this slowly to our guide.

"The tractor replaces too many people," he explained.

I didn't agree with this, but I didn't tell him. Cows pulling the oldest kind of plow in the world was silly. Look at the light industries Egypt was skipping over for one basic industry—steel. Steel was for implements, yet this country bought parts of automobiles and assembled them here but didn't create a single car of their own, didn't make enough chairs, enough brooms, didn't manufacture any refrigerators, vacuum cleaners, bicycles, wagons, and a thousand other needed things. If these essential industries were developed, they would need plenty of manpower. But people needed to be trained for industry. Technicians were brought from Germany. The Russians were building their dams. And here

were Egyptian children learning ancient methods of farming. Tremendous potential lay right in these classrooms.
Here was Egypt's future.

What was lacking was management, planning. Small industries had to come. They should come before guns and
army trucks and tanks and planes.

Why weren't all those loafing teen-age boys I saw in the
village in high school or in technical schools, learning to
make doors and window screens and gates and tables? Our
students learned these things at McKell High School, even
though it wasn't really a technical school. This elementary
school was a beginning. They had just laid a foundation for
what should follow—what had to come for any country to
survive in this modern technical world.

"You've been very kind," I said to the teacher-guide. "We
thank you."

Carl took some pictures, and then Muhammad went to the
car and brought the remaining candy for the pupils and gave
it to the headmaster to distribute before school closed. We
shook hands with our friendly fellow teacher hosts. We
thanked them over and over, for they were delightful hosts.
No hosts can excel the Egyptians when they like you. They
liked us because we were friendly and we complimented
them highly on what they were doing. And they were doing
a job too. And schoolteachers of all countries have a firm
brotherhood. We understand each other and work together
better than the uneducated politicians.

When we got back to the car Muhammad's uncle was
waiting for us. He had a reception committee there in the
road. We had to have coffee, sodas, or plain water with him
—no alcoholic drinks, for these people are of the Muslim
faith. Not to accept their hospitality was a sign of a breach
of faith. So we drank soda, coffee, and water toasts to each
other.

Muhammad's uncle learned we had not eaten lunch, and

he was going to take us back to the village to have some mutton. Here was where Carl Leiden's diplomacy came in. "He is on a diet," he said, pointing to me. And this was true. "We must get back to Cairo. He must take medicine."

Finally Muhammad's uncle believed us and let us go. He was a handsome elderly man. His hair was white, and he wore a long, clean white galabia. He couldn't be nice enough to Muhammad's friends. Then more handshaking with everybody; we must have shaken hands with everybody at least a half-dozen times.

We got in the little car. Then we waved back to our village friends as we drove down the dusty canal road. Before we got out of sight, I looked back, and the crowd was still in the road waving to us.

"I wonder why more tourists don't come to Egypt," I said. "I can see more different things here in one mile than I can see in ten miles in any other country I've ever visited!"

The Bent Pyramid and the crowd of lesser ones loomed up now against the blue, afternoon Egyptian sky.

"Yes, advertise the villages and tell the truth," Carl said. "They'd bring tourists by the millions! These people are Cheops' children, and they live as they did in his day and time!"

"Yes, thousands come to Pompeii," I said. "There is no one living in Pompeii—and Pompeii's not two thousand years old. We are told by a guide how they once lived there. Over here we see how they lived five thousand years ago!"

"No, no, we don't want that," Muhammad said. "People are poor. We don't want to show that!"

"Your village is a part of Egypt," I said. "Isn't it? Why not see it?"

"Villages all be gone in ten years," Muhammad said. "We have new one, we have new life. We be like you! Clean Americans." He smiled broadly. "In ten years villages be gone, and we live clean like the Americans. We have cars and everything and better schools."

TO TEACH, TO LOVE

We passed a loaded camel train on its way toward Cairo. Men dressed like those from another world looked down on our little car as we breezed past them. Even these strange beasts with pig-heads on long giraffes' necks looked strangely at us, as if we were the strangers from another world intruding into their own private world. These wise old prehistoric beasts of burden seemed to be inquiring why we wanted to change the world that had existed, just as we saw it that day, for several thousand years.

Muhammad yearned for change, but not all Egyptians did. A student in my class wrote a paper calling for the education of the fellahin, the farmers along the Nile, and one of his classmates protested vehemently. Laila Enan, a young lady in the front seat, interrupted Sayed so often as he was reading his paper I had to ask her to keep quiet until he had finished.

"He's wrong," she said. "You know you are wrong. You know we can't educate the fellahin. It would be suicide for our country."

Laila always sat in the front seat, and she took issue with everything in the text or anything said in class. I thought of her as the god-bird Horus; the falcon who guarded Egypt's ancient dead. Only she guarded a way of life in Egypt that I thought was over. And she was a spokesman for Egypt's young. She took issue with Sayed Rashid.

"Mr. Stuart, the fellahin have been on the land for five thousand years," Laila said. "Why educate them to farm the land?"

"They would make better farmers," I said.

"You don't know us, Mr. Stuart," she said. I thought she would rise up from her chair. "When we educate the fellahin they think they don't have to work any more. They want to come to Cairo or go to Alexandria and get jobs in the city."

"Educate them in agriculture," I said. "That is if they want to study agriculture. Instead of those short-handle hoes they dig with, as they have done for five thousand years, give them tractors."

"They'd never learn to use tractors, Mr. Stuart."

"In our agriculture classes in high school our students learned to use tractors."

"We have land, Mr. Stuart. We had tractors. They tore them up. We had no one to fix them. So they went back to using their hoes."

"Now, if they had been trained to handle tractors in secondary schools as our students were, they could have repaired the tractors."

"Mr. Stuart, how could a fellah use a tractor on one or two acres?" she asked me. "We have canals to irrigate, you know!"

"Fill up those deep ditches," I said. "Put the acres into ten-acre fields and use the tractor."

"Ten families use one tractor?"

"Yes—why not, and save that back-breaking labor."

"But what about crossing the irrigation ditches?" she asked. "Crops have to have water."

"Yes, I know," I said.

"Mr. Stuart, you're not a farmer," she said.

"I live on a farm," I said. "I grew up on one. I own one thousand acres of land. One of our acres is just a little less than your fedan. And I have tractors. We plow, ditch, dig postholes, and pull loads with them."

"But, ah, Mr. Stuart," she came back at me, "pumping water is a big problem!"

"It wouldn't be if you'd use new methods," I said.

I had been warned not to criticize in my teaching in Egypt. But how could I teach if I didn't criticize? I wasn't going to be inhibited, even if I were fired.

"I saw two men turning the Archimedean screw pulling water up to a higher level. Now, Laila, when did this Greek inventor, mathematician, and physicist live?"

"Mr. Stuart, sometime before B.C.," she said. "I believe from 287 B.C. to 212 B.C."

"You're right," I said. "I just checked the dates last night. Think of his invention of over two thousand years ago still being used. Laila, I had students in my high school, who, if they lived on these farms, would have rigged up pumps from automobile engines. They'd never turn a screw and lift water with their hands. I wouldn't either."

"But we have more men than we have jobs!" she said. "If the men didn't turn the Archimedean screws, drive the oxen at the water wheels, and use the short hoe on the land, what would they do?"

"Laila, that's a good question," I said, while Sayed smiled. "Why not a factory to make pumps to pump water from the canals onto the land? Why not factories to make tractors? Why not a factory to make plows, harrows, corn planters, and hay rakes—and all the other farm equipment—even to long handles for the hoes? This would use much of the surplus labor!

"Laila, we're getting into problems of national economy," I said. "But let me ask you. Do you make the lipstick you wear on your lips in Egypt? Do you make the shoes you wear here? Do you make the dresses?"

"Yes, we make the dresses, all right, Mr. Stuart, and we make the shoes," she said. "But I don't know about the cosmetics."

"Find out," I said. "If you don't, you form a corporation and start an industry, and you'll be rich."

Laila didn't know that I had found out she was from one of the wealthiest families in Egypt. She didn't have to start an industry. She was already rich. And the dress she wore probably came from France. Her shoes and cosmetics came from Germany, where she had been to study ballet and music after she had persuaded her parents to let her go. If they had not been liberals in family tradition, she could not have gone.

The bell rang. Another class was waiting outside to come into our room. But the arguments between us grew warmer.

Sayed and I believed in mass education. Others in the class didn't.

"Education can change Egypt if you give it free to everybody," I said. "Education is the only thing that will change you. And, Laila, you could help change Egypt."

"Not, sir, if she doesn't believe in education for the masses," Sayed said.

Right in my class was the problem that confronted Egypt. Laila Enan belonged to one strain and Sayed Rashid to another. We left our classroom with Sayed and Laila arguing. They argued all the way down the stairs. I was grateful, for I had found two natives interested enough and fearless enough to be outspoken in what was the hope of their country's future.

In my creative-writing class, I had Ibrahim Nimr, a large friendly Sudanese who sat in the front row. I also had him in one of my education classes. He was as dark as a moonless winter night, with the gentleness of a lamb. I was very fond of him. He had not enrolled in my writing class but had not missed a class since it had begun the second semester. When a student read a poem he liked, he was all smiles, showing a mouthful of white teeth.

I made it a point to get better acquainted with him. I learned he was a member of one of the 140 tribes which made up the twelve million population of the Sudan. I learned his 140 tribes all spoke different languages too. And I learned Ibrahim was a schoolteacher. But I wondered why he liked our writing class so well.

"May I ?" he asked, handing me a sheaf of something at the end of a class. "I'd like to show you."

"Sure," I said. "I'd like to see."

I opened the sheaf, and I got a stack of two dozen pen-and-ink sketches of the Sudanese. This man was an artist.

"Where did you study art?" I asked him.

"I never studied art, sir," he said. "I just like to draw in my spare time."

"Have you been the one doing all the drawings on the blackboard before this class begins?" I asked him.

"Yes, sir," he replied.

"What else do you like to do?"

"Write poems and stories!"

"Have you got any with you?"

"Yes, sir, but they are written in Arabic."

"Can you translate them?"

"Yes, sir, with some help. My friend Omar El Reedy is helping me."

Omar El Reedy, a Muslim despite his last name, was writing some of the finest lyric poetry written in all Egypt. He was in this class too.

"How much verse have you written?"

"Enough for two or three books if it's good enough to be published."

"And what about your stories?"

"I have many."

"I would like for you to join this class and make credit hours," I said. "I'd like to have you. You're the kind of student I'm trying to find."

"I'd like to be in here," he said. "I'd like to register if I can."

"I think this can be arranged," I said. "I'll see the registrar."

He was pleased.

I went to the registrar's office, where Dr. Freeman Gossett told me to write a letter explaining this and to have Ibrahim Elawam Nimr (whose name translated means Son of the Tiger) write a letter applying to register in this course. I was so anxious to have this Son of the Tiger in my class that I wrote the letter on the spot. Son of the Tiger wrote his, and we gave them to one of the secretaries.

Now, A.U.C. has twenty-nine committees, and one of these committees is the Committee on Committees, which keeps the others functioning. When I wrote this letter, I never dreamed it would go before the Committee on Student Standing. I had forgotten about the red tape of A.U.C. I'd already taken his drawings to the editors of our A.U.C. literary magazine, and three were immediately accepted. I thought he would be a shoo-in. For me, he was a must. I wanted him.

In one week a copy of a letter to him was put in my mailbox. I was so furious when I read it, I didn't want to see a member of this committee. I didn't know what I might say. I had already spoken my mind too freely on rules and regulations that restrict men's minds. The report read as follows:

March 11, 1961

To IBRAHIM ELAWAM NIMR

The Committee on Student Standing received your petition to take English 325 for credit but cannot accept your request. There are a number of irregularities:

(1) a student cannot add a course for credit after the first week of class;

(2) an auditor must place his request to audit a course before the end of the first week of class and must receive an auditor's card from the office of the registrar before a teacher admits him to class;

(3) when a student drops below twelve credit hours, he must pay an auditor's fee for the course which he is auditing.

Therefore, I am sorry you cannot receive credit, but this matter should have been settled during the first week of classes.

E. FREEMAN GOSSETT
Chairman
Committee on Student Standing

Son of the Tiger came to the door of the English class. He stood in the corridor.

"Come in," I invited him.

He smiled and walked in. I didn't tell I had received a copy of the committee's letter.

After the class was over he walked up to my desk smiling.

"Now, you come back to this class," I said. "You don't get credit when you audit. You don't pay. You just be my guest."

Son of the Tiger understood.

When my creative-writing course was offered for the second semester, Omar El Reedy, a young man who had met me every schoolday of the first semester and had shown me one of his poems, was the first to enroll. Omar was Muslim and Egyptian, and his people were landowners and farmers in the rich Nile Valley. Although there was much responsibility on his shoulders, since he was trying to run his farm and trying to pass science courses at A.U.C., he found time to write poems. Writing came first with him. He was a delightful young man. He was a born poet, and I welcomed him as my first student in the second-semester class. Omar was a science major. My students in the first semester were majoring in English, drama, and philosophy.

Jane Stuart, our daughter, had been promoted from her freshman class by Miss Mildred Ware, a teacher from Dublin, Ireland, who said Jane was wasting her time in her class and needed more advanced English. I had tried to avoid having her in one of my classes. She had been writing since she was six. She was very much like Omar El Reedy, one who was compelled to write. Her poems had been accepted by a few small magazines in America. She wrote poems in English, French, and Latin, and short stories in English and French.

Not one of my students had ever had a course in creative writing. I'd gotten some interesting work the first semester. With Omar El Reedy and Jane, both prolific natural-born writers, as a nucleus, I thought I could get others started writing creatively about what they wanted to write most and

in whatever form best suited them. I took only one period of
the first day to explain what I expected of them. I made very
few suggestions.

At the second meeting of our class I called on Omar to read
first, and here is the poem he read:

THOSE BLUE SPECKS OF DUST

Hate not the dust that blew in your eyes,
Hate not the wind that made it;
Hate not those specks, the birth and the rise,
The home that your soul evaded.
Hate not the pillow that will cushion you when
You've trodden the dusty road.
Be kind for it will own you again
In that dark and lovely abode.
The arms of the dead that once loved you,
Reach out with longing devotion;
Pale lips now dust, red lips made blue
Are kissing without emotion.
When you're the earth you'll cling to their feet,
With longing affection and cries,
This wind will come up now wonderfully sweet.
Then you'll be dust in their eyes.

Omar was about six feet tall, olive complexioned, with
dark eyes that sparkled. He was nineteen, a sophomore, and
he spoke four languages fluently. Sitting in a chair and facing
the class, Omar read six poems which he unrolled from a
sheaf. The reaction of the class was electrifying. The students
applauded Omar.

Next I called on Jane, who read a half-dozen of the dozen
poems she had brought along. One of the poems she read,
"Summoned," was written on the Sunday before our class
met, when Jane, her mother, and I spent a Sunday afternoon
visiting the City of the Dead, sixteen square miles of Muslim
cemetery in the heart of Cairo, a city of approximately four
million people. Perhaps this City of the Dead held this many

of the deceased. In addition, approximately one hundred thousand people lived among the tombs. The poem:

In the blue winds of dusk, with their backs to the moon,
And their white tangled hair in their eyes,
They came chanting and wailing and winding their way,
From the depths of their dark Paradise.

Their wax faces were grim, their thin fingers were thrust
In the skirts of their gray pleated gowns
From a chain at their waist, keys heavy with rust,
To the tombs of the damned, dangled down.

Their sad songs sealed my sleep as I felt those hands twine
Tiers of black, shrouds of black, to my bed
And I knew, when I woke, that I'd walk beside you
In the streets of the City of the Dead.

A German girl, Regina Weingartner, had brought a score of short poems. She was the girl I had least suspected of being prolific or creative. She was a slender, blue-eyed blond who was a part-time student at A.U.C. But she ran into much criticism from her classmates for her stubbornness, even arrogance.

When I asked for volunteers to read, all hands went up. I certainly had misjudged this class. I had fourteen original young men and women in this class.

Since I had suggested to the class that they write about what they knew best and wanted to write about, I received varied and surprising papers—a reflection of the numerous nationalities, religions, and political faiths they represented. I received scores of poems and dozens of stories and articles and a few plays. I never knew there were so many new literary forms and so many different methods of writing as my fourteen originals were showing me. Each student in this group not only spoke from two to eight languages but read books and magazines in these varied languages.

There was always a race among Omar El Reedy, the Egyptian; Regina Weingartner, the German; and Jane Stuart, the American. Competition rose to a great height in this class, and excitement ran high. Jane invited Omar to our apartment, where they read their poems to each other and discussed revisions. Several times I listened to them read their poems. Then I'd get some of my poems and read with them. All over the campus students from this class would get together and read their work to their classmates and discuss it before they came to class. Jane Stuart admitted she had never been in a class as exciting as this one, her father's. And her father will add that she was never in a class where she had such competition. She learned there were other young ambitious writers in the world, youth who grasped at a straw to improve themselves. Jane, being an American, had never seen a girl faint when she was given a B instead of an A.

Regina Weingartner set the pace in this class, with forty-four poems, twelve short stories, and a play in less than two months. I never had a class that worked me harder trying to keep up than this one. But poor Regina, due to a love affair, was sent back to Germany by her father in the middle of the semester. According to rules and regulations of A.U.C., I could not give her a grade. But at the end of the semester I gave her an A anyway, hoping that one of the secretaries would copy it on the permanent record card by mistake. Being from a war-devastated and cruelly divided country, she was vitally concerned with the freedom of the individual. I'll never forget this poem:

FREE

A leaf that lay on the ground
Wanted to be back on the tree
But there it lay
Torn off, tossed away
And it knew:
Life was through.
When it had been on the tree

It often had longed to be free:
It had wanted to fly around
Blown by the wind along the ground—
Yes then it had longed to be
Free, Free, Free!

Then, there was big Ibrahim Nimr (Son of the Tiger), my Sudanese auditor. He was one of the most talented men I ever had in any class. He wrote a fine story about his grandfather, the Old Tiger, which he read in class. I told him not to turn the story loose but expand it into a book. He had sheafs of poems written in the dialect of his tribe. In addition to his writing stories and poems, he could make anything out of clay with his hands. His notebooks, filled with drawings of his native Sudanese, coming from this untrained artist, filled his classmates and teachers with delight. He had found an appreciative audience anyway—new-found classmates and a sympathetic teacher who encouraged him to do more.

I never got to give Ibrahim Nimr an A legally, but I put his name with an A plus on my list of grades and sent it to the office. I hoped somebody in that office would make another mistake and record his grade.

The literature that impressed these students of the Near East was that of the old and new French writers; new and old Italian writers; books by the nineteeth-century Russian writers; classics from Norway, Sweden, and Denmark; books by Near Eastern and Oriental writers from Egypt to Japan. Books written by Greeks, old and new, in drama, poetry, and philosophy, were still their favorites. Many, many books I had never heard of.

Each of my students had his own theory of what literature should be like. The fourteen students had fourteen theories. Often they discussed among themselves, when arguing a point about a story or poem, how ancient Greeks felt about a certain way of writing. I let them talk. I had never taught a class when I didn't learn as much as one of the pupils. I was only the director of this class, trying to pull the best from each student.

On June 10, after the graduation exercises were over and I was ready to walk through the A.U.C. gate for my last time, Najat Sultan came over smiling and said: "Dr. Stuart, I want you to meet my father and mother, my brothers and sisters." When they were standing on the steps of the administration building and while I was meeting her father and mother, her seven sisters and brothers, Sayed Rashid, one of my education students, pulled at my sleeve. "Sir, I have been looking everywhere for you," he interrupted me. "I wonder if you will write me a letter of recommendation to the Kuwaitian Oil Company."

"Just a minute, Sayed," I said. "I don't know about the Kuwaitian Oil Company, but here is Mr. Sultan, who is from Kuwait, and maybe he could tell us where to write."

"I am the Kuwaitian Oil Company," he said.

Now, I knew why his talented Najat had only smiled when I had suggested that she send her poems to an American woman's magazine, where, if one was accepted, she would get from one to two Egyptian pounds per line.

Here is one of the many poems Najat read in our class:

EPITAPH

he saw a star
and tried to reach it
and they chided him.
he heard the music
and tried to touch it
and they scoffed at him.
he felt the love
and died in pain of it—
and they dismissed him,
and they buried him,
and they wrote on
his grave—ADOLESCENT.

TO TEACH, TO LOVE

At A.U.C., I had taught the sons and daughters of millionaires. But I didn't know this at first, since they didn't display their wealth. Over there, their names would correspond—on a smaller scale—to the American names of Rockefeller, DuPont, Ford, Kennedy, Getty, Mellon, and Slocum. I had taught the descendants of kings, many of whom had pharaonic blood in their veins.

I had taught students from twenty-nine countries and five continents. I had taught students from twenty languages and a dozen dialects. I had taught Christian, Muslim, and Jew. I had taught all colors, from the whitest to the darkest. I had taught students from countries with all forms of government, from monarchies to dictatorships. And nowhere, at any place and time, had I ever taught a finer, down-to-earth, more creative group than my fourteen originals.

Long after I returned to America, I saw the work of one of my A.U.C. students, Aly Mahmoud, who was working for the Associated Press in Cairo. There were three articles he had written in one newspaper on one day. I wrote him a letter of congratulation and here is his reply, which gave me such pleasure:

Dear Jesse,

I loved your letter, but may I make a protest? You asked if I remember you. The question should have never been included in your fine letter. For one thing, anyone who claims to be educated must know Jesse Stuart. For another reason, I have been educated and befriended by the great Jesse Stuart. How could I ever forget you, sir. You are one of the greatest men I know today. Your wife is one of the greatest, most charming ladies I know today. Your daughter is one of the most personable young ladies I know today.

I remember the fine quotes you gave me for the feature story I had done on you several years ago. You mentioned a few suggestions to enhance tourism in Egypt and to preserve the immemorial villages of this ancient country. I can now recall that you said the villages should be maintained as they are and that the lurid modernism should never be permitted to blemish the romantic feature of these picturesque places. I'm glad to inform you that the Egyptian government is now doing exactly what you had suggested eight years ago.

I remember you describing my great-grandfathers, Thutmose, Ramses, Ikhnaton, Cheops, and others as "kings who swayed empires and worlds."

My beloved professor, I do remember you—the way you talk, the way you walk, your words and your phrases. Or how do you think I have reached the position of deputy bureau chief for the Associated Press in Cairo—how do you think I have become a capable writer mainly for millions of American readers throughout the United States and many more around the globe—how could I achieve such scores without remembering and often imitating Jesse Stuart. Yes, sir, *The Thread That Runs So True, The Trees of Heavens,* and many others are still with us. You will not be surprised to know that a small congregation of Jesse Stuart students often meets in Cairo to discuss one subject—Jesse Stuart.

Omar El Reedy, myself, Hatem Dali, and many others are members. In another letter I hope to have the chance to write to you at length on what we think and what we write and discuss. I'm sure you will enjoy every bit of it.

Thank you for the clipping. What made me very happy and proud is the fact that what I write did come to your attention. I hope you liked them. I often travel in Egypt and the Middle East, primarily for news coverages. But I always love to develop feature stories and photographs on the different aspects of human endeavor in these lands. I would appreciate if you would permit me to write to you every time I have something interesting to tell you, or whenever I need my professor's advice to achieve the superiority I cherish for myself as a writer and a poet. Yes, sir, I'm a confirmed Arabic-language poet. I also have a few poems in English.

Please convey my sincere greetings to Mrs. Stuart, whom I love and respect so much, and to Jane, and above all to yourself.

Sincerest salaams

Yours very faithfully,
Aly Mahmoud

Recently I read that this fine young Egyptian had been arrested by his government as an Israeli spy. And still later I learned through Carl Leiden, who has since returned to the United States and is now teaching at the University of Texas, that Aly Mahmoud is to be hanged. Among the charges against him is his having studied under certain members of the A.U.C. faculty, for the Egyptian government has decided they are dangerous radicals.

What a tragic reflection on the terrors that beset dictators, that the government of Egypt should determine to take the life of this gifted, educated young citizen of theirs on such flimsy charges as they have made against my student, Aly Mahmoud!

As much as I loved my students in Egypt—Muslims, Jews, and Christians—Christians of all denominations and colors— as much as I loved the mighty Nile River, which gives of itself more than any river in the world—water, water, for thirsty people and animals, water shuttled into canals to grow food for the people and feed for animals—as much as I loved antiquities of this fabulous land, perhaps the very Cradle of Civilization, there was one thing being a man from the free Western world I could not understand. I could not understand one man's rule, what we call dictatorship.

I counted in one issue of an English-printed paper twenty-six pictures of Gamal Abdel Nasser. In each published daily paper, Arabic, French, and English, there would be from a half-dozen to a dozen pictures. And in each store, dozens of pictures of him hung everywhere on the walls, except in the little Greek and Armenian stores, which might display one.

When we took a trip to Alexandria, one of the most beautiful cities in the world, we had to check with police before we left, and at the point of our destination, and when we returned. Even when I went to speak in Alexandria, Port Said, and Asyut, I had to check with police. They had to know where I was going and what I was doing. When Dr. Carl Leiden and his wife, Mary, and their small children took Naomi, Jane, and me with them on Sunday drives, at crossroads near villages there would be a parked car with a man who took Carl's car's license number. Nothing ever came of this as far as we knew, but it was unnerving.

Our police take license numbers in America only when they pursue criminals, and I was no criminal in Egypt or anyplace else I have lived or visited.

The Egyptians are friendly—I used to say "too friendly" —and a lovable people. The students loved us, and we loved them. The big differences were in our governments—ours a free society and theirs dictatorial. For instance, I received a notice from an Egyptian bank in Cairo that money was being held for me. I didn't know how the money got there, so I went. Yes, there was money for me. *Taps for Private Tussie,* my novel, had been accepted for publication in Czechoslovakia for which I had received an advance of $150, less a ten-percent agent's fee. This had left me $135, but when the Egyptians took out taxes, I had $92. They had lifted my check from the mail—I didn't know it was in Egypt until I was informed at the bank.

Then, my incoming letters were censored. Naomi and I are Christians. We are Methodists. But unfortunately for Egypt, our first names, Naomi and Jesse, are Old Testament names. They were Hebrew names. So our letters were opened and read.

I couldn't stand up and voice my opinion about what was right and wrong the way I could in America. I would have been arrested. No one could speak against the government. It had the final say, the final word. And my wife and I, before we could teach there, had to become temporary citizens of Egypt. This was so our earnings could be taxed.

Even our school paper and magazine, *The Scarab,* had to be read and censored before publication. These young and old Americans who bellyache about freedom in America should try being in a dictatorial country such as Egypt now and then. One simply doesn't criticize the Egyptian government, or President Nasser, who is the Egyptian government.

I disposed of the notes I used in my classes even though they contained nothing critical about Egypt. Since our fireplace wouldn't work, I took them down to the Nile, right in front of our home, where Moses was said to have been found in the bulrushes, and here I cast my notes upon the water. I left no traces of my scribbled handwriting. I learned fast. I learned the color of the galabias the Egyptian CIA wore. They were very often on our campus. I learned to take taxis for home behind the campus and not at the front gate. Too often the taxi taking me home would be trailed. And I knew to do this in a hurry when the riots began against "imperialistic America." We were really not imperialists, I was told too often, but we were guilty in our associations with Great Britain, France, Belgium, Holland, Portugal, Spain, Italy, and Greece.

Products from these countries which the Greek and Armenian merchants managed to smuggle in, such as Danish and Dutch butter and cheese, had to be sold under the counter. Before we left Egypt dozens of stores, banks, and newspapers had been "nationalized." And these included stores run by Muslims. We who have lived our whole lives in America find such things difficult to believe. We read about them in the newspapers but suspect someone is making up a story to entertain us.

I loved the masses in Egypt. The fellahin who have farmed the Nile Valley for five thousand years are the best workers in the world. All they do is work. They hardly know they have a government. When the masses in Egypt become educated, Egypt will change. It has to change to keep pace with an ever-changing modern world. I wonder what students I taught there thought when Apollo 8 went around the moon. I am sure they rejoiced and remembered that a free man from a Western-world society was for a time in their midst.

Chapter 10

WE ARE FORTUNATE TO HAVE been born IN America. But what brought our country into existence?

Did God have something to do with finding a continent for those oppressed peoples of old Europe? Those who sought to leave the oppression of monarchs and later dictators who have controlled much of Europe? Did God select and direct to a new land those people who sought religious freedom in a new world? The tough, the ambitious, the aggressive, the unfortunate yet finest people of many lands came.

The early migrants were so elated with what they found that they believed God helped them, and many of their descendants have continued to thank God for what they inherited in the southern half of this North American continent. We have the soil and climate to grow almost all staple crops —crops as varied as cotton and corn! We have practically all kinds of timber and fruits. Almost everything that grows, we can grow on our topsoil. Under our soil, we have found rich veins or ores, coal, and stones. We have rivers, two oceans, abundant rainfall. We have everything. It isn't any wonder we rose to a world power.

Perhaps another people could have taken the southern half of this continent and would not have risen to a world power. Then why did we? Those who settled our bleak New England shores were generally frugal, and many attained great commercial wealth. But these peoples attained a more distinctive achievement.

New England sponsored a new kind of wealth. The little town Concord, Massachusetts, gave abundant riches to all the world. Emerson, who influenced my life in high school, Thoreau, Hawthorne, James Russell Lowell, Whittier, and others grew up there. Learning reached such high levels that people paid just to hear men talk.

The great families of the state of Virginia, Mother of Presidents, did not seek fortunes alone. They found a greater ideal —a greater richness—and that was education. Out of this came the names that will outlast the names of great wealth: Washington, Jefferson, Madison, Patrick Henry—to mention only a few. Out of this aristocratic living came the idea for the public school system, the most democratic of all of our institutions, and it came from a Virginian, Thomas Jefferson.

George Washington is said to be father of our country, but I cannot reject the idea from my mind that it was Thomas Jefferson. We need men in America today like him. He was a man of many intellectual facets, and one of his greatest was his belief in the American people and his idea of education for all. He believed that out of our masses would come greatness. How right he was!

Today it is a shocking fact that in America approximately forty-eight percent of our elementary and secondary pupils drop out of school before they reach or finish the twelfth grade. Parents, teachers, and the general public are alarmed. In my state of Kentucky the dropout figures are much higher than the national average. We have, according to reports, approximately a sixty-five percent dropout. Educators are trying to learn the causes in order to effect some sort of cure. And they are finding the going difficult. They have suggested that the age limit of compulsory school attendance be raised two more years. Some of our people who believe money is a cure-all for all problems pay their children to go to school with bonus bribes for passing simple high-school courses and additional bonuses for higher grades.

Now, the reason parents too often give for their children's leaving school is that the teachers are inefficient or the school plants are inadequate, or the cafeteria food isn't any good. Sometimes it is that "old mean teacher" who fails everybody. Very often parents will come to the school (at least they did when I was principal) and demand that teachers "up" the grades so their children can pass. One year in a local high school parents tried to sue two teachers who failed to pass a boy and a girl in a subject, which kept them from graduating. One of these teachers was my youngest sister. Since local attorneys would not take these suits, the parents went to a large city and sought the advice of attorneys there. Failing again, they took their charges against these teachers to the state Department of Education, who passed the buck back to the county superintendent and local school board. This is an indictment of our people. It also has a demoralizing effect upon our teachers. But the sorry attitude of a minority of parents is not the single cause of such a high percentage of dropouts.

I have spent the best years of my life as a classroom teacher or as a school administrator. These years, for the most part, have been spent in secondary schools, and I have come to know the secondary pupils very well. And to know them is to love them, regardless of their virtues or faults. The so-called "teen-age" years are, in my estimation, the most wonderful years in the life of man. I have heard silly people condemn and bemoan this age, but there isn't a week in my life that I do not wish to return to it. And this is a wonderful time for teachers and parents to mold and shape adolescents into useful men and women.

It is most unfortunate that American parents who blame teachers, school plants, cafeteria food, and other things for their children's dropping out of school cannot travel to some other countries just to learn about the general superiority of American teachers and American schools. We Americans are prone to boast about having the best of everything. We can truly boast of telephones, bathtubs, automobiles—gadgets that make life easier, more comfortable, and softer. However, we can no longer boast of the better automobile, for the German, British, Italian, and French automobiles are replacing our cars over the world. We can no longer compete in some areas of world trade. There are other commodities which we used to export that have been replaced, mainly by Japanese and German competition.

But there are professions in which we are at least a half-century ahead of the world average. American-trained schoolteachers, doctors, dentists, nurses, health officers, engineers, and agricultural technicians are in demand over all the world, except in a few European countries; our agricultural technicians have worked in nearly all of the countries overseas. My students who were trained in agriculture in our county high school could serve as agricultural technicians and soil conservationists in many of the seventy-four countries I have visited.

The fundamental philosophy of our public schools is "the greatest good for the greatest number" and "educating for their needs." This is a sound philosophy that has paid dividends. Each youth is entitled to a free education up through twelve grades; he is not only free to go, but compelled to attend up to a certain age. In addition to this great public school system, there are excellent private and church schools all over the United States. There is no question that we have the finest school system on earth. Then why do we have forty-eight percent dropouts?

Perhaps Americans who have taught in American-sponsored missionary universities, colleges, secondary and elementary schools overseas are better qualified to answer this question than teachers who have taught only in the United States. American doctors, nurses, agricultural experts, building technicians, and Peace Corps members should have some excellent answers. And I believe the answers from all of these groups might have a common denominator. But first, let me admit that after teaching a year in the American University in Cairo, Egypt, I have almost become a "spoiled" American teacher. I have changed my ideas about begging students in America to finish high school and college. They should, if they have any sense at all, know the value of an education, of head or hand or a combination of the two.

When I went to the American University in Cairo I couldn't conceive of their having a wall around the campus, a large gate and padlock where a bowab (keeper of the gate) allowed the students and teachers to go through only upon identification. Everybody wanted to go to the American University, which was staffed with teachers from ten countries, American and Egyptian teachers in the majority.

My students were eager. They asked me questions that were hard to answer. With the exception of three American students and one Canadian, not one of my students spoke fewer than three languages. I learned that their being able to speak, write, and understand English was the main criterion of their acceptance; that of every six who applied, only one was chosen. Here were the best and most eager students I ever taught in my life. The schoolteacher was the most respected person on earth. They were especially fond of American teachers. A few Americans among us would not be considered outstanding teachers in American schools, but they were considered wonderful there. A lemon teacher in America is a sweet apple over there.

The majority of the students were Muslims. If anybody ever taught better students than the Greeks and Armenians (who are of minority Christian groups in a Muslim country) or Muslim girls, who for the first time are beginning to fill the colleges and universities, I would like to listen to that teacher. "Dropouts," unless because of sickness or poverty, are unheard of there. These youth will fight to get into school. When the teacher walks through the gate onto the campus, the students stand. The graduates of this small school in Cairo who receive scholarships for America go to such institutions as Harvard, Yale, M.I.T., Columbia, Vanderbilt, University of Chicago, Princeton, Duke, Emory, University of Illinois, Indiana University, Ohio State, University of Iowa, University of California, and the University of Minnesota. Secondary schools are few and far between in Egypt. Most of the students I taught had been educated in missionary schools: Presbyterian, Catholic, Orthodox, Coptic, Greek, and Armenian. They go anywhere they can to a secondary school. So the Egyptian youth cannot understand "dropouts." The whole populace would be educated in a few years if they had our school system in Egypt.

From September, 1962, until February, 1963, I went around the world as a specialist for the United States Information Service (USIS), a branch of the State Department. I lectured to university, college, and secondary-school groups, to teacher and writing groups in Iran, Egypt, Greece, Lebanon, West Pakistan, East Pakistan, the Philippines, Taiwan (Formosa), and Korea. I learned much about the young people by talking directly with them and with their teachers. Although I imparted knowledge to them, I received more from them than I gave. Poor as these countries were by our American standards, these millions—yes, a billion people—were on the rise. And they are working first to equal and then to surpass

America. It was a thrilling experience to see them advance and to note how proud they were of their small achievements.

There were conditions that broke my heart too in these countries. Youth were crying to go to elementary schools, to secondary schools, to colleges and universities. There were not enough schools and teachers to accommodate those eager for an education.

All we need to do is to give these eager young people teachers. Let the physical plants come later. American parents, never satisfied, who complain about the schools and teachers, should see what the American teacher can do for the unspoiled and bright children of other lands. If the youth of these countries where I visited had American teachers, with a hot lunch thrown in free, there would not be even three percent dropouts. Can any American doubt the integrity of young people who sit on the doorstep of a school that is bursting at the seams, waiting for a student to move away or die so they can fight for his place?

I do not mean this to wind up a heavy-breathing advertisement for the American teacher. Teacher strikes leave me cold, in fact downright freezing—though I believe in the union and how it has helped raise teachers' salaries. I scorn graduate degrees earned merely to raise the pay another notch. Teachers who don't have the calling aren't worth your good tax dollar—and I use the word "calling" in the old-fashioned pulpit sense. A good teacher has either to love his kids or his subject. A great teacher loves both and marries the two. As the spirit has seeped out of the schools, teacher attitudes have changed.

So what has happened to our people in America? Why do we have almost fifty percent dropouts before our young people reach the twelfth grade? It cannot be denied in America that our main motive in education is to "make life easier." We have tried to replace all labor with machines, even machines to think for us. We have even tried to invent a teaching machine to replace the teacher. We have mechanical slaves to do ninety percent of our work. Each day we read in the papers, or hear over the radio, or see on TV that some person has devised a way by which one man can do the job of twenty.

We read or hear daily that our country is heading toward socialism. That isn't true; we're not heading that way, for we are already there. There's not another country in this world where the supposedly poor can drive automobiles to haul their free commodities home. Some of the people who don't work live about as well as some who do. In New York City alone we have a million people on welfare.

No wonder our youth drop out of school! What is there for them out there in our bleak future? Why become a number, a zip code, a cipher? This new way of life is tearing the very guts and hearts out of our youth, deadening their brains, killing the greatest inheritance a youth can have, incentive to do, incentive to have, incentive to compete. We look askance at people who are eager to work, who like to save, to build fortunes. We have a name for these people: Eager Beavers! We soft-pedal competition. Yet competition, academic and athletic, is present in every country on earth. Americans love to compete, and millions pay to see them compete.

In the Kentucky mountains some have drawn their dole so long, they perhaps will never work again. They don't know how!

What do you think has happened to their children who attend public schools? What ambition will they have? When a tree fell across the road, we used to take axes and saws, maybe a mule team or a tractor, and remove the tree. Today we call the state Department of Highways. So what is so strange about youth's demanding unearned grades from teachers so they can graduate?

When they look into the future, what do they see? Is it

better to work or not work? It doesn't matter much, for if they don't work they may fare about as well as those who do. Incentive, ambition, and competition are almost archaic words in our language. Our present and future generations will demand and get as long as we can give, while the pauper countries of the world, whose youth are eager to rise, will work and rise up like long-submerged islands in the sea. My father used to say the third generation was a shirt-sleeve generation. The first generation worked to make it, the second generation spent it, and the third generation were in shirt sleeves again. Will our future generations be shirt-sleeve generations?

In our Kentucky area this summer twelve thousand youth applied for work to help them defray college expenses. Of this number, only eleven hundred got work. These were the ambitious ones. Tell youth something is out there for them if they will only work for it, and ninety percent of them will. Yet, we haul them free to school by bus. We give them a free noon meal if they can't pay for it. We buy their books, and we pass laws to protect them from labor. We give them everything, even money to stay in school and money to make grades. We try to buy them. Money can't turn the trick.

We forget the human spirit and its response to challenge. We have forgotten incentive and competition. These are dirty words, but how the people of the world love them. A Greek girl I taught at the American University in Cairo couldn't get a scholarship (she couldn't get money out of Egypt) to come to America. I thought she was a good student, although she didn't have the best grades there, and I recommended her for a scholarship, which she didn't get. She actually begged me to say a kind word for her in America, and I did. An institution of higher learning accepted this twenty-one-year-old girl, who had taught school one year for a pitifully low wage. All she could do was pay her way over and bring a few clothes. She was ambitious and determined. Of the eleven grades she received, nine were A's and two were B's. She got her M.A. degree in one year, youngest in the class of 275, and with the highest grades.

This is the spirit of youth. Give them a challenge, and they accept it. They want to work. They want to do. Give each boy and girl a goal to work for; give him or her a challenge, and I'll guarantee that only sickness or death will make him or her drop out of school. We might even equal or surpass Japan's record of 99.7 percent that remain to finish the free elementary and junior high schools.

And the purpose of education must not be purely materialistic. It must not have value only in dollars and cents.

My purpose in going to college was not to expand my earning power. I had teachers who taught me that knowledge was the greatest thing I could possess, that a college education would awaken the kingdom within me—help me expand my heart, mind, and soul.

Then there was my father. "Amount to something," he often said. And my mother once told us: "I want you children to live so I will never be ashamed of a one of you. And you, Jesse, I want you to amount to so much that when you are in a crowd, you will be singled out and someone will say: 'He's Martha Hilton's son.'" I never forgot her words.

There were many things between me and my college. The main one was dollars.

But I pursued my dream, and I learned both in and out of the classroom. For one thing, I learned to apply Ralph Waldo Emerson's kind of self-reliance I had read about in high school. Somehow, I learned that most men sometime must accept defeat. I wanted a first place on our track team, but never got it. But I learned if one wanted a first place in something that he could not get, the next best thing was to try to excel at something else.

In August, 1969, forty years will have passed since I received my diploma at Lincoln Memorial. Was the seedbed carefully prepared in college? What of the harvest?

Materially, I have done better than ever I expected. My birthplace was a one-room shack; as an itinerant farm-boy worker, I earned twenty-five cents a day. Now I live in a comfortable home and own the farms where my father and mother rented and sharecropped in my youth, a thousand acres in all. I have made over one hundred thousand dollars in one year. But these are not the important things. They are the by-products of my dream—education and enlightenment, and awakening of the kingdom within.

As a teacher, I have tried to go beyond the textbooks into the character—stressing honesty, goodness, and making each life count for something. I have written thirty-two books, nearly four hundred short stories, two hundred articles and essays, and two thousand poems, trying to share my dream. I have tried to arouse and awaken our people through more than five thousand lectures. I shall do more.

Surely, I owe more than mere gratitude for God-given talents and energy and for the privileges, opportunities, and freedom this country has given me to develop them. And the only way I can repay my debt is to work with children. No joy runs deeper than the feeling that I have helped a youth stand on his own two feet, to have courage and self-reliance, and to find himself when he did not know who he was or where he was going.

Yes, I have tried to follow my dream—and it has led me to dedicate much of my life to an effort to be an awakening teacher, one like so many of those I knew in my own youth, like so many of those who taught me and, later, studied under me.

Let me tell you about one more such teacher.

When eighty-four percent of the Greenup Countians voted to eliminate sixty-six rural schools for ten consolidated ones, Nina Mitchell Biggs was one of the dissenting sixteen percent.

Nina Mitchell Biggs, a former teacher, taught her first school in Greenup County in 1881. She was fifteen in 1881 when she taught the Raccoon Rural School.

She taught big boys, too, but discipline wasn't her problem. Her problem was keeping the sheep out of her school.

Colonel Bill Worthington, lieutenant governor when William O. Bradley was governor, had purchased the denuded acres that made up the entire Racoon-Furnace area. Colonel Bill figured the best thing to do with his newly acquired acres was to raise sheep.

When he clashed with the spirited fifteen-year-old teacher Miss Nina Mitchell, Colonel Bill was a man of state and national reputation, attorney, political figure, soldier, and dominant personality. That didn't keep Miss Nina from using the broom more than once on his sheep. She wouldn't let him use her school for a barn.

Miss Nina continued teaching until she married Maurice Biggs in 1886. She moved onto her husband's farm, which was a part of the Bigg's family estate. Nearly seventy years later, long after a bond issue was voted by Greenup Countains to build consolidated schools, Miss Nina, long a widow of great wealth, was forced to leave the home where she had lived almost three-quarters of a century. Industry had taken the acres the Biggs family had owned since the Indians had been chased out by the white settlers.

Within a quarter of a mile stood the neglected Frost School, its pupils transported by bus to the big consolidated McKell Elementary.

Miss Nina could have purchased the finest home in Fullerton or South Shore, but she had another idea. The acre where the Frost School stood reverted to her estate when the school was discontinued, so she purchased the old schoolhouse. She employed two carpenters. Miss Nina and her daughter stood by directing the work.

They built a new home over and around the Frost schoolhouse. Her daughter, Mrs. King, drew the plans.

"I'll see that this one-room school doesn't go," Miss Nina said. "I hate to see the old schools go. But most of them have and we have lost something. I associate them with the old *McGuffy Readers.* They will live forever with me."

The old one-room Frost School became Miss Nina's living room. Visit her and she'll point out to you where her desk used to be. She'd show you where so-and-so used to sit and now he has retired from business in Ashland or Lexington.

She had memories of her pupils—where they sat in the room and how they played on the schoolground, which is now her yard.

When her former pupils came back to see her they visited their elementary alma mater too. When her own children, now grandparents and great-grandparents, returned, it was alma-mater homecoming for them and for Miss Nina, who was still spry and chipper at ninety-two.

She was determined not to let what she believed in pass away. She was determined to hold on to her rural school so long as she lived.

In Kentucky today, the one-room school, where teachers taught all eight grades, belongs to an age gone by. In portions of our state, especially in the eastern Kentucky mountains, we held on to the one-room school longer than any other state in America, unless it was the mountain areas in West Virginia, Tennessee, Virginia, North Carolina, northern Georgia, and northern Alabama. Still in the mountains of eastern Kentucky and West Virginia there are areas which are using the one-room schools. These schools are in isolated mountain areas where modern highways have not penetrated, where youth cannot be transported by bus to consolidated schools.

Now, in Greenup County, Kentucky, our pupils have been transported by bus to consolidated schools for years. There used to be eighty-two one- and two-room schools in Greenup County, and now only two of these are left. One, the Claylick School Building, which I visited as a young county school superintendent back in 1932, is still left standing because Greenbo State Park has purchased the grounds. This school-house is now a showplace. And the other is Cane Creek School, where my sister Sophia began teaching at seventeen. Older people with a nostalgic longing for the past drive to this school, sit in parked cars, look at it, and dream. They get out of their cars and look in the windows at the potbellied stove, which is going to rust, and at a few of the old seats that are still left.

These people fondly remember the age gone by. And I remember the years gone by too. I remember them so well that with the permission of the Greenup County school su-perintendent I hauled the old seats where my pupils sat in 1923 to a building on my farm, where I have them stored. On many of the seats I have found carved initials. I am glad they are on the seats now, but it wouldn't have done for me to have caught a pupil carving his initials on a seat in 1923. Initials are all that a few of these youngsters left to remember them by. In this landlocked and poor rural area, youth back in 1923 had little chance of higher education or making a mark in life. They had such small chance of improving themselves. Today they have equal chances with youth over most of this coun-try.

Now with highways penetrating approximately ninety percent of what used to be inaccessible mountain areas, school buses can haul pupils to large consolidated schools. This new consolidated school, with better-educated and more-sophisticated teachers, superior health practices, and more recreational opportunities, is quite a contrast to the old one-room school. One teacher can teach his or her particular grade or specialty without other pupils listening in. Often one grade is divided and subdivided and there are several teachers. And there is a principal, an assistant principal, and a second assistant principal, not one of whom teaches a class; there is a guidance counselor who doesn't teach but who steers pupils in the right direction according to the results of his testing. We used to talk about Big Business! Now we have to talk about Big Schools. They are going to get bigger, no matter what we say.

Maybe there is a reason why people today in our area and others have a nostalgic feeling for the one-room school, which has disappeared into that bygone era of American life, like the oxcart, sled, saddle, horse and buggy, rubber-tired fringed surrey, jolt wagon, express wagon, hug-me-tight, and the bull-tongue, cutter, bottom, and hillside turning plows. Even the passenger trains are going, and we are taking to wings and to three cars a family on the broad highways that thread this nation.

The one-room school had some advantages which the con solidated school cannot give its pupils. One was walking to and from school. Then, the roads were not crowded with automobiles. We walked over hills and up and down valleys where there were only footpaths. And in July, when our country school began, we walked barefoot along the dusty footpaths. We got caught in summer rainstorms. Often we got soaked. We waded streams barefoot. We got to know the names of wildflowers, shrubs, different species of trees. We had books in school (very few), but there was another kind of book all of us had to read, Earth's Book, which was filled with many pages and many delightful paragraphs.

Autumn along these paths was more interesting. The acorns dropped like big brown heavy raindrops from the oaks; the chestnuts dropped to the leafy ground from their satiny burrs that pricked our bare feet. The papaws ripened after the first frost. And the trees were loaded with persimmons, which we tried to get before the possums got them.

Then, there were hickory-nut trees everywhere. Mornings we left home very early to try to beat other pupils who traveled the same path to the chestnut trees, papaw groves, and hickory-nut trees. We didn't race for the persimmon trees, for there was always an abundance of this ripened fruit on the ground. We couldn't pick all that fell from the trees. We gathered white and black walnuts and cracked them between rocks under the trees.

I remember animal and bird tracks in the snow. Winter was a great time too. I couldn't keep from tracking a rabbit, fox, possum, mink, or weasel even if I was a little late for school. And I learned how hard it was for animals and birds to live in winter on the scanty food left for them, most of which was covered with snow. Many times I tracked a rabbit to a shock of corn on a hill slope which I shook with my hand to watch the rabbit run out. Many times I found a covey of quail hiding under falling grass where they could gather a few weed seeds to eat. I learned a lot about rain and snowstorms that I couldn't have learned on a school bus. But the pupils today who ride school buses are not to blame. This has happened in our changing world. We were the more fortunate because we could walk to and from school. Anybody who ever walked to a one-room country school will tell you about his experiences in the schoolroom. These are dear experiences that will never come again. Youths who visit the few old school relics, bird- and bat-filled belfries where there used to be a school bell, who stand and gawk at these relics of the past, do not know what they have missed. No one fought harder than I did to see our one-room schools go in Kentucky and consolidation come. A country must progress and must move from the past into a modern world; our schools had to move in this direction. But this is what we must never forget: There was a day and time when education was considered a priceless gift.

And what is wrong with such an idea today? Such an idea

in a youth or a community, a state or a nation, cannot become outdated.

When I make a speech and tell the young today about the teacher who taught all the grades from first to eighth in six hours, many of them laugh. I know what they are thinking. But they do not know what I am thinking, and it is hard for me to tell them. What I believe we had then in the one-room school was what is called today "The Accelerated School Program." If a student was alert and eager to learn, there was no problem. If a student was not alert and eager, to sit in this schoolroom and hear others recite in classes ahead and behind alerted him. He had to learn to study when there were others reciting or had to study at home. When I went from one grade to another in my scanty schooling at Plum Grove, I could have skipped the grade ahead of me. I had already listened to others ahead of me in their recitations and discussions. My brother James, who attended the Plum Grove school, learned so much so quickly that when he was ten years old he entered Greenup High School and finished when he was fourteen. In his last year at Greenup he made all A's and read all the books in the Greenup High School library and many of the encyclopedias.

The youth of today who attend departmentalized consolidated elementary schools should never laugh when they look at one of the one-room schoolhouse relics now on exhibit in state parks. They ought to know what transpired between pupils and teachers in these one-room schools. They served a day and time in America, and they served it well.

One teacher taught all eight grades and usually enjoyed it. At least I did. Education to them and for them was idealistic and the greatest thing they could pass along in life. The children I taught were, more often than not, unspoiled, eager, and ambitious. And they managed to convey the impression that they enjoyed my classroom. Maybe they were faking it—but you know I don't think so.

We've lost something we've got to get back. Not the one-room schoolhouse, but the spirit of the one-room schoolhouse. I am incurably optimistic about young people and have boundless faith in the kind of people who go into teaching. We'll get it back.

About the Author

JESSE STUART is recognized as one of the most important voices of America. Poet, short-story writer, and novelist, he has written over thirty books, all of which have immortalized his native Kentucky hill country.

Besides being one of our best-known and best-loved writers, Mr. Stuart has taught and lectured extensively. His teaching experience ranges from the one-room schoolhouses of his youth in Kentucky's mountainous regions to the American University in Cairo, and embraces years of service as school superintendent, high-school teacher, and high-school principal.

Mr. Stuart and his wife, Naomi Deane, make their home in Greenup, Kentucky.